# METABOLIC MISSION

THE INCREDIBLE TRUE STORY OF ONE MAN'S SEARCH FOR ULTIMATE HEALTH IN A WORLD OF MEDICAL TRADITION

## DR. CURTIS R. KUHN

Certified Metabolic Therapist, Ecological
Lifestyle Advisor, AA, BS, MS, PhD

Foreword by William Donald Kelley, D.D.S., M.S
Founder of the International Health Institute

Copyright © 2023 Dr. Curtis R. Kuhn.

All rights reserved. No part of this book may be reproduced, stored, or transmitted by any means—whether auditory, graphic, mechanical, or electronic—without written permission of both publisher and author, except in the case of brief excerpts used in critical articles and reviews. Unauthorized reproduction of any part of this work is illegal and is punishable by law.

ISBN: 979-8-88640-705-1 (sc)
ISBN: 979-8-88640-706-8 (hc)
ISBN: 979-8-88640-707-5 (e)

Because of the dynamic nature of the Internet, any web addresses or links contained in this book may have changed since publication and may no longer be valid. The views expressed in this work are solely those of the author and do not necessarily reflect the views of the publisher, and the publisher hereby disclaims any responsibility for them.

This book and the therapies described within does not claim to be a substitute for a physician's care. The programs described are solely nutritional in nature and do not intend to diagnose a health problem nor propose in any way to cure, treat, mitigate, or prevent any illness or disease. To obtain advice on medical recommendations you should consult with your physician.

One Galleria Blvd., Suite 1900, Metairie, LA 70001
1-888-421-2397

To my Grandmother, Anna Kuhn, who always taught me to seek the truth. She also once told me as a young boy that in this life, man can take everything away from you except your mind and soul. Therefore she stressed that I should always strive to better myself academically and feed my eternal spirit. To her, I not only owe my life but also all of the talents that she encouraged me from day one to explore and cultivate.

## Special Tribute

The following pioneers of metabolic science, have contributed not only to metabolic typing but have ultimately given me a second chance at life.

Dr. Roger J. Williams, as proponent of the concept of biochemical individuality.

Dr. William Donald Kelley, who coined the phrase "Metabolic Typing" and who may very well be recorded in history as the father of metabolic medicine for his establishment of the autonomic nervous system as the basis for metabolic typing.

Dr. George Watson, for his research on the effects of oxidation in psychophysiology.

Dr. Henry R. Harrower

Dr. Henry Bieler

Dr. Melvin E. Page and Dr. Elliot Abravanel, for their respective work with metabolic individuality and the endocrine system.

And all of the noted visionaries and researchers such as Dr. Royal Lee, Dr. Weston A. Price, Dr. Joel Wallach and Dr. Francis M. Pottenger Jr., who all recognized the importance of whole natural foods and saw the wisdom of building health rather than treating disease.

# CONTENTS

The American Death Ceremony ..................................................... vii
World Research Foundation Fact Sheet ........................................... ix
Foreword ............................................................................... xiii
Preface ................................................................................. xv

1  Too Sick to Have Cancer ........................................................... 1
2  Rebuilding and Recalling ......................................................... 13
3  Rediscovering the Rhythm of life .............................................. 21
4  Transition ............................................................................ 43
5  Must I Die to Get Better? ........................................................ 71
6  Please, Doctors, Only One Diagnosis! ....................................... 97
7  From the Country to City and Healthy to Sickly ...................... 118
8  $10 Million Only a Phone Call Away ....................................... 139
9  From Clinic to Branson and then Vegas! .................................. 151
10 Born Again ........................................................................ 183

Epilogue ............................................................................... 211
A Few Personal Testimonials .................................................... 219
A Comment on Dr. Kelley's System of Metabolic Typing .............. 225
Bibliography and Suggested Reading ......................................... 227

# THE AMERICAN DEATH CEREMONY

The death ceremony started as a crude ritual back in the days of witchcraft. In recent years it has been developed into a science. It usually takes from ten to fifteen years; however, modern scientific advancements are shortening this period of time.

It starts with one simple aspirin for a simple headache. When the one aspirin will no longer cover up the headache, take two. After a few months, when two aspirin will no longer cover up the headache, you take one of the stronger compounds. By this time it becomes necessary to take something for the ulcers that have been caused by the aspirin. Now that you are taking two medicines, you have a good start. After a few months, these medications will disrupt your liver function. If a good infection develops, you can take some penicillin. Of course the penicillin will damage your red blood corpuscles and spleen so that you develop anemia. By this time all of these medications will put such a strain on your kidneys they should break down. It is now time to take some antibiotics. When these destroy your natural resistance to disease, you can expect a general flare-up of all your systems. The next step is to cover up all of these symptoms with sulfa drugs. When the kidneys finally plug up you can have them drained. Some poisons will build up in your system but you can keep going quite a while this way.

By now the medications will be so confused they won't know what they are supposed to be doing, but it doesn't really matter. If you have followed every step as directed, you can now make an appointment with your undertaker.

This game is played by practically all Americans, except for the few ignorant souls who follow nature.

By Dr. L.I.
Reprinted with permission from:
Cancer Control Society
2043 North Berendo
Los Angeles, CA. 90027

# WORLD RESEARCH FOUNDATION FACT SHEET

In the United States in 1987, 1,323 people per day died of cancer—about one every 65 seconds.*

From 1950 to 1982, cancer-related mortality in the U.S. (age adjusted to the 1980 population) rose approximately 60% among nonwhite males, the most rapid rise of any sector of the population.**

More than 200,000 cancer patients receive chemotherapy in the U.S. each year, yet the number of patients who are being cured can hardly amount to more than a few percent of those who are treated.***

Of 1,248 patients in a series of phase 1 clinical trials coordinated by the National Cancer Institute, "The complete plus partial response rate was only 2 percent. Moreover, only two patients (0.16 percent) achieved a complete remission."

A study by the National Center for Health Statistics put overall medical costs for cancer at $71.5 Billion for 1985.*

Notwithstanding this national outpouring of money and resources, a major study found that, "Age-related mortality rates have shown a slow and steady increase over several decades. In this clinical sense we are losing the war against cancer."*

The main conclusion we draw is that some thirty-five years of intense effort focused largely on improving cancer treatment must be judged a qualified failure.**

---

\*   The American Cancer Society, ACS Cancer Facts and Figures; 1987.

\*\*  J.C. Bailar & E.M. Smith, "Progress Against Cancer?" The New England Journal of Medicine, 5/8/86.

\*\*\* John Caimes, "The Treatment of Disease and The War Against Cancer," *Scientific America*, Nov. 1985.

- 999 out of 1,000 people today are malnourished.
- Birth defects in the U.S. have tripled since 1956.
- About 80 percent of the modern western world's population suffers from degenerative conditions.
- The National Cancer Institute found that diet and nutrition appear to account for the largest number of human cancers.
- Only a few years ago, accidents were the major cause of death in children under the age of fifteen, but today the number one cause is cancer.
- Degenerative disease conditions, such as cancer, diabetes, heart disease, hypoglycemia, eczema, emphysema, arthritis and ulcers occur in more and more children each year.
- Chronic illness is responsible for more than 80 percent of the total cases of disability in the U.S. and England.
- Each year, the United States drops lower and lower on the list of "Health of Nations."

Statistics compiled by Dr. W.D. Kelley

*The doctor of the future will give no medicine but will interest his patient in the care of the human frame, in diet and in the cause and prevention of disease.*

—Thomas A. Edison

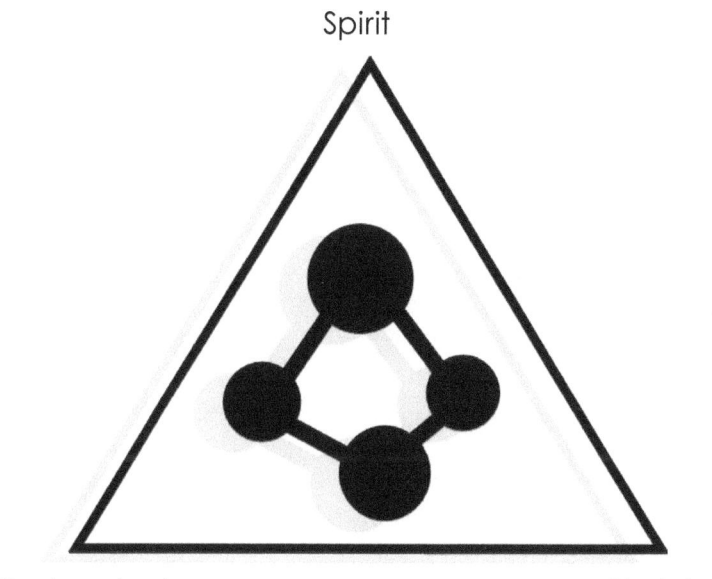

# FOREWORD

In changing the course of medicine from the witchcraft of modern therapeutics, that is treating disease, to the health building of our metabolic paradigm, it will take the trauma of ill health of millions of individuals as the author brings to your attention in this book. But more than that, it will require the attrition by death of thousands of physicians, possibly two or three generations, deceived by the fraud, ignorance, greed, plunder, and murder paradigm of the multinational pharmaceutical conglomerates.

In choosing to possess health, those who obtain it must realize it is a lifetime "Do-It-Yourself" procedure. No one can "Do-It-For-You." Like the dawn of a new day, the realization that your physician does not know any more about health than you do and certainly has no concern or interest in your well-being is the first step on your road to optimal health.

As in the author's experiences, health is a lifelong process of caring and respect for this magnificent temple your soul inhabits. As the author has well established in this book, taking care of your palace by building and maintaining with the perfection of truth is imperative.

May *Yahweh* our Father God Almighty extend his loving kindness, protection, and blessings in all ways—always!

Respectfully,
Dr. Kelley
William Donald Kelley, DDS, MS
Administrator; College of Metabolic Medicine

# PREFACE

*So we fix our eyes not on what is seen, but on what is unseen. For what is seen is temporary, but what is unseen is eternal.*

—2 Corinthians 4:18

Throughout the ages, *truth* has been the burning ember that spurred the theologian, the scientist, and the physician toward knowledge and acceptance of all things occurring within the universe, whether biochemical, structural, or spiritual. Without this pursuit, where would man be now, or perhaps should we ask, would he even be?

Truth is, and always will be the same. It is like our planet, which continues on its eternal axis, shifting slightly but destined to continue in time and space. So it is *truth* that I must share with you, for without this simple yet complex paradigm, I would not be here today to share myself and my incredible biological adventure with you.

My story may even be similar to your own or someone close to you, but there is one unequivocal element that has separated us, one from another. That element I will call the *metabolic truth*. It is this dynamic truth that has provided me with renewed strength and profound knowledge and compelled me to share it with every soul I can encounter.

Throughout your life, many doctors, food fads, shaman, herbologists, etc. may attract your attention and cause temporary distractions, but the science of *metabolics* will put all of the pieces of the human puzzle together. Once you have determined your functional and metabolic subtype, you will no longer have to guess at what your nutritional needs are at the cell level. For the first time in your life, you will experience what the right combination of foods, food supplements, and detoxification will do for you.

Think about that for a moment. When you walk into a health food store or pharmacy, there are literally hundreds if not thousands of formulations on the shelves. Do you know exactly what you need for your type? What herbs, vitamins, minerals, pancreatic enzymes, coenzymes, hydrochloric acid combinations, etc. do *you* need for *your* specific metabolic type?

I have been on a program since 1985 and although I claim to know quite a bit about this science, it would be incorrect to state that we have *all* the answers, yet every day I hear of another magic bullet in the media—such as shark cartilage, or antioxidants or bee pollen and etc. We must realize that the human body is the most complex organism on this planet and address it as such.

Assuming that we all have the same exact nutritional needs is like saying that we all should wear a size 6 shoe, it just won't fit! Biochemical individuality is the core premise of metabolic typing and is the basis for each individual program. Years of research has helped us to understand this genetic proposition. For instance, we were talking about and utilizing antioxidants in the 70s, years before the term was even coined.

I could stand on my metabolic platform and probably preach a good sermon at this point, but I'll save that for a later chapter in this book. But I would like to state that during the past thirty eight years, I have carried my metabolic cross across the plains of Kansas and the searing heat of the Las Vegas desert and still hold true to what I believe and what has happened to me and thousands of others. May this book mark the beginning of an era whose time has come—a time when we no longer have to succumb to our ecological imbalances and become human byproducts of this diseased planet. A time when we can control the biological fate of ourselves, our families, and the ones we love the most.

# 1

# TOO SICK TO HAVE CANCER

*Therefore each of you must put off falsehood and speak truthfully to his neighbor, for we are all members of one body.*

—Ephesians 4:25

As we glided along the highway toward Dallas, my mind wandered back to that small health food store in Arkansas City, Kansas. I could still see the brilliant green cover of that book staring me in the face as I browsed through hundreds of supplement formulations, searching endlessly for some answers, anything that could help my body to rebuild and balance itself! Not even knowing why, I scurried over to a bookrack, picked up a book, and carefully read it's glistening cover "Metabolic Ecology."

*This is interesting*, I thought, while thumbing through the pages. As I began to skim its contents, the owner of the store approached me. Trying not to lose my place, I glanced over my shoulder and gave her a puzzled look.

"What is this about?" I mumbled.

"It's a documentary on a nutritional approach toward cancer and all other types of degenerative diseases. I actually went to grade school with Dr. Kelley, as he grew up on a farm near here. That man is a *genius*."

As she brushed past me, I focused on a case history of a terminal cancer patient that had completely recovered and was living a fulfilling life, all because of this "Metabolic Therapy." Flipping toward the back of the book, a boldface title caught my eye—supplements, dietary, and detoxification procedures. Now this was more up my alley, although I wasn't familiar with detoxification. I had been searching and studying the effects of vitamin and mineral supplements upon the body and mind since my second year in college! In fact, I had been looking for answers to my health problems for the past decade—from clinics to hospitals, MDs to neurologists and even chiropractors. With so many extreme and serious symptoms, my physiological dilemma had puzzled many doctors and specialists for years. In fact, I felt as though I had become part of some bizarre experiment!

There were times when I was so tired that I would sleep all day, times when my memory would go blank, and times when my behavior would suddenly reverse from relaxed to an extreme hyperactive state. Finally, after being referred to a well-known neurologist, I was submitted to a morbid prescription of chemicals—Valium, then Thorazine, Stelazine, Compazine, and SK Pramime. What a mess! He even told me that I may have to take these drugs for the rest of my life! Thank God I was wise enough to get a second opinion from a general practitioner, who simply encouraged me to throw my drugs into the trash and pursue a more *sane* approach to my health and well-being. Little did any of us know that one day, this same neurologist would lose his practice, family, home, and become a street person.

Questions—answers, doctors—quacks. Ten years of my life and here I was, still looking for an answer. Closing the book, I shuffled over and laid it on the counter as I searched for my wallet.

"Is there anything else today, sir?" she asked, smiling with her eyes.

Pausing for a moment, I scanned the supplement shelves but tired at the thought of trying to find what my body really needed. That was a mystery that still was unsolved.

"No, I think perhaps this book is about all I can digest for the time being. Maybe it will open some doors that I haven't discovered yet."

Handing me my change, she looked at me a little funny, as if I had said something strange. Had I? Walking toward the door, I turned back and winked at her, commenting one last time.

"I haven't read any great books for a while, maybe this one will actually change my life." With that, I turned and walked out into the cold Kansas winter wind. Little did I know that from that moment on, my life would *never* be the same!

As we entered the suburbs of Dallas, my wife Cathy slowly opened her eyes. It was almost five o'clock and the traffic was bumper to bumper. As we searched along LBJ freeway for our exit, snow touched lightly on the windows of our new Honda.

"At least it's warmer here than back home," Cathy muttered as we edged along the packed freeway. It was hard to believe that February was already here. So far, 1985 seemed like a bad dream that wouldn't end.

Looking for our hotel, my memory automatically took me back to my last conversation with Dr. Kelley, after I had a left canine gum graft at my local dentist's office. My gums had been receding for the last year and I had already scheduled another graft for my right canine within the next couple of months. But Dr. Kelley assured me that this next surgery would probably *not* be necessary, once I started a metabolic program. Although this would be *great*, I just couldn't wrap my head around such an *incredible* possibility!

When Cathy finally spotted our hotel, we checked in, ate, and went to bed. I was totally exhausted from the six-hour drive and felt like I was running on what little adrenalin that was left in my body!

As I drifted into the first stage of sleep, I recalled Dr. Kelley's theory of cancer and his book "Metabolic Ecology." I had taken his four-week enzyme test and was confused with the results. The first week I had felt like a million bucks, but during the last three weeks, I became very sick, in fact sicker than during the past ten years. I had obviously made the correct decision by having the blood work done along with the metabolic survey but the results of the blood profile were scary. The lab stated that my liver enzyme levels were indicative of malignancy and a severe liver dysfunction and that I should see my physician immediately! But I had no family physician. I had given up on the medical profession a few years back. The only reason I had the blood work done was for Dr. Kelley and his metabolic program.

While sleeping, I began to dream. I was talking with Dr. Kelley although we hadn't met yet. As he spoke to me, his soft words became thorns as they penetrated my body and soul.

"I'm sorry, Curtis, but you don't have much time. The cancer has been growing too long. We can only make you a little more comfortable for a short time."

As his final words echoed throughout my body, I jolted upright in bed, mumbling in some language that I couldn't understand. As Cathy sat up to comfort me, she noticed the sweat that was dripping from my face and chest. Something quite unusual, as I hadn't been able to sweat during my workouts for the past few years!

"Another bad dream again, honey?" She tried to console me as she got a cool washcloth for my forehead.

"Ten years I've been searching for answers to my health problems and soon I may meet the man who can finally put all of the puzzle pieces together. And you know what? I'm confused and anxious, not only about the truth, but of what happens next."

"But you've searched for so long and have learned so much. You should be optimistic about this workshop, it will help you to finally end your journey."

"I guess that's what I almost *fear* most of all, the one piece of the puzzle that may finally come into place, the predominant word that has kept me searching for the last decade—*truth*."

After a fitful sleep, the alarm went off at 6:00 a.m. I wanted to turn it off and sleep for another week! The virus I was fighting had totally plugged my sinuses and every inch of my body ached terribly! After Cathy and I dressed, we walked slowly to the restaurant, as our conversation focused on the workshop we were about to encounter. I knew little about the International Health Institute, other than they were sponsored by the World Health Organization. But for some strange reason, I had a good feeling about this Dr. Kelley, his program, and the metabolic workshop at hand.

As I sipped on some nasty-tasting coffee, a woman without any hair caught my eye, obviously a victim of chemotherapy. For a moment, I tried to picture myself without any hair, like Marine Corps boot camp all over again, not a pleasant thought! As she sat across from us, Cathy recalled when she worked on the hospital Oncology ward in Wichita. She had grown accustomed to the strange side effects of all those caustic chemicals they were injecting people with. Personally, I was thankful for the opportunity to meet Dr. Kelley and his staff.

First to arrive at the meeting room, we checked in and sat toward the front. As others trickled in, I thought about the metabolic survey I had filled out a few weeks earlier. It had taken me *over* fifteen hours to complete and had *over* three thousand questions. It took all of the energy I could muster just to finish it. And then, when my blood work came back with the bad news, I was beyond stressed out, I could have exploded.

The first speaker, Dr. Ty Minton, welcomed everyone to Dallas and the Institute. There were people here from all over the United States, Europe, and even Korea. Dr. Minton then asked us to introduce ourselves, giving a brief history of our malady and why we had chosen metabolic therapy. As each person shared their personal story, a feeling of compassion and deep remorse came over me. Everyone there had some form of cancer and many had already tried the traditional route of slice, dice, chemo and radiation therapy!

I'll never forget a young Korean girl who was suffering severely from bone cancer. Her sister had brought her hoping to find a quick cure. She didn't return the second day, for time had finally ran out for her. There seemed to be more women than men, some who had already undergone radical mastectomies from breast cancer. Liver and pancreatic cancer were also prevalent with colon cancer close behind.

Now I understood why the workshop was called "A Resort to Health." It was a last resort for many people there. As I glanced around the room, I noticed that even people who were terminally ill looked as healthy or healthier than I did! As I shared my own personal story, I pondered what I was going to learn about my condition. There I was with a high fever, sinuses flowing, lymph glands bulging and pulsating with my blood pressure near the roof! I already felt dead, just bury me before I begin to rot!

Most of the first day focused on the metabolic health program and why people developed cancer and other degenerative diseases. I learned that lifestyle, diet, stress, carcinogens, genetics, and even spirituality played a significant role within each individual. "Balance" was the key to regaining an optimum state of health. Dr. Kelley's theory of metabolic typing was presented to us in the form of a basic triad—structural, biochemical and spiritual.

As Dr. Kelley spoke of his own struggle and victory over liver and pancreatic cancer, I was amazed. Although his cancer was considered "incurable" twenty years ago, he was still alive and well today. Not only did he invent a logical tool to combat disease, but he actually experimented on himself from the onset, opening the door for others to heal themselves.

After lunch, a slide program took us deeper into the theory of metabolic typing. The autonomic nervous system was the main focus for typing each individual. At conception, we all have an eye color, skin color, hair color etc. But just as all of these physical properties are predetermined so is the autonomic nervous system. Then depending on which mode of this system is dominant, will determine which internal organs, glands and systems will have strengths and weaknesses. The three modes of the autonomic nervous system are the sympathetic, parasympathetic and the balanced of the two. The sympathetic tends to be more of a vegetarian, while the parasympathetic is more carnivorous, and the balanced type has the best of both worlds, with equal access to all foods. Likewise, the sympathetic has a leaner, more linear build while the parasympathetic has a larger body mass with a much stronger digestive system.

As I saw the next slide, I was reminded of Dr. Sheldon's theory of somatotyping. The slide had three figures; one was lean, the second had a medium build and the third was stocky. These represented the three body types of the sympathetic, parasympathetic and the balanced, similar to Sheldon's three types; the endomorph, ectomorph and the mesomorph.

Sheldon was a psychologist from the second World War era who had formulated a theory of personality based upon a person's physical characteristics. Like the parasympathetic, the endomorph was heavier set, with dominance of the right part of the brain, which is more creative and intuitive. This type was more carnivorous genetically. The ectomorph, like the sympathetic, was left brain dominant, more of a linear analytical type thinker, and more of a vegetarian. The mesomorph, like the balanced metabolic type, had equal access to both halves of the brain and also to the widest variety of foods. Little did he know that his theory would someday be expounded upon, although metabolic typing would eventually far surpass even these basic categories for typing!

As the day drew to an end, I tried to recall all that I had learned. This program seemed very scientific, yet quite practical and easy to apply to oneself. After we adjourned for the evening, my wife and I ate dinner and talked about the results of my own metabolic program, which I would learn about the next day. Looking through my notes, I began to compare some of my symptoms with those of the metabolic types—dry skin, weak immune system, hypoglycemia, severe digestive problems, diabetes, calcium deposits, high blood pressure. I had apparently shifted from a parasympathetic dominant to a poorly functioning sympathetic. When I was much younger, in grade school, I tended to be a bit chunky, easy going, creative, athletic, with a strong immune system, like a parasympathetic. But throughout junior high, high school, and my 20s, I was always on edge, had extremely dry skin, brittle graying hair, terrible gas, memory loss, and was sick all of the time! My body obviously had some severe imbalances to restructure!

As the waitress announced fried ice cream and cake as the dessert special for the day, I just rolled my eyes to indicate that it sounded good but wasn't on my internal menu. I hadn't been able to digest dairy products and fats for years.

Day two of the workshop focused on nutrition as well as supplement and detoxification therapy. I was surprised to learn that most supplements on the market were laced with dicalcium phosphate to enhance shelf life.

This factor could have helped contribute to my raging calcium deposits on my lumbar spine and fingers! Even vitamin C was sometimes cut with sugar to make it go further.

The statistics on water were downright gruesome—only 4 percent of the world's remaining drinking waters were pure! Then what the heck had I been drinking all these years? Sediment, chemicals and human waste! Some definite changes had to be made here in America and abroad.

When the discussion shifted to the detoxification program, the coffee enema procedure was explained thoroughly. This method was used not to enhance a bowel movement, but rather to stimulate the liver, lymph, kidneys, and blood to dump metabolic debris, toxins, and chemicals that had built up over many years. Then the "greenies" were shown on the screen. These were soft and hard gallstones that accumulated inside the gallbladder and were finally dumped during a liver-gallbladder flush.

The coffee enema was actually administered to most new patients before surgery at the famous Lahey clinic in Boston way back in the 1930s. It was even used on the battlefields of the civil war when a medic would run out of morphine. It was well known and recommended for its calming effect, especially during an amputation. Coffee, although thought of as a stimulant because of the caffeine, is actually an alkaloid. It will at times pull the blood chemistry more alkaline, which will cause the individual to become calm and sedate, at times putting one to sleep.

As the slide show ended, Lanny Smith, founder of the Ultra-Life Supplement company, shared the startling story of a woman who thought she had passed her colon after a coffee enema. She had called him and hysterically announced that "it was in the stool." But after rechecking, she discovered that it was not her colon at all, but a three-foot string of *black-green* mucus that had taken on the convolutions of the colon!

After lunch, Dr. Kelley began to counsel each person that had taken the metabolic survey. As I anticipated my turn, I listened to his comments to those with cancer. It made my skin crawl.

When he finally called my name, my heart pounded so hard I knew it would explode. Sitting next to him, I was engulfed by his warm and comfortable aura, which helped my heart and blood pressure to settle a bit. As he studied my metabolic index, a puzzled look crept over his face.

"You were raised on a farm, weren't you, Curtis?"

"Why yes I was," I announced. "How did you know that?"

"Because your index indicates that you have a very strong constitution, which tells me that you grew up on whole organic foods without many chemicals. The soil was still black in Kansas when you were a boy during the early fifties, which meant that the minerals were still there. Today that same soil is brown, most of the minerals have been farmed out with the abuse of herbicides, pesticides, fungicides, nitrites, and nitrates. You are from one of the last groups of people to grow up in the Midwest eating pure food and drinking pure water. I'm afraid the next generations will not be nearly as fortunate!"

While he thumbed through my program, I briefly stated my own theory pertaining to my present condition.

"Actually, Curtis, at least 85 percent of all cancers can be attributed to an overabundance of protein in our diet. The human body has only so many pancreatic enzymes from birth, and when they are depleted, a malignancy can form. This combined with genetics, imbalanced hormones, other carcinogens in the water, food chain, air, and lifestyle can allow a foreign mass to develop."

Contemplating what he said, I explained my results of the four-week ultrazyme test. His answer again took me by surprise.

"The first week of the test, your body began to absorb nutrients that hadn't been assimilable for years. During the last three weeks, many toxins were released into your bloodstream, including sloughed off cancer cells, which made you feel depressed, goopy sick, etc. Now I have good news and some bad news for you. First, you're too sick to have cancer, and secondly, you may have to die to get better!"

Speechless, I sat there not knowing quite how to respond! "Doc, I may be a little off base, but I can't see much good news in your diagnosis!"

"Curtis, your blood work did indicate malignancy. However, your metabolic profile shows me that you actually have worse problems to contend with, although your biochemical foundation is very strong. You are lucky to have a second chance! Your body has over fifty trillion cells and each one is like a miniature trash can, but unfortunately, yours are all filled to the top! Although you may feel half dead, your body has survived the years of punishment quite well. Your adrenal glands are completely worn out, causing the severe hypoglycemia and erratic blood pressure. I recommend that you take a year off and rebuild your liver and adrenal glands!"

"A year! Why I couldn't take off a week let alone a year. I lift weights and run every day of the week! I've got to stay in condition."

"Curtis, if you don't rest and rebuild, you won't live to see your 31$^{st}$ birthday! On the other hand, if you start this program and do repair and rest for a year or two, it will take *twenty* years of hard living to break your body down again!"

That last statement struck me hard. I actually had to quit working out to rebuild my entire body.

"Curtis, you've been living on adrenalin and beta-endorphins for so long, you don't know what homeostasis would feel like! Those high intensity workouts over the past decade have depleted your body tremendously! It's like running on a treadmill and never getting anyplace. You wouldn't know what normal felt like if it slapped you in the face!"

I had never thought of it that way but it did make sense. I did seem to live on an adrenalin high most of the time. In fact, the only time I ever felt human was when I would pump weights for a couple of hours. But every day, after an exhausting workout, I would go home and collapse, as my blood sugar would drop dramatically. But that never stopped me from working out! Instead of resting when I was weak, or when my diabetes was acting up, I would go to the gym and force myself to work out. This was the only time that I felt like my body could function halfway normal.

As Dr. Kelley consulted with Dr. Gonzalez, a medical student that was doing a case study of several of Dr. Kelley's cancer patients, I pondered what he said about me having to *die* to get better. That didn't sound good. However, I already felt half dead most of the time!

"Dr. Kelley, exactly what did you mean when you stated that I also had to die to get better?" The doctor smiled at Dr. Gonzalez then returned my question with a sheepish grin that made my stomach quiver.

"It's taken years of abuse to get you where you are now, and it will take some time to climb back up the spiral of health. It won't be easy, but if you discipline yourself you can eventually enjoy a state of health you haven't known for a very long time! Within the first year, there will come a time when you will *feel* like you are going to die, but you won't." At that moment, I had the feeling that the next few months would definitely not be a picnic.

After we finished consulting with Dr. Kelley, the group formed a large circle and talked casually about the program and some of our own personal health experiences. One young lady with breast cancer was enthusiastic about the program but didn't think she could afford all the supplements, although she had already spent thousands of dollars on orthodox treatment. Yet the few hundred dollars for the program and supplements was trivial compared to being treated by the medical establishment. Besides, how could one put a price on life itself? She obviously needed to get her priorities straightened out.

As the workshop came to a close, we discussed the spiritual aspect of the metabolic triad. From my own studies of theology, psychology, and physiology, I truly felt that our psychological and spiritual outlook could enhance the healing of our physical bodies. Much was still to be learned by the scientific community in regard to this phenomena.

As I flipped through my notes from the first day of the workshop, it read, "Metabolic Typing is intended to consider the *whole* person, not just the symptoms themselves." All of my own problems were only symptoms, just as an ulcer, diabetes or even cancer are all only symptoms of a more complex metabolic disorder. I was finally going to get to the core of the problem and not fool around any longer with all of the symptoms!

While waiting for the last few people to leave, I silently prayed for everyone I had met at the workshop and also myself. Although I felt good about this program, I had no idea as to what the next few months had in store for me. As we said our goodbyes, I especially thanked Dr. Kelley, Dr. Minton, and his wife.

"Dr. Kelley, this may be a bit premature, but I think I should thank you for saving my life, and I can honestly say that if I *live*, I'm going to *tell the world* about your program."

As I shook his hand, Dr. Kelley smiled and said, "We need more people like you, Curtis, but don't be too thankful yet, remember, you still have a lot of rebuilding and repair work to do. It has taken your body years to break down, so it will take some time to climb back up that spiral of health. It won't be easy, but the results will be lifelong!"

# 2

# REBUILDING AND RECALLING

> *Why spend money on what is not bread, and your labor on what does not satisfy? Listen, listen to me, and eat what is good and your soul will delight in the richest of fare!*
>
> —Isaiah 55:2

Seek therefore, a large trailing gourd having a stalk the length of a man; take out its innards and fill it with water from the river which the sun has warmed. Hang it upon the branch of a tree and kneel upon the ground before the anger of water and suffer the end of the stalk of the trailing gourd to enter your hinder parts, that the water may flow through all your bowels. Pray that the angel of water will free your body from every uncleanness and disease. (*Essene Gospel Of Peace*, a book written from the Dead Sea Scrolls)

When the alarm blared at 7:00 a.m., I wanted to throw the clock across the room and fall back into a lifeless void! The past weekend in Dallas had drained what little strength I had left. As I showered and dressed, it occurred to me that I had forgotten to purchase a colon tube while at the workshop. Big mistake! This item was necessary for detoxification. The supplements were already ordered and would arrive today, but I needed that colon tube. I wasn't sure how I would deal with it after I had it, but it was necessary.

Before Cathy left for work, I slipped out into a snowbank, warmed up the car, and skidded across town to the local drugstore. It must have snowed seven inches over the weekend.

As I browsed through the medical supply area, a middle-aged pharmacist brusquely offered to help me out.

"Yes, sir, I'm looking for a colon tube that fits on an enema bag kit." Looking a bit puzzled, he steered me toward a display rack with a few different lengths of colon tubes.

"Exactly what are you going to use this for?" he asked suspiciously.

"For detoxification, of course," I replied.

"Is this prescribed by a physician?"

"Sure, Dr. Kelley in Dallas is my metabolic doctor. It's part of the metabolic protocol." When I said this, his eyebrows raised and he stepped back about a foot.

"Are you talking about that so-called cancer therapy, by chance?"

"Why yes, that's what it's best known for."

"Then you are aware that Dr. Kelley is only in remission, aren't you?" For a moment I hesitated, my mind went blank, but then I regained my composure.

"Twenty years is a pretty incredible remission period if you ask me," I blurted out as I stomped toward the door. Turning around, I stopped to throw in one last word. "Thanks for your help, and by the way, orthodox medicine has established that five years without any sign of cancer means *cured* not *remission,* fella!"

Walking briskly to the car, I replayed the scenario that had just taken place. Lordy, Dr. Kelley was a little more popular around here than I thought. He had lived here in Winfield, Kansas, but that was over twenty five years ago.

By the time I arrived back at the house, Cathy had already gone to work. The supplements I ordered were setting neatly in a box by the door. As I counted all the different types of supplements I was overwhelmed. There were "before," "during," and "after" pills for two meals of each day, more "during" pills to be taken with a third meal and even "bedtime" supplements.

As I began to separate the different types of supplements, I remembered what Dr. Kelley said about the caloric intake that a day's supply of supplements contained, sometimes up to six hundred calories. Obviously there was some mega nutrition in these tiny pills!

After two hours of bagging the different supplements, I nearly collapsed. I had so little energy, even the smallest task would drain the reserves I had tucked away! When I woke up, it was two in the afternoon, time to drive to Arkansas City and give my boss final notice at the insurance company. Might as well start getting rid of all these other stressors in my life.

Charlie's jaw dropped when I gave him the news. Even after I told him I had to rebuild my health, he just couldn't understand. But at ninety pounds overweight himself, I guess it would be hard to believe that a skinny kid like myself could actually be sick! I wanted to suggest he do a program also but instead just held my tongue. Charlie also had extremely high blood pressure and a severe case of gout.

With my two-week notice behind me, I shuddered at the thought of looking for another job. My bachelor's degree in psychology was a door opener but insurance was what I knew best for the past few years. But then again, I could use a few weeks off to jump-start this metabolic program.

When I arrived back at the house, I decided to brew some organic coffee for my first detoxification enema. I would have to use the standard enema kit short tube end, until I ordered an actual colon tube. After it was brewed and cooled to lukewarm, I lay on my left side and slowly let it flow into my colon. Cathy said that she would help me for the first couple of times but I was pretty independent and a little self-conscious. Being a nurse, she was used to doing things like this, but I surely wasn't!

I had added some black strap molasses to help with the cramping, which worked quite well. Laying quietly in the hallway upstairs, I could see the snow falling outside, which gave me a serene feeling deep inside, a feeling of timelessness. As I watched each snowflake sink into the roof, my mind began to meander back to the time when I lived on my grandparent's farm. My winters then were filled with carefree spirits and the blessings of a body endowed with tremendous vitality. In fact, I never missed a day of school for the first five years of elementary school. This changed when I left the farm to live with my father and his new wife in Great Bend, Kansas. This dramatic change in lifestyle and environment was a precursor to my current health problems. I shifted from whole foods grown in our garden and pure poultry raised in our barnyard, to all store-bought items, sweets, preservatives, along with the petrochemicals in the city water supply. Great Bend was an oil boom town that dumped tons of chemicals into the water supply over several decades.

Rotating to my right side, I silently thanked God for those first twelve years as they were undoubtedly the building blocks of my life, biochemically, structurally, and spiritually. I also had a very strong genetic background consisting of both the German and Welch ancestry.

That first week on metabolic therapy was one I would not soon forget. I would grind up the supplements before each meal and follow the detox procedure each morning. Although initially, the detox coffee would stimulate my adrenal glands, after a few days it had a calming effect. There were even times when I would fall asleep for a minute or two during the event!

After twenty years of intermittent constipation, my bowels began to move like clockwork! My colon was finally *beginning* to do the job it was designed to do.

As my body began to adjust to the sudden ingestion of concentrated nutrients, my psychological and mental abilities went through many various stages. Cycling off the supplements after eight to ten days helped my body and mind to remain in a semi-balanced state. I was rebuilding at such an incredibly fast pace; my body could not get rid of all the metabolic waste. Dr. Kelley was *absolutely* correct when he said that all of my cells were like miniature trash cans, that were filled to the top. I was beginning to realize that it was going to take some time for the rebuilding and detoxifying process to take place. After so many years of abuse, I knew that this wouldn't be a picnic!

In late April of 1985, I went back to my dentist, to have my right upper canine tooth grafted with skin from the roof of my mouth. I was ready for this second surgery, although the gum tissue surrounding the tooth did feel differently than it had a few months earlier.

After checking in and sitting in the dentist chair, his assistant came in to look at me before the surgery. As she began to probe the upper portion of my mouth, a puzzled look came over her face.

"Are you sure that you are scheduled for this surgery?" she exclaimed.

"Yes, the left canine was done in December, and Doc told me that this other one had to be done in a few months."

Shaking her head, she quickly left the room, as I silently snickered, remembering what Dr. Kelley had said a few months earlier. Finally, after several minutes passed, the doctor entered. As he slowly and methodically checked my mouth, he also seemed a bit uneasy. "Well, it looks like you don't need this surgery after all, at least not at this time."

Thanking him on my way out, I was compelled to *shout* out why this surgery was *not* necessary, but I kept my composure. When I got home, I called Dr. Kelley and shared my newly discovered news. Laughing a bit himself, he just confirmed what he had told me before starting his program. To him, it was just another side effect of this *incredible* protocol. But to me, it was truly an *amazing* testimony to the healing powers of the human anatomy and physiology!

During the next few months, I meditated as I experienced the detoxification process. With each session, I was drawn back in time, often reliving all the good and sometimes bad times of my childhood. As the rebuilding was taking place dramatically at all levels, my memories were somehow strangely connected. It were as though the liver was slowly unlocking these memories as it was rebuilding, along with many deep emotions.

Drifting back in time, my thoughts automatically took me to my favorite place in the world—that little brook in Reece, Kansas. The first and best years of my childhood were spent there at Spring Creek, fishing and enjoying life with my two dogs and all of the flint hills. The country was always beautiful, no matter what season. It's serenity was like poetry gently flowing through my mind, arousing all of my senses, a serenity that was to be the major building block of my future emotional and spiritual outlook on life.

The school I attended was very small, with grades one to four in one room and five through eight in another. The old high school was next door but they tore it down when I was in the fourth grade to sell and reuse all the bricks.

I remember Grandma with her sparkly blue eyes and witty sense of humor. She was always playing little tricks on someone but only in fun. She didn't have a mean bone in her body.

Grandma definitely had her hands full when she agreed to raise me. I couldn't count the number of whippings she gave me, but I have to admit, they were all substantiated! I wasn't a problem child, but I was a trifle headstrong and independent. When she went for the Chinese elm tree, I knew that a good thrashing was near!

Grandma's sixth sense was highly developed, a fact that everyone in the family knew but didn't really talk about. Like the time that her great auntie died when Grandma was a little girl. Grandma said she heard something hit the wooden floor in her auntie's bedroom, so she went to check. At first she assumed it was her false teeth, but they were still on the dresser, and the floor was bare except for her shoes set neatly near the closet. As she checked closer and saw that her auntie wasn't breathing and was cool to the touch, she concluded that the thump was her soul leaving the body at death, on its journey to another dimension!

Probing deeper within, I recalled a conversation with my Aunt Mary Ann during my college days. After several beers between all of her friends and myself, I asked her about Grandma's uncanny sixth sense. "Mary, how is it that Grandma knew so much about the things I did and even thought about as a child?"

"She had a keen sense of *vision*," Mary replied. "For example, do you ever remember using an alarm clock all through your grade school years?" I glanced around the room, then returned my aunt's stare.

"No, I don't, but what's so unusual about that?"

"She woke you up every day with her mind! That's why you didn't need an alarm clock, Butchy boy!" (Butch was the nickname Dad gave me at birth.)

"You are kidding, aren't you Mary?"

"And that's only the beginning, she had more control of your life than you ever knew!"

*Good grief,* I thought, it did make sense, Grandma always did seem to know what I was up to or thinking about.

Finishing up another daily detox, I shifted to my right side and thought about other psychic powers Grandma may have had. I shivered at the thought of myself also having this strange but wonderful gift. There had been a few times in my life that I was partially aware of something unusual taking place within my psyche, but ill health and an unbalanced biochemistry had surely stunted this ability! Perhaps, by rebalancing my body chemistry, this ability, if it was there, could actually grow stronger! Only time could answer such a profound question.

My mind was crystal clear after the detox, just one of many benefits of all systems functioning at normal again. The human body was similar to electric current, it functioned at many different levels or "watts," depending upon organ integrity, genetics, cellular strength and metabolic toxicity levels throughout the entire body. This also held true for the central nervous system and the brain. If this system were overloaded with toxins and environmental chemicals, combined with several metabolic nutritional deficiencies, it would function at a much lower capacity than usual. This would in turn cause nerve impulses to misfire and slow down the communication process. But if it functioned properly, it ran like a tremendous power plant, with millions of high wattage light bulbs all firing simultaneously!

Stumbling down the stairs, I was struck suddenly with a marvelous insight into the reality of this program. If psychic phenomena were based upon the complexity, structure, and ability of the brain to function at a very high capacity, this program could release and increase that ability! It would be similar to adding a few trillion volts of electricity to an already highly functional electric plant! The results could be very astonishing!

Thinking back to my grandmother again, I remembered something she told me as a boy, something that had always remained in the back of my mind.

"Butch, they can take anything away from you in this life that you own, but no one can ever steal your mind, remember that!"

Although I had only been on this program for a short time, I could already sense that my body was changing at an incredible rate, and at many different levels. As my immune system strengthened, my blood sugar began to stabilize and my mind was working at a much higher capacity. I was slowly beginning to sense a paradigm shift within my body and soul, a shift so dynamic that it almost seemed euphoric at times. It was similar to a butterfly emerging from its solitary cocoon, a type of metamorphosis, a "metabolic metamorphosis."

# 3

# REDISCOVERING THE RHYTHM OF LIFE

> *I tell you the truth, if you have faith as small as a mustard seed, you can say to this mountain, "Move from here to there," and it will move. Nothing will be impossible for you.*
>
> —Matthew 17:20

Quickly handing some money to the attendant for my gas, I glanced around the convenience store. In the back stood a video game, "Galaga." My favorite. Having some time, I decided to challenge this electronic gizmo. As I dropped in the first quarter, I remembered my highest score, which was around 22,000 points. Within the first two minutes of playing, I noticed something peculiar happening. My fine motor reflexes were incredible. Could it be the supplements I was taking? My hand and eye coordination was functioning at a remarkable rate compared to the past.

After about twenty minutes of playing, I glanced at the score: 76,000 points, unbelievable! I felt almost like a kid again. When the machine finally defeated me, I was again amazed at the final score, 97,000 points. Those supplements were powerful! Even though I had many other metabolic problems, my central and peripheral nervous systems were already under major construction. I felt like screaming to the world that I was coming back, I had been given a second chance and nothing could keep me down this time.

During the next several weeks, I began to sense a gradual increase in total body energy, as though a master switch were turned on at a great central power plant. My mind was much more alert, I was sleeping less and even had some energy left at the end of the day. Even my sex drive was coming back. After years of sporadic functioning due to diabetes, hypoglycemia, adrenal and liver dysfunction and polycythemia, this system was finally starting to function again.

One Friday, I began the procedure for my second gallbladder-liver flush. I had tried one a couple of months earlier but did not get any significant results! Just a few very small lentil-sized green stones. Two hours after lunch, I ingested two tablespoons of Epsom salts with a couple of glasses of water. Two hours later came the coffee detox with a half cup of Epsom salts mixed in. This loosens up the smooth muscles of the internal organs and stimulates the liver and gallbladder. I fasted until bedtime, then drank half a cup of pure extra virgin olive oil to stimulate the gallbladder and liver and for the bile duct to expand and contract strongly, dumping accumulated metabolic debris, gallstones, and chemicals.

Laying on my right side in bed, I began to sweat and shiver. My gallbladder area was cramping severely, and I wanted to puke! Then around midnight, after only an hour or so of sleep, we got a call from the hospital. Cathy's great aunt was in the emergency room. She had a large tumor in the abdomen, and it seemed that it was growing at an exponential rate. We had known for months that she had cancer, and she actually was doing pretty good, but there were times when the tumor would grow and cause her a lot of pain.

When we arrived in the small emergency room at Winfield Hospital, her aunt's voice could be heard way down in the lobby. She was moaning terribly, which actually sounded about the way that I felt. With a high fever, chills, and migrating aches and pains, I lay down on the couch in the lobby as Cathy assessed her aunt's condition. After two hours, it was decided there was nothing more that we could do, so we went home. The only thing the hospital could do was give her some strong drugs to help ease the pain. The way I felt, I could have used a few of those drugs myself!

All night I tossed and turned, occasionally waking Cathy. My dreams were in vivid color but all nightmares! The toxicity levels of my blood were extremely high because of the biochemical debris being released from the gallbladder and liver.

One dream took place in a huge room which appeared to be an ancient latrine with open pits in the ground overflowing with urine and fecal material! I could smell the toxins as I walked beside the cesspools, trying desperately to find a way out. Dream after dream engulfed me as I endured that first *effective* gallbladder-liver flush! As each dream became stranger and nastier, I assumed that by morning light, I would surely be dead!

When the sun finally began to beam through our terrace window, I knew that the nightmares were over. Pouring myself out of bed, I felt a sudden urge to let my bowels release themselves *forever*! Half stepping toward the bathroom, I felt as though I had been beaten up at some point in the night. My body felt like one huge bruise, and my head pounded exactly like one hangover that I experienced back in 1974, in the Marines, after gulping down way too many rum and cokes!

After preparing my morning detox coffee, I sank down in my easy chair for a few moments of silent meditation. When I finished, I picked up a book that I was almost finished reading, *The Shroud of Turin*. Could this actually have been the shroud that Christ was draped with before his resurrection? This was still another mystery behind the teachings of Christianity.

With the coffee brewed and cooled, I started the detox procedure. Laying there, I was not prepared for what was about to take place! The previous night was rough but I was still alive, I was thankful for that.

After expelling the coffee, I was astounded by what was passed! Some were the size of golf balls, and there were several hundred of them! Cathy didn't believe me until she saw for herself. Some of the gallstones were metallic green, some dark green but the largest ones, about nine in all, were white! They ranged from the size of a pea to that of a golf ball!

Cathy was amazed! She had worked on the oncology ward for years and had never seen anything quite like this. Obviously, these stones had been forming over the past several years. In addition, many toxins had been hiding around, inside and under each of those stones. The white stones were probably milk based, as my extreme milk intolerance had been a problem all of my life. In fact, in 1974, when I began serious bodybuilding in the Marine Corps, I had taken a milk-based protein drink that caused many of my metabolic problems. These stones obviously were never detected although I had been tested and x-rayed several times from 1975 to 1985! My liver dysfunction along with all of my other metabolic deficiencies and malignancy were surely connected to this phenomena!

When breakfast was over, I called Dr. Kelley in Dallas and told him what happened. He wasn't too surprised. Because of my rare condition, he felt that almost anything was possible. We discussed all of the thousands of needless gallbladder surgeries performed every day, and how metabolic therapy could help so many people with any type of degenerative condition.

After our conversation, I thought about the methods used for cancer patients in most hospitals. After being diagnosed, a patient was sometimes given a certain amount of time to live. To me, that seemed like signing a death certificate. It is sad and disturbing that disease is always looked upon as being hopeless and negative. I saw this disease as a wake-up call. A second chance to change my lifestyle and rebuild my body, mind, spirit, and life. With the mega nutritional help of this program and varied forms of detoxification, I could finally have control of my own life, mental and physical well-being.

One evening while thumbing through the paper for a job, the phone rang. When I answered, an old familiar voice said hello. I couldn't place the voice until he told me where he worked. It was Steve Dreiling, an old high school friend that now was the agency manager for the Farm Bureau Insurance company in Winfield.

"How would you like a job, Curtis?" Surprised, I hesitated and stated that my insurance days were over. But after twenty minutes of convincing, I finally agreed to meet with him and take a "personality test" as a prerequisite for a sales position. Actually, I enjoyed taking any type of personality test, as my emphasis in college was on psychometric testing in the psychology department. I tested all of my friends with the MMPI, Myers-Briggs-Introvert-Extravert Tests, IQ tests and so forth.

After arriving at his office, we chatted about our high school days in Great Bend. Then he passed a check to me, stating that it was his monthly renewal check, written on business a few years ago. Glancing at it, I handed it back to him nodding my head, indicating that was nice. Looking at me a bit puzzled, he handed it back to me, asking me to take a closer look at it. Again, I glanced at the check, which I *thought* was for $2,800. Gasping, I bolted to my feet and shook my head as my jaw dropped.

"You're kidding right? $28,000 in one month's time?"

"Curtis, that's after six years in the business. Those numbers are very realistic for you also. You could possibly become an agency manager during the next few years." He definitely had my attention now.

Scoring high on the personality test, I agreed to work for this insurance company. Eventually, I was to be licensed in homeowners and auto insurance along with my current life and health insurance license.

Because of my affiliation with the Methodist Church, I was asked to teach vacation Bible school at the end of the summer. It turned out to be a terrific challenge, as it reminded me of my teenage years growing up in a house full of nine kids! This small town community was a great place for kids to grow up in, contrary to life on the big city streets for kids in other parts of the country.

With training under my belt for the insurance company, my goal was to eventually lead the company in sales. I wanted to be the best. Deep down I knew that fighting this disease wouldn't be easy, but my newfound energy gave me an optimism I had never known. My health was slowly coming back, at times in spurts, so I wanted to utilize each and every ounce of energy to get ahead. Just as they had conditioned us in the Marine corps to "lead, follow, or get out of the way!"

That summer, I sported a rich tan and dropped five pounds, although I was pretty skinny already! I started to feel like I was in my twenties again! Even my libido was coming back! I also had begun training in Dallas to become a metabolic therapist, as it was Dr. Kelley's *final* course that he was teaching. I wanted to become part of this elite group of therapists scattered throughout nine different countries. He had trained several hundred in his career, and I wanted to be part of this scientific team, a group that was easily at least a hundred years ahead of the orthodox medical community!

Although my strength was slowly coming back, I still had many months of rebuilding and metabolic debris to get rid of. Every few days, my body would expel mucus that had been forming for the past twenty to twenty-five years. It was heavenly to actually breathe again! I had suffered from asthma and allergies from birth, and for the first time in years I could breathe freely and deeply without coughing! As my immune system strengthened, all of the metabolic imbalances were gradually correcting themselves. This was what Dr. Kelley spoke of when referring to nonspecific metabolic therapy. Each system would rebuild itself, in a hierarchical fashion, from the inside out, and from head to toe. Thus cancer, and all other degenerative diseases, were only *symptoms* of a more complex metabolic dysfunction. Quite the opposite of what we were taught in any premed classes in undergraduate school.

I began training in the summer of 1985 in Dallas at the International Health Institute. The classes were very extensive, covering all phases of the metabolic types, including their general and distinctive characteristics. Detoxification was a crucial area of study also, as this was the life-taker of a person fighting any degenerative disease. One can rebuild the body with all the supplements and foods in the world, but if the sloughed off cancer and other cells cannot be eliminated, the patient will die of toxicity! Just as in my case, I was rebuilding tissue at many different levels daily and helping the liver to get rid of the excess garbage with the coffee enema. But because of my already diseased liver and gallbladder, the process would take a longer period of time. Any and all tumors and growths would have to slowly be broken down by the pancreatic enzymes and then passed on through the liver to be expelled.

Specifically with cancer, the diet was created to rebuild organs, glands, and systems but reduce the animal protein intake as cancer is fueled by animal protein and sugar.

This process cannot be speeded up too quickly as the patient will not be able to handle the massive amount of broken down cancer cells waiting to be eliminated through the blood and then liver. That is why many chemotherapy patients die, not from the cancer, but rather the dead and dying cancer cells that cannot be expelled fast enough. A dynamic equilibrium must be maintained at all times throughout the metabolic rebuilding process.

As we studied further, I was amazed and saddened to learn that most fruits and vegetables were repeatedly sprayed with chemicals, such as pesticides, fungicides and herbicides to enhance their shelf life and increase production. These chemicals could not be washed off! Soaking them in apple cider vinegar helped, but they still contaminated the human body when ingested. Bananas were reported to be lethal! An ongoing study conducted recently linked pesticide spraying of bananas to leukemia in most of the natives that sprayed them! And they had to be sprayed several times, even when being loaded on ships for export. A slide then appeared in the slide presentation showing a small child sitting in a shopping cart chewing on the skin of a banana. My stomach began to churn as the old blood pressure elevated. I was angry, not only at the heavy use of chemicals, but at mankind. Man was destroying himself, all in the name of what? Profit? Was the almighty dollar really more important than a human life?

As the lecture continued, the truth about our country's ecological problems permeated my mind and soul—toxic waste dumps, contaminated waters, human cesspools, carcinogenic sprays. We are living in a chemical world. No longer could man evade this brutal reality. It truly was a miracle that I was still alive. My body wasn't just fighting a sewage backup, it was also fighting all of the many toxins it continually came in contact with! It made me mad. How could anyone's body remain balanced in such an unbalanced environment? What was the answer? Obviously I was sitting in the midst of it. Metabolic therapy seemed to hold the key to this complex and wide spreading problem linking man and his ever-eroding environment. Science still had much to learn about the human body. We were only beginning to scratch the surface.

As more statistics were given to us toward the end of this first school, I was again taken back. We were shown documents that focus on the risks of pesticides released by the National Academy of Sciences (NAS) and the Environmental Working Group (EWG). The NAS study points out the inadequacies of governmental regulations on pesticides and explains why children are at increased risk.

The EWG report analyzed 19,000 samples of fruits and vegetables over three years to get residue data and documents its findings in relation to children. The EWG report found that the average child exceeds his or her lifetime cancer risk by the first birthday, based on exposure to residues of eight pesticides which were found on the food studied. Obviously, the food choices you make now will impact your child's health *for life*!

The Environmental Protection Agency (EPA) estimates pesticides—some cancer causing—contaminate the ground water in thirty-eight states, polluting the primary source of drinking water for more than *half* the country's population.

Many pesticides approved for use by the EPA were registered long before extensive research linking these chemicals to cancer and many other diseases had been established. Now the EPA considers that 60 percent of all herbicides, 90 percent of all fungicides and 30 percent of all pesticides are carcinogenic. The bottom line is that pesticides are poisons designed to kill living organisms and are harmful to humans.

A National Cancer Institute study found that farmers exposed to herbicides had a six times greater risk than nonfarmers of contracting cancer. In California, reported pesticide poisonings among farm workers have risen an average of 14 percent per year since 1973, and doubled between 1975 and 1985. Organic farming seemed to be the only resolution to this growing epidemic. The soil had to be rebuilt and nourished as it was in the beginning, long before the chemicals had been invented!

Toward the end of this first series of schools, we focused on the psychological and physical components of the twelve basic metabolic types. As we talked about the sympathetic dominant, I thought about my wife. Her blood chemistry tended to be a bit more "acidic" most of the time, which coincided with her body type which was similar to the sympathetic. She was thin and tended to be quite logical, hard-driven, and a bit temperamental at times. Her diet leaned toward high alkaline foods such as green leafy vegetables and fruits, with occasional grains and some poultry. Conversely, my metabolic program was designed to pull my acidic blood chemistry more alkaline, toward a parasympathetic dominance. Although my body was quite lean, I was genetically a strong parasympathetic, that had completely flipped metabolic types. I had blown out the parasympathetic side and was functioning erratically on the sympathetic side. My diet and all of the supplements was designed to rebuild the parasympathetic side while my blood chemistry became a bit more alkaline as it shifted in that direction. I was eating very minimal amounts of animal proteins, purines, liver, beef and a variety of root vegetables instead of the green leafy type. I also had begun to experiment with many different types of grains, lentils, and legumes. Carrot juice was now a part of my daily regimen, with organic freeze dried powdered liver stirred in. This was a tremendous blood and liver healer! I also had to keep my daily protein levels at a bare minimum for the first few months, so as not to feed the malignancy. Over the next several years, Dr. Kelley took a much more stricter approach to ingesting *any* type of animal protein, until the tumors were definitely showing reduction!

I was becoming more even-tempered, relaxed, creative and had even started to gain a little weight evenly throughout my body. I was currently a type 3, which was the bottom number of the metabolic chart. That was why Dr. Kelley stated that I was "too sick to have cancer." As a type 3, I was clear at the bottom of the metabolic chart, whereas most cancer victims functioned at the type 4 level. Cancer was only one malady that I was fighting, combined with diabetes, polycythemia and several related metabolic digestive disorders. I had a long way to go to the top which was a 10, if that was even possible!

Reviewing my notes, I closed my notebook and joined the class in an open discussion of the past few days material. Much was covered, but many more months were ahead of us. This program was constantly being updated, tested and retested. With thousands of patients already to his credit, Dr. Kelley definitely had his hands full most of the time.

Then, during our last break, I pondered the idea of a world with far less degenerative disease! What a thought. If this program were incorporated into mainstream medicine, it could actually happen. But what about the money factor? Today, if I walked into the hospital and got on the liver transplant wagon, a price tag could almost be stuck on my forehead. And how much would that be? $250,000-$400,000, or maybe even more! That's one heck of a lot of money for an organ that was donated by someone for *free* to the hospital to replace in someone else! Somehow that just didn't make much sense. You would think that the family of the organ donated would get a big chunk of that money, wouldn't you? I mean, let's call a spade a spade here. And then there's metabolic therapy. At an initial cost of a few hundred dollars to run a program and purchase all of the supplements, there's no comparison. To rebuild a liver, or any other organ would not be profitable at all, period.

So guess what, I think I already answered my own question. Would this or any program similar ever be incorporated into every hospital and clinic in America? Probably not. I wanted to believe that was not true, but today most hospitals were deeply entrenched in corporate America, and corporate America wasn't built on cutting profits drastically. And besides, what about the mighty prescription pad. Would nutritional supplements ever equal the power of the drugs taken every day in this country? Of course, if they were to *control* nutritional supplements like a drug, and charge incredibly ridiculous prices, then it could maybe become a possibility.

With the last few people saying goodbye, an old memory flashed back to the anatomy classroom at Marymount College in Salina, Kansas, in the fall of 1981. It was my last semester before an early graduation, and I had been working on the cadaver for the last two semesters. Our instructor, Dr. Zeakes had just finished an in depth lecture on the reproductive systems, and we were faced with the chapter on metabolism. As my friend Mick thumbed through the text, he whistled. "Man this is some heavy biochemistry. The krebbs cycle, glycolisis and some deep physiology. It looks pretty tough!"

Nodding my head in agreement, I looked up just as Doc started to speak again. "Class, I have some good news and bad news today. The good news is, because of its complexity and nature, we will be bypassing the chapter on metabolism. The bad news is, we do not even study this in medical school. In fact, to date, this still is not required to be taught or learned in medical school."

"Thank God," Mick mumbled under his breath as the rest of the class let out a sigh of relief. But although I was also somewhat relieved, I knew that this information was the key to my current health maladies. If only I could someday understand how the body utilized nutrients, I could help it to correct it's deficiencies.

After class, I stopped Dr. Zeakes and shared my concern about medical school and the fact that I would *not* learn how to rebuild the body. "Curtis, that is a decision you will have to make. Give it some thought and be honest with yourself." As Dr. Zeakes walked away, I bowed my head, shuffling down the long quiet basement corridor at Marymount College. How could I pursue a career where my thirst for truth would never be quenched?

The answer was obvious, keep looking and sidestep the medical school idea. With the decision made, I already felt a sense of control over my life and health.

Bidding a farewell to Dr. Kelley and the rest of our metabolic research class, I made my way to the parking lot. I was again thankful for this unique and gratifying opportunity. Not only was I starting to finally rebuild my body, but I was also learning exactly how it was taking place and why. What better subject to experiment on than myself!

Driving back to Winfield from Dallas was a pleasant but long journey. I had a lot of studying to do during the next several months, plus refresher courses in biology, genetics and biochemistry. My memory and mental abilities were increasing at an uncanny rate, which encouraged me to pursue this schooling and become certified. I was eager to help "save the world."

At 6:00 a.m. the next morning, I awoke and prepared my coffee. Having some extra energy, I decided to do a few sit-ups before doing my detox. This, combined with a few different forms of stretching exercises, was the extent of my daily workout. I wanted to start running again and lifting weights, but that wouldn't be for at least another year. These spurts of energy were a little misleading as my adrenal glands were rebuilding and constantly repairing. I had lived on adrenalin for so many years that whenever there was some extra, I would immediately use it up and then feel exhausted. I had to learn how to maintain balance within all of the systems of my body. My dream of competitive bodybuilding was still only a dream that may never materialize. I had to rebuild my liver, adrenals, and several other organs and systems before that could even be a mere possibility.

Most of the day was spent at the office doing paperwork and calling a few prospects for life insurance. I had already won the county sales contest and took second place in the state for most production written in a five-week period. I enjoyed the income, but the work was a little dry. It involved a lot of mind work but not the same kind as our school on metabolic typing. I already was planning on a major career change although the insurance industry was a stable business to settle in to. I knew that change was gradually taking place. It was evident whenever I would write up a policy of any type, the conversation would turn to metabolic therapy and how I was doing on the program. I'd spend an hour writing up a policy and two more talking about this incredible science I had discovered.

That evening, I began studying the metabolic training manual and started a course in biochemistry and genetics. After putting in a ten-hour day, I still had some energy left for a few more hours. It was as if I had a new body and brain. Old neuronal cells were coming to life again, the cobwebs being swept away with other garbage accumulated internally over the past thirty years. Not only was my mind clearer and quicker, but physically I felt like I did about three years ago. It was as if I was slowly going back in time, regaining certain sensory perceptions and senses. Even old thought patterns were coming alive. This sparked my first concrete idea for a new "theory of personality." I had spoken with Dr. Kelley about this idea, and he agreed that it was a valid one that should definitely be expounded upon. I remembered Dr. Sheldon's theory of somatotyping, way back during the 1940s. This old personality theory had set the prototype for Dr. Kelley's advanced paradigm of the twelve metabolic types. The three modes of the autonomic nervous system were seen by Dr. Sheldon in the three major body types. Eventually I wanted to study the correlations and give credit to Dr. Kelley's extensive work. With my background in psychology and especially physiological psychology, I decided to put this ambition on the back burner until I had obtained my MS from the institute. Then depending on how the research had evolved, I would start working on my doctorate degree. It could focus on this *new* theory of personality, future clients, and also myself.

After dinner, I leafed through my own program and read about the psychological changes that were going to take place. I could already feel my temperament and general personality changing to a more goal-oriented, social individual. It also stated that sometimes, as a person regains one's health, old relationships die and new ones evolve. That would seem logical considering the tremendous difference between a sick, weak, toxic person compared with a vibrant, robust, energetic individual. It would be like night and day. Reading this made me consider my relationship with Cathy. I could already sense that we were growing apart, although that had started before I had discovered this program. I wanted to bridge the gap we were experiencing but wasn't sure how to do it. She was very supportive of this science, in fact she had initially encouraged me to do a program. She was pretty smart. There were times when she used to laugh at me when I would buy supplements at the health food store, which only made me mad. But before beginning this program, she told me that she was laughing because there was no way humanly possible that I could know what my body needed nutritionally. Especially if I was fighting any type of degenerative disease. She compared it to giving the *wrong* drug to a cancer patient when she worked on the oncology ward. That patient could possibly *die*. Concentrated supplements could also do extreme *good* or could affect an individual *severely negatively*. She was very impressed with metabolic typing and felt it took a logical and scientific approach to finding out what each individual person needed. It wasn't a guessing game as played by some doctors she had worked with. She also didn't speak too highly of several she had worked for over the past few years.

The months that followed passed quickly, each day bringing me closer to a stronger, self-sustaining, *whole* body. Some days were good and some were not so good. At times, instead of extremely high blood pressure, it would actually drop lower than it had ever been recorded at. This indicated that the blood flow and supply to the liver and gallbladder was finally coming back to a half way normal state! When this would occur, a feeling of "goopy sick" would accompany it, which was another sign of major repair taking place at the cellular level and a high level of toxicity. I learned to realize that this was only temporary, and that it was a good time to cycle off the supplements for a few days.

The weekend before my next trip to Dallas, I experienced another detoxification procedure called the "purge and fast." This was designed to clean out each cell and flush the lymph system, kidneys, and the liver. It was easy to do and gave me a temporary boost in energy. To initiate this one day cleanse, I squeezed six lemons, twelve oranges and six grapefruits with a gallon of purified water. I then drank two glasses of water mixed with magnesium sulfate (Epsom salts). For the next twenty-four hours, I sipped on this drink. It was also called an alkalinizing punch, as it tended to pull one's blood chemistry a bit alkaline, although it sounded like it was an acidic drink.

After a day of this drink and no food, I felt a surge of energy and a mental clarity beyond what I had already experienced to this point. This, combined with the coffee detox really jump-started my liver and lymph systems to dump accumulated metabolic debris at an elevated level.

This would be my last trip to Dallas for a few weeks. I had been traveling back and forth for several months and was close to finishing school.

Most of the material we covered this time focused on the structure and genetic origin of each metabolic type. Like a blood type, your genetic metabolic type was set, but it could and often did change as the body became deficient and diseased. Once it had changed, this was considered to be the "functional" type, or the type that was currently functioning for that individual. Once that had taken place, the goal of the program was to bring the client back up the "spiral of health" to the original genetic type. I could use myself as a prime example of this metabolic type shift. Before this program, I was basically functioning like a sympathetic, I couldn't digest fats, any dairy products, and even had a hard time assimilating any type of protein such as beef, pork or even chicken. My skin, hair and even my personality was very dry. Instead of my right brain being dominant, I was functioning in the left brain mode most of the time, like a sympathetic.

During the past few months, my body was repairing the parasympathetic side of my autonomic nervous system. This meant that my right brain was kicking in again and those organs that were parasympathetic dominant were beginning to function at a much higher level again, as when I was a young boy. My posterior pituitary gland, lungs, pancreas, adrenal cortex, liver, gall bladder, stomach, duodenum, small and large intestine, digestive, immune, lymphatic, respiratory, and excretory systems were all functioning like they had years earlier. Also my fat, carbohydrate, cholesterol, protein and starch metabolism were all functioning at a much higher level. My skin and hair were actually getting some oil again and my nails were growing like crazy. Even my voice was dropping a few notches as I was finally assimilating calcium at the cell level, along with my hormones rebalancing.

Now I could sweat at the drop of a hat, compared to all those years that I would rarely sweat even after a grueling two-hour workout. It felt so good for all of my internal organs to finally function like a normal human being. I had been constipated off and on for several years and was constantly plagued with gas at both ends. As all of my organs and systems regenerated I was amazed, but it was the physical growth of my bone and muscle structure that was truly amazing. Although I had been on this program for several months, without even touching any weights,

I was still very lean and was actually gaining a little muscle mass. After sharing this with Dr. Kelley, he offered the logical answer to this phenomena. After ten years of religiously pumping iron, running cross country in college and basically killing myself, the trillions of cells in all of my muscles and bones were virtually impregnated with a memory of all this activity. But because of massive nutritional starvation at the cellular level, the opportunity to reach maximum growth potential was never reached.

This, combined with a milk intolerance, a severe blow to the head in high school, years of alcohol abuse and a slight hormone imbalance, had set the stage for my present condition. So now at thirty-one, I was starting the rebuilding process that should have finished in my late teens or early twenties. I was still five feet nine inches tall and weighed 155 pounds. After ten years of pumping iron, eating all kinds of protein and protein drinks, one would assume that I would be much bigger and healthier than I turned out to be! (During the next few years my bone and muscle growth was actually incredible. I reached a point that even Dr. Kelley could not have known, but you'll find that out later in my story!)

During one of our many slide presentations, we discovered how internal organs could vary dramatically in size and shape from person to person. This attributed to some clients needing up to ten times more of a specific nutrient compared to another person, especially if any degenerative condition were present! There could even be a tenfold variation in hydrochloric acid from one stomach to the next. No wonder my own metabolic rate had stepped up so much.

The enzymes combined with the different stages of hydrochloric acid I was taking were finally helping my stomach to work again. It was functioning at an optimum level. It was almost like a kid's stomach, I was eating everything in sight and still looking slim and trim! After living on Mylanta and antacids for a decade, it was great to stop taking all the drugs.

That evening was dedicated to the viewing of a special report filmed by the BBC in Europe about a few alternative therapies for cancer and other degenerative diseases. We watched the uncut version and were told that the final clip had been grossly edited to the point that three cancer patients had been completely left out of the final tape! All three had terminal cancer at one time in the form of Hodgkin's disease and leukemia. Seven years had passed and all were completely recovered. Their stories were fascinating, as I remembered reading about them in Dr. Kelley's book, *Metabolic Ecology*. Most of the show seemed to lean toward misleading the public about all forms of alternative therapies. And we thought the media in America was jaded!

The more I learned, the angrier I got. The power of the AMA and our government was choking the life out of all forms of alternative therapies! Granted, some were a bit unorthodox, but there also were others that worked and helped people to finally help themselves. Obviously, holistic medicine, in particular that which dealt with degenerative diseases, needed to be researched more extensively and taught to the masses here in America! All other forms of medicine practiced by physicians, such as emergency, surgical and certain therapies would always be needed, but teaching the general population how to take care of their own health was truly becoming a necessity. We were paying all of the wrong people for help. It showed in increasing insurance rates due to inflated medical charges and malpractice insurance.

Instead of transplanting an organ, the patient could learn to rebuild it. It would take time and discipline, but is that so much to ask of someone? Especially if the rebuilding process will help them to become a better, more productive human being? Think about that for a moment.

As this final class ended, I made the decision to write my book. I would start soon and try to finish it within the next four years. I would have to extend it for this period of time in order to experience the many levels of rebuilding that Dr. Kelley had explained to me would take place.

Before we adjourned for the weekend, Dr. Kelley asked us if we had any particular questions about everything that we had gone over. When the final question was asked, I slowly raised my hand, pondering the question that was heavy on my mind. As usual, I was always trying to look far down the road, anticipating many of the *mega trends* that our country was going to experience over the next few decades!

"Dr. Kelley, cancer hits about one out of every five people today here in America, isn't that correct?"

"Yes, that is the current statistic for 1985."

"Well, given that cancer is a pancreatic enzyme deficiency, combined with a slight hormonal imbalance, wouldn't it be accurate to say that over the next few decades, cancer here in America will grow almost *exponentially*?"

As Dr. Kelley reached for his calculator, a few of the doctors and students in the class mumbled to each other about my question, obviously quite curious to hear his response. As I was taught in undergraduate school all questions are *valid*, even if they do seem a bit unusual at the time.

After a few minutes of silence, his response took us *all* by surprise! "Over the next twenty-five to thirty years, cancer here in this country will affect one out of every two people!" *Gasping*, the entire class was taken back by his answer! With many hands suddenly shooting into the air, Dr. Kelley began to explain and validate his numbers. Although it did seem surreal at the time, Dr. Kelley's prediction, turned out to be yet another *extremely* accurate realistic set of numbers that no one in the medical community could have known or been aware of so many years in advance!

As fall transformed into winter, the leaves were gradually covering our entire yard, front and back. I had picked up my twelve-string guitar again and was practicing it whenever I had a few spare minutes. Our minister at the Methodist church had asked me to perform on Sunday, so I had to try and build a few callouses on my fingertips again.

After my performance, I was invited to speak and play at another function at the local university for a group called the Baha'i faith. I didn't know much about them except for the fact that they were involved with the pursuit of world peace, a pretty tough mission to undertake.

The following Wednesday, after my performance, the sponsors thanked me again for sharing my faith in God and my music with the group. It was an honor to be there and share something with others that was very personal and real to me. It was kind of strange, but as my body and mind were healing, my spirit was also experiencing a certain type and level of growth and regeneration. As the *temple* was cleaned out and rebuilt, the spirit seemed to have more room and ability to function at a higher and stronger level!

With the arrival of winter, I spent much of my time driving up to Manhattan, Kansas, where the home office was for our insurance agency. There was always another school to attend, as if I wasn't already overloading my brain cells on metabolic typing! But it all seemed to come quite easily. For the first time in years, I was actually hungry for knowledge again. It felt *fantastic*!

Insurance people were a great crowd to hang with but they did tend to party a little too hard at times! My drinking days of the Marine Corps were far behind me, besides, as my liver was rebuilding, I could not tolerate even the slightest amount of alcohol. But I did enjoy the social life and the dancing. Just as my mother once said, she would rather dance than eat as a kid, I also had felt that way during my late teens and twenties.

After each trip to Dallas or Manhattan, my lower back would go out. This was due to a gymnastics injury I sustained during my senior year of high school. I had fallen off the high bar while attempting a *giant*. After spinning completely around 360 degrees *three* times, my spotters said I dismounted *perfectly*—but upside down! I had become completely disoriented, as the spinning around affected my sense of balance. I had forgotten to also put any handguards on, so it ripped the skin off my palms as I spun around. I shot past them, missing the mat and landed upside down on the left frontal lobe of my head on the gym floor! This compressed my spine like an accordion! Then like a dummy, two days later I flew off a 25-foot embankment on my new Suzuki dirt bike with it landing *directly* on my back!

After again seeing the same doctor in the emergency room, he told me that I was lucky not to have broken my back and neck. He also said that there could have been some damage to the base of my brain which could cause some growth, hormonal, and metabolic disorders later in life. Of all the doctors I have seen in my lifetime, he was the closest to knowing the severity of this accident.

When I would return from each trip, I would visit good old Dr. B. He had just finished chiropractic school and could always fix me right up. I was finally beginning to feel like a man again, not an ape. I hadn't been able to touch my toes without bending my knees for years!

When I had let Dr. B. see my X-rays of my back, he gasped, "Your spine has almost grown together in the lumbar area, Curtis. You've got a lot of repair work to do here!" Nodding in agreement, I explained a little more about metabolic therapy to Dr. B. From what Dr. Kelley had told me, the calcium deposits in my spine and fingers would break down and dissolve over the next one to two years.

"I'll set you up for some more X-rays in a few months, Curtis, and we'll see how things look then." As he finished checking my adrenal glands, he adjusted my back and neck. "Your right foot is about an eighth of an inch shorter than your left, did you know that?"

"I wasn't sure if it was shorter, but I know that I was supposed to wear braces as a child because of a 'serpentine' leg. But Grandma said that I would eventually grow out of it, in fact I still hold two track records from junior high school!"

"Well, I'll put a lift in your right shoe for the next several months and I think we can fix that uneven leg."

"Sounds good to me, Doc, I'm trying to rebalance the rest of my body, so go to it!"

While chatting with Doc's wife and paying my bill, I noticed a sign on the wall that stated, "Did you know that your chiropractor has had more hours of training in some areas than an MD?" I didn't even know that. I read the comparisons out loud as I skimmed over the chart. This was quite a surprise!

> Anatomy and Physiology Medical-508 hours
> Chiropractic-520 hours
> Physiology Medical-362 hours
> Chiropractic-420 hours
> Bacteriology Medical-114 hours
> Chiropractic-130 hours
> Diagnosis Medical-324 hours

Chiropractic-420 hours
Neurology Medical-112 hours
Chiropractic-320 hours
X-ray Medical-148 hours
Chiropractic-217 hours

"Sure," agreed Dr. B. with a little smirk. "Most people just are not aware of that, so we like to remind them. Chiropractic has come a long way in the last ten years."

As we discussed metabolic therapy, he agreed that it should be incorporated by the medical community but stated that it would take some time and political clout to create such a change in the present system! I knew he was right. It was only a few years ago that the entire chiropractic community was labeled as quacks and treated like they were one step above a sorcerer or charlatan! My, my, how times were a changing!

As the snow fell and my body continued to change, I studied for my final exam in metabolic science and finished a course in biology and biochemistry. I was also brushing up on my anatomy and physiology. Many things had already changed since my college days. Science was constantly updating new data, through experimentation, intensive study and research.

With December in the air, I shivered as another blanket of snow covered our little town. It would remind me of the winters I spent in the country at Grandma's. They always seemed more majestic there. The Flint Hills stood like a backdrop, softly calling me, whispering, telling me stories about the animals and people that had once lived in their midst, a long time ago. They stood like silent guardians, making sure that all was well and in order.

Their trees glistened like alabaster in the winter and their streams flowed like liquid crystal. I would often sit on a distant hill and ponder about the awesome powers of God and nature. Was this life only a beginning, a stepping stone to something much greater? Was space infinite or did it stop somewhere? Why was I still alive and living here instead of somewhere else? The entire concept of life puzzled me at a very early age. It was so multidimensional.

I was also disappointed with the things man had done with life—abused it, enslaved it, bought it, sold it, even took it away. Man seemed to be trying very hard to play God's role and he was continually failing. He needed to stop and look at himself, the heavens and all of life. He must reconsider all the decisions he has made and would make again, for they affect us all. Each life touches another as we travel through time and space. Our energy never ceases but transforms itself from one type of molecule to another. Just as snow becomes rain, then nourishes the earth, our souls become part of the cosmos as they leave something old to join something new and different.

The circadian rhythm of life is infinite. Like the movement of the earth and sun, the body and spirit also follow a path, a winding path that one day will return the spirit to its origin, a path that we all must walk sometimes together—but many times—alone.

# 4

# TRANSITION

*Stand firm then with the belt of truth buckled around your waist, with the breastplate of righteousness in place.*

—Ephesians 6:14

With Christmas 1985 approaching, business at the office was booming. Our agency was trying to win the state contest, which would end December 31st. I was still having some heavy toxicity days on my program, but my health was taking on a *totally* new dimension. The gray in my hair was all turning dark brown again and my skin was smoother and moister than it had been since my early teenage years. My oil and sweat glands were finally working normally again also!

My allergies had also almost disappeared, except for my intolerance for any milk products. We were doing some extensive research at the institute pertaining to this malady and found that a condition known as candida albicans overgrowth was a by-product of this allergy. If a person did not have enough of the friendly lactobacillus bacteria in the intestinal tract, this otherwise semi friendly pseudo-parasite-bacteria-type fungus would proliferate and eventually compromise one's delicate immune system.

Since I had been milk intolerant from birth, this condition was a major battle for me to constantly overcome. Because of my weak immune system, years of antibiotics and a compromised diseased liver, this parasite would at times grow exponentially, if given the correct environment. Once this happened, it would travel in the lymph system, the mucus membranes and could even change its structure and enter into the blood stream. If this happened, many severe physiological and even psychological symptoms could manifest themselves.

By combining the correct supplements with a diet that restricted such things as sugar, alcohol, fermented foods, dairy products, monosodium glutamate, some fruits, and anything containing large amounts of yeast, even some breads, I was learning to control this microscopic alien! The blurry vision, anxiety, sugar cravings, chronic fatigue, mental confusion and intestinal bloating and discomfort would recede when I followed the protocol closely.

Nutritional Science was just beginning to understand this condition which seemed to be epidemic throughout our western society. Everyone has this type of yeast within their gastrointestinal tract, but many people are afflicted with its overgrowth. Research was suggesting that chronic candida albicans overgrowth could cause many illnesses, such as multiple sclerosis, schizophrenia, multiple allergies, lupus, and many others related both to the body and the mind.

Lying on my left side, I began another day's detox. I had cut this procedure back to about five times per week unless I was really toxic. Thumbing through the Bible Cathy gave me for our anniversary, many ideas began to spring from its pages. This would be a great reference for the book I was about to start writing. For the last several thousand years in history, food, health and spirituality had been linked together. It had the market just about cornered on *truth*!

Drifting slowly back in time, I tried to picture the many events that had taken place in my life since my adventure in Los Angeles in the spring of 1979. That was a year to remember. After graduating from Barton County College with an AA in communications in Great Bend,

Kansas, I somehow got the notion to move to Los Angeles. I knew that I could stay with an old friend from Maine, so I sold my '73, Mach 1 Mustang, bought my mother's old 65 Ford Galaxy and drove to Los Angeles. With only $300 to my name, I was ready to take on the big city and "Be discovered."

The trip was great but it was a miracle that I made it in one piece! That Ford used more oil than gas, but it did survive the long haul. I topped the spectacular mountains east of Los Angeles just as the sun was rising. The blue of the ocean blended into the sky, like a huge majestic painting! It was breathtaking! Never before had I experienced such a moment in time. With my heart in my throat, I began the descent toward my new home, Los Angeles—"City of Angels."

When I reached the downtown area, the traffic mesmerized me. It was crazy, like ants trying to reach some destination during a thunderstorm! I finally found South Catalina street in the Vermont-Wilshire District, parked my car and strolled toward the apartment building. It was still early and not many people were moving around. When the elevator stopped at the third floor, I quickly stepped out into the hall and almost ran into my friend Linda! "Why Curtis Kuhn, what in the world are you doing here?" As we hugged I explained to her what I had done.

"I would have called but I knew you all liked surprises!"

Linda and I had dated when I was stationed in Brunswick, Maine, in the Marine Corps. But after my time was up, in the fall of 1975, I had moved back to Kansas. We had kept in contact and had even talked of marriage, but we weren't really sure of what we both wanted to do with our lives. So she had then moved to LA with her sister and cousin and now was living with a tennis pro.

After unpacking my meager bags and meeting her boyfriend, I decided to see this city again under more relaxed circumstances. I had spent a weekend in Hollywood while in combat training school, but that didn't count. Now I was a civilian, and a soon to be actor-musician. I was ready for the challenge!

My first few days in LA were great with sightseeing, touring Disney Land and Universal Studios. There was so much to do! Being with

Linda again brought back many good memories of our relationship and all of the people I had met in Maine. I had very fond memories of all the times we had spent out dancing in Lewiston and the foggy moonlit nights we had shared together near the ocean, feeling the breeze in our hair and the fine mist of the Atlantic Ocean. She was a woman that I would never forget, her beauty still radiant, with that little sparkle still dancing in her soft brown eyes.

She knew me so well. Every little emotion, each memory of us together still made my body tingle. It were as though our souls had met years before our flesh did. But time had passed, and she was happy, I could also see that in her eyes, and I was happy for her. She had a great job, a good man and lived in LA. What else could she ask for!

After a few days of tourism, I decided to find a job. I wanted to get my own apartment and start pursuing an acting and singing career. With only an associate degree in communications, I knew that I wasn't qualified for many jobs. I wanted to break into the entertainment world but didn't know beans about the industry, so I hit the streets and played it by ear. Reluctantly, after another week, I finally took a security job in Beverly Hills, at the Wilshire Estina, a fancy high roller condominium complex on Wilshire Boulevard. I worked the night shift from 8:00 p.m. till 6:00 a.m. The doormen were from British Honduras and smoked hash a lot but were still pretty cool.

The cars people owned in that complex were incredible! 1940s Rolls Royces, Jaguars, Mercedes, almost everyone in mint condition. As I walked the perimeter each hour, I began to envy the amount of money a person would have to make just to own such an incredible piece of machinery. Obviously LA was already enticing me to someday become as successful as all of the people that lived here!

During the day I scanned the newspaper looking for acting or singing auditions, anything to get my foot in the door. Finally, I got an appointment with a video casting company. They would audition me on tape for two minutes and use it for directors in the movie industry. The next day, running ten minutes late, I opened the door to the office building on Hollywood Boulevard and wiped the sweat from my forehead. But just as I took my first step, a familiar face by the elevator caught my attention. We both stopped, stared at one another and pointed.

"Hey, you're a Marine, aren't ya?"

Taking off my mirror sunglasses, I answered. "Platoon 3069, right?"

"Private Kuhn, right?"

"Yeah, Compton, Brooklyn, New York, Golden Gloves, right?"

"Right. Kansas boy aren't ya?"

"Absolutely."

It was definitely an *uncanny* but most appreciated meeting. Chris and I were in the same platoon in 1973, during boot camp at San Diego. Now, six years later, we were both in LA pursuing acting and music careers. This just couldn't have been a mere coincidence. We had some catching up to do.

The video casting agency was a farce, but at least my meeting with Chris was positive. He knew all about the various casting magazines and how to get your foot in the entertainment door. Now I had a friend to struggle through the hard times with and believe me, they did get hard and lean! I could barely make the rent on my security salary and had to sell that old car for grocery money. But that was okay, I kind of liked taking the bus everywhere, it was affordable and very convenient.

I ate lots of Chinese food and drank only bottled water. It was common knowledge that the tap water was pretty funky! Come to think of it, it did smell like my toilet at times! My diet, combined with the pure drinking water, started a mysterious chain of physiological events that made me feel kind of alive again!

I dropped ten pounds of excess fluid, didn't experience hypoglycemia as much and my energy levels increased. My circulation also greatly increased, but that was due to walking several miles each day. Sometimes, what little money I had left went for food, so I'd walk instead of taking the bus. And talk about suntan. People were always asking me questions in Spanish, thinking I was part Mexican. Each morning after work, I would fall asleep on the roof of my apartment complex, as the sun was pretty easy to take.

Even though we were poor, Chris and I always had a good time. We'd go dancing at "Circus" in Hollywood for hours. It was a huge disco that was all dance floor. Being a Kansas farm boy, this scene was definitely a new experience for me. But I loved the music and met a lot of pretty unique and interesting people there.

Chris Compton and I spent hours talking about our future careers in showbiz. He was dedicating his life to it. But I was just giving it a fling. In the back of my mind, I knew that college was still calling me, enticing me to quench my thirst for knowledge. It burned day and night, never letting me forget its importance. It seemed as though something mystical was behind it all, an energy I couldn't see but always felt deep within my mind and soul.

With an October chill in the air, I walked briskly to an evening rehearsal. I had finally been casted in a musical written by William Cousher, *Ice Cream Alley*. Not only that, but I was the only white member of the group and had a lead solo in the show. It was an African American musical, with its roots from their Motherland of Africa. It was my favorite type of music to sing, as all of my recitals in voice class were old spirituals. We had only two more rehearsals before we showcased for the LA Jazz Festival that took place downtown. This was an annual event. Our director was optimistic that a producer from New York would like his showcase enough to take it to Broadway. Everyone here had a dream, that was what Hollywood was all about.

The day I first auditioned for William actually turned out to be a bit unusual. I had seen the ad in the Hollywood Reporter, called and set the appointment, but somehow didn't realize that it was a musical with an African American theme, which called for an "entirely" Black cast. So when I arrived, he brought up this overlooked fact on my part. At first I apologized, but then, asked him if I could still audition. Scratching his head, he handed me some sheet music. Reluctantly, I scanned the music, then handed it back to him, stating that my sight reading skills were not that good yet. As he set the music down, I shuffled toward the window, cleared my throat and stated "I could do a song I sang for my final recital in voice class last semester, but without any music. It's an old spiritual."

Nodding his head, he smiled, stepped back a few feet and asked me the name of the song. "The Blind Man Stood on the Road and Cried," I blurted out, as I felt that old familiar internal nervous *monster* overtake my now stiffened body.

As I began to sing the song, I noticed that his arms were folded in front of him, but slowly they began to loosen and drop. Then when I got to the verse "These shoes I wear are the gospel shoes," I slipped off my sandals and took a step back. As I ended the song, he walked toward me with a big grin, shaking my hand and saying, " I believe you have the part, in fact I believe that you have the *lead* role and song."

That was a day that forever permeated my mind, body, and soul. This Kansas farm boy got his first gig in Hollywood. At least it was a beginning.

The day before our performance, I arrived at the studio early. Receiving no answer to my knock, I slowly opened the door. William was sitting crossed-legged in front of a statue of Buddha. Occasionally he rang a bell and chanted something in another language. Incense filled the room with a warm, flowery yet musky scent. I wanted to catch his attention but wasn't sure how. Instead, I drifted off into my own little world, enjoying the calmness of the moment. I was glad I had witnessed this event, it planted a seed in my soul that would again replenish my own Christian spiritual hunger.

When we did finally perform downtown, we all were excited, hoping that someone would want to take our show to Broadway. But unfortunately, it didn't quite make the cut. So as they say in Hollywood, "That's showbiz."

My next couple of weekends were still spent at the Circus disco in Hollywood, but as the mid-October air chilled my skin, I longed to go back home.

A week before I returned to Kansas, Chris and I took an overnight trip to Tijuana, Mexico. Like Las Vegas, this city partied all night long. We danced most of the night in several different clubs and watched the sun come up as we walked along the beach with two cute senoritas we had met earlier. It was truly a beautiful sight. The city was not very clean but this moment made up for all of that.

On our way back to LA, we stopped at the Marine Corps Recruit Depot in San Diego. Gazing across the massive parade deck we both heard that old familiar sound pounding in our ears. Eighty pairs of boots simultaneously hitting the ground, as though controlled by one body. This was the United States Marine Corps. Walking through the main gate, I saw those familiar words, "Semper Fidelis," Latin for "Always Faithful." Thirty minutes of old memories proved to be enough for the both of us. Those days were thankfully…gone forever.

When we got back, I gave my father a call. With only a few bucks to my name and three days till payday, I was desperate. I had never borrowed money from him before but this did seem like an emergency. Luckily, he was home and agreed to send enough money for bills and to catch a Greyhound home. Dad and I never talked much, I guess those early years with my grandparents had caused a gap between us. Hopefully, someday, we could become father and son again.

Two days before I returned to Kansas, I took a trip to Santa Monica. I loved the ocean and the different types of people that it attracted. The beach was usually crowded, but the gray October sky had thinned out the tourists and sunbathers. Only kids, a few scantily clad women, and some homeless people were left.

Strolling along the storefronts, I was impressed by the array of swimsuits and the bodies they barely clung to! California women weren't as modest as Midwestern girls! Turning my head, I scarcely missed a head-on collision with a gorilla! At least he looked like a gorilla, shorter than myself, but outweighing me by at least seventy pounds. Actually, he had a tremendous physique which was surely the result of years of pumping iron. As he bounced into the gym, I looked up at the marquee—"Gold's Gym." This was a pretty famous old place. Anybody that was somebody in the bodybuilding world could usually be found here.

Hesitant to walk in, I stepped slowly through the front door. The smell of sweat and grease pierced my nostrils, bringing back memories of all the gyms I had worked out in over the years. Scanning the area, I began to see familiar faces and bodies, the Metzner twins and Franco Columbou. I was hoping to spot Arnold Schwarzenegger, but no such luck. The energy of the place was electrifying.

My reluctance to speak was broken when the manager shook my hand and introduced himself. His easy manor made me feel right at home. As we walked around, several guys greeted me, shattering the tough stereotype I had planted in my brain. These guys were pretty down to earth. As I watched them work out, I yearned to someday possess such a body. I had trained almost religiously with weights for years but could never make any significant gains. I knew that my body had several metabolic disorders, but every time I saw a doctor, another malady would appear. It had gotten to the point that my trust in the medical profession was almost completely gone.

As I sat there with my head in my hands, I silently prayed. "Lord, if I can ever find out the origin of my physical problems, please help me to correct them and strengthen my body as they do here." Since I was fourteen, I had dreamed about becoming a world famous boxer or bodybuilder, but since 1973, that dream had slowly drifted into my subconscious. Only occasionally would it resurface, reminding me that it still existed.

Walking toward the door, I glanced over my shoulder once more, drinking in the beauty of the metal and smell of the gym. This was a high that couldn't be matched. Drugs and alcohol were only temporary but the gym could make you *fly*!

For the next twenty-four hours that gym was all I could think about. I knew that I must someday identify my deficiencies and try to rebuild myself. Purified water, combined with lots of walking and oriental food seemed to help my body to function better, but I also knew that I was deteriorating faster than normal and needed to somehow rebuild!

The night before my bus left for Kansas, I decided to celebrate a little, so I bought a gallon of cheap Rhine wine and knocked on my neighbor's door. Being Latino, she didn't speak much English, but that was okay. She was quite curvy and very interesting to talk with, always referring to her native culture and their customs. We had never really sat down and spent any time together, so we stayed up most of the night.

By 5:00 a.m., I expressed that it was time to catch a cab to the bus station, so we said our farewells as she gave me her phone number and kissed me once more for the road!

The ride back home was bumpy and long. Finally, after two days, we stopped in Liberal, Kansas, for a two-hour dinner. Feeling dehydrated, I decided to have a drink at the tavern across the street. Scooting up to the bar, I ordered a red draw. With a funny look, the bartender nodded and filled up a frosty mug, straight from the cooler, with tap beer and tomato juice. My hair was past my shoulders and my skin was a very dark brown. My genetic combination of German and Welch definitely showed, as my skin was incredibly dark from the past several months in LA. There were a lot of Mexicans in Liberal that worked at the meat packing plant, so he probably thought I was also Mexican.

Gulping down my beer and tomato juice, I noticed a black man sitting at the edge of the bar. Flashing him a smile, I nodded hello and then glanced around the room. Three big, ugly cowboys were playing a game of pool, whooping and hollering, obviously drunker than skunks! As they finished their game, I listened as they walked toward the door. When their footsteps stopped behind me, my fists became clenched and my heart began to pound hard. These guys were about to start messing with me and I surely wasn't in the mood! After two days on a hot, stinky bus and a *Godzilla*-sized headache, I wasn't in the talkative spirit!

Before I could even blink, two grabbed me while the other one confronted me with, "Hey, boy! Are you a nigger?" Stunned for a moment, I was slightly confused. Then I glanced at the black man at the bar and shook my head, as he also hung his head and mumbled under his breath.

"A what?" I asked, pretending to be confused.

"I said, are you a nigger?" Although I was about to blow a gasket, I quickly answered with a big smile.

"Now, fellas, do I honestly look like a Negro?"

Looking at each other, they burst out laughing, releasing me as they headed toward the door. Slowly sitting down, I could feel the sweat beading across my brow! This was crazy. Here I was, just back from LA, a city plagued with crime and racial problems and I almost get assaulted by three drunk cowboys! After all of the nights I walked in downtown LA and Hollywood, not once was I even *close* to being mugged! And to think my dream as a small boy was to someday *be* a cowboy! Welcome back to Kansas, Curtis!

That evening, as we passed Kinsley, Kansas, I thought about Bill Brokar, my high school boxing coach. He had moved there back in the early seventies. Bill had been a heavyweight contender at one time. He had made his way to the National Golden Gloves competition, although he never won the title. When he trained me, although I was a scrawny welterweight, he taught me to throw body punches like a heavyweight. This strategy, combined with the speedy hands of a welterweight, gave me an advantage. I was proud to say that I had never been knocked down in the ring. I was just too bullheaded!

I had been downed a few times in street fights, but the rules there were different, there weren't any! I never lost a street fight, but there were times when it looked like I had. Broken noses, black eyes, even a cracked cheekbone were all reminders that no one ever really wins a street fight! You just don't get hurt as bad as the other guy.

The next morning, our bus arrived in Larned, Kansas, where my mother lived. My plan was to find a job quickly and try to get back in college. Second semester was only eight weeks away. Mom was surprised and glad to see me again, considering that I didn't call before I dropped in.

After borrowing money from the local bank to buy an old three-quarter ton Chevrolet pick-up, I got a job working in the oil fields again. I had worked for Halliburton, an international oil company, the summer before as a dry bulk cement truck driver. This new job was with a wire line company that used blasting caps to back off stuck drill pipe and used a variety of other tools for checking drill pipe at different depths.

The work wasn't very hard but the Kansas wind and snow was a killer! The cold I had caught on the trip back from LA progressed into a good case of tonsillitis. I was also starting to have more problems with indigestion, vision loss, hypoglycemia and fatigue. The glasses I had gotten in early 1979 were not as effective as they initially were.

After my third week on the job, I paid a visit to a local chiropractor, who persuaded me to take a five-hour glucose tolerance test to check my blood sugar stability. After the third hour of the test, Dr. Eaton came in to share some news. "Curtis, you have diabetes, with unusually *extreme* hypoglycemia! We will finish the test, but I wanted to let you know the facts."

Over the next two hours, as my blood sugar dropped dramatically, a deep depression came over me. I hated diabetes! It ran in my family, and I wasn't ready to become another of its victims. Then at the end of the test, Dr. Eaton came back with another diagnosis. "Curtis, you have type 2 diabetes, which I believe can be controlled by diet. I have tested hundreds of patients over the years, but you are the first to ever test out so erratically!" As he explained the blood sugar graph, he also stated that my severe hypoglycemia could possibly be stabilized with my diet and the correct supplementation.

At this point I was exhausted and didn't care what he had to say! Maybe I wasn't insulin dependent yet, but if he came up with any more surprises, he may see my darker, toxic side, which didn't take kindly to another doctor playing with my mind and body!

"Curtis, your adrenals, pancreas, liver and gallbladder aren't functioning well at all. Also, your thymus, thyroid and pituitary glands are working at minimum capacity. This, combined with too many red blood cells, is also causing your high blood pressure and blackout spells! You definitely need to keep giving whole blood every few months, to keep your blood from becoming too thick. I'm writing you a prescription for nutritional supplements to rebuild these organs and give you much more energy. Your blood sugar should also begin to adjust gradually. It's just a matter of time and effort on your behalf. No one else can do it for you. You must take charge of your own body!"

Hmmm, where had I heard *that* before? At least this time I wouldn't have to take a *morbid* combination of *drugs* to try and fix my problems! I may *actually* live, although my *quality* of life was still a *huge* question mark! The way I felt, anything was possible.

Shelling out what money I had, I bought all the prescribed supplements. Little did I know that Dr. Eaton had his finger on a pretty amazing program. It wasn't based on a person's metabolic framework, but only on organs and systems that were depleted.

During the next seventy two hours I recognized an inner strength and a sudden explosion of energy that hadn't existed for years. My body was starting to absorb and utilize all of the vitamins, minerals, glandular and pancreatic enzymes that I was taking with each meal!

Almost overnight, I felt new life in all my muscles and my mind began to half-way function clearly again. These standard process supplements were really putting the life back into my entire body!

During the next few weeks, I planned for my move to Salina, Kansas. Marymount, a private Catholic college had accepted me for second semester and also gave me a grant. It was a small school, that had only a few years earlier been an *all-girl* nursing school, that had finally opened its doors to the male species. The ratio of girls to guys was about five to one, something I could live with. I wanted to finish my BS degree in psychology and minor in world theology with a premed emphasis. It meant cramming four years of psychology into two, but I was up to the challenge. The old Marine Corps discipline was still there.

The drive to college in January of 1980 was refreshing. With two years of veterans benefits left, I was up for this adventure. During that first week, I consulted with my advisor about changing my major to psychology from communications and pursuing the premed field. It was a big change, but my search for answers to my own health problems was beckoning me to reach within myself and discover why the mind and body function as they do. Almost every class would have to be relative to psychology, anatomy and physiology, biology and theology. I wanted to take more dramatic arts and music classes but there just wasn't time.

That first semester went fast, as I still was in a couple of plays and was running on the cross-country team. The ten-mile workouts each day were tough, but I adapted. The only real problem was nutrition. I was running out of the supplements I had and the food in the school cafeteria was all starch and sugar. The protein content was minimal and at times, nonexistent.

By February, I was out of supplements and couldn't afford any more on my V.A. income. Gradually, I began to feel like I had before I started with Dr. Eaton. My immune system and blood sugar levels were falling back to the way they had been before.

At the end of the semester, I moved to Wichita, Kansas, and spent the summer with my Aunt Mary. I worked for manpower and picked up other odd jobs whenever I could. I also spent a lot of time dancing in the clubs and swimming out at the lake. I even took a part-time job dancing in a male review but never did feel completely comfortable about the atmosphere and the moral implications. With my Christian background, as well as my scholastic search for *truth*, it seemed to contradict the very *core* of my being! But my experience in gymnastics and the year in LA dancing *every* weekend definitely got me the job! Even my Aunt Mary disliked this novelty job, although she had herself been a Go-go dancer in California twenty five years earlier!

During this time, I bought supplements at the health food store but could never duplicate what Dr. Eaton had done for me earlier, which was a mistake. But I was stubborn and presumed that things would get better, although they didn't.

By the end of summer, I was ready to start school again. The next year would be a tough one, especially if I wanted to attend graduate school. I was living in the dorm again but this would be my last semester for that. I would get an apartment by second semester.

The day before I left Wichita for college, I did decide to do something that at the time was definitely *not* the social norm across America. I got my ear pierced! When I got back to the Marymount campus, several of my friends began to quiz me about my decision. "Curtis, are you *gay*?" Laughing, I would just shake my head and assure them that my *left* ear was pierced, meaning that I was definitely *straight*! I was the first male on campus to do such an unusual thing especially for 1980! Looking back, I can say that summer my self-esteem had definitely been boosted, although my health was still at times *unpredictable*!

It was on the weekend of October 17, 1980, that a very strange thing happened to me. On Friday evening, Michelle, a girl I was dating, went with me to a campus theatrical production of *Camelot*. After the play ended, we chatted with the cast and then went back to my room. Then for no apparent reason, I began to cry. Not knowing its origin, I was embarrassed. The play had left a radiant warmth in my soul, but now I felt my heart was suddenly laden with sadness.

For almost an hour I wept, making us both a bit uneasy. Finally, as quick as they came, the tears were gone. By the end of the weekend, I still couldn't understand what took place. It was strange.

On Monday morning, it all came together. At eight o'clock, our dorm leader knocked on my door. As usual, I was studying for a test. Her manner jolted me when she practically barked the news. She was so impersonal.

"Curtis, we tried to find you Sunday afternoon but you weren't around. Your grandfather in Reece is dead." The words hit me like lead. "He died Saturday afternoon and the funeral is tomorrow. I'm sorry."

With the words spoken, she closed my door. I was stunned. Turning around, I walked to the window and looked across the wooded area behind the campus. Slowly, dropping my head into my hands, I wept again. Although we weren't that close, Grandpa was like a father to me as a child. He and Grandma were all I had until I was twelve.

After collecting myself, I thought again of Friday night. Could I have somehow known about his death even before it took place? Never before had something like this happened to me. Maybe all of Grandma's stories about her sixth sense were true. And just maybe I had genetically received this mysterious gift. The remainder of that semester I read everything I could about the mind and its many powers, above and beyond what science and human reasoning had already discovered and documented.

As fall drifted into winter, I spent several hours each week at the library studying the effects of different nutrients on the body. Most of my reading material could be found in the college library, but I would also visit the local health food store. I was still searching for that missing link, that exact combination of foods and supplements that would restore my body and mind. I knew the answer was out there, somewhere.

One book that fascinated me, written by Dr. George Watson, was *Nutrition and Your Mind*. If what he said was true, human behavior could be altered by diet and supplementation. This guy was years ahead of anything we were studying there at Marymount.

During Christmas break, I moved off campus into a very old apartment building. It was perfect. I had to force myself at times to go out and socialize. The atmosphere helped me to study and meditate for days at a time. The changes in my eating habits were also for the better. Now I didn't have to live on pasta and carbohydrates. I started to eat fresh vegetables, fish, and poultry.

Immediately I sensed a change in my body, especially during my cross-country workouts and the times I pumped iron in the gym. But these changes were quite minimal compared to the rebuilding that needed to take place.

As spring semester continued, I found that my spare time was minimal. Between my classes, anatomy and physiology lab, studying and workouts, I had just enough time to rest. I didn't even have enough time to go to Red Cross and give blood, which had become a routine since the spring of 1977 when Dr. Liggett told me I had polycythemia. This was a disorder that somehow triggered the body to make too many red blood cells when the oxygen levels got too low. I had to give blood every two months to lower the red blood cell count and bring my high blood pressure down. Sometimes this, combined with my severe blood sugar problems, would cause me to black out for a few minutes. It didn't happen very often, but it had become a nuisance.

During this semester, I volunteered to help dissect the cadaver in our anatomy class, for extra credit. The subject was a sixty-five-year-old man who died of a massive coronary, but after opening him up, we could see that his liver was almost gone. As Dr. Zeakes questioned us on various internal organs, he stopped at the liver. "Students, if you will look very close, you can see that this man's liver was barely functioning at the time of death." Looking closer, I could see that the entire organ, which was huge as he was a big man, was a gray color except for one spot about the size of a quarter.

Pointing out the spot, Dr. Zeakes exclaimed, "This one small area of stroma cells was keeping this man alive. Isn't that fantastic?" Nodding our heads, we all agreed. Everyone wanted to get out of there as quickly as possible. The formaldehyde was causing our eyes to water and a few students were gagging.

After the class dismissed, a fellow female student and I stayed to finish dissecting the right forearm. During the past three weeks, I noticed that each time I worked on the cadaver, my blood sugar would drop dramatically. I couldn't put my finger on it but I knew that it had something to do with the formaldehyde. I had no idea that I'd find my answer in a few years, it was Candida albicans overgrowth!

The following week I received a letter from the Veterans Board in Wichita, Kansas. In November of 1980, I had attended a hearing to petition the V.A. for all of the medical bills I had paid since my honorable discharge in October of 1975. Thousands of insurance and personal dollars had been spent for testing and retesting at several clinics and hospitals. Before I even opened the letter I innately *knew* the outcome. As I silently read their decision, I sat and pondered the broader scope of their finding. I had to be *completely* honest with myself. I *couldn't* blame the Marine Corps for my health issues, no matter what I was faced with. It was *ultimately* my *choice* to take all of the dairy-based protein in 1974, when I had started my bodybuilding program. That, combined with my very strange immune system, had caused all of the medical problems that I now faced. Granted, the Navy doctors on base could never figure out the causes for my high blood pressure, passing out spells, ulcers, and digestive issues, but my case was very unusual. Even any type of specialist at the time would have been thoroughly *confused*!

I had to take a moment and reconsider the *positive* aspects of my time in the Marine Corps, as there were several. They had given me a *true* purpose in my life, at a time when I was a teenager without direction, like a ship without a rudder. I had become a significant component of the most *elite* fighting machine on this planet. I *survived* the grueling *pain* of boot camp and *excelled* in combat training school, as the *only* private in the entire company that was a squad leader. Which earned me my first stripe when I graduated with *honors*!

As I dropped the letter on my desk, I thanked God for all of the obstacles that I had already overcome in my life. I would *keep* searching, reading, praying, looking, and *finding* the answers to all of my physiological problems!

At the end of the semester, I decided to enroll in summer school so I could finish at midterm. I still needed classes in experimental psychology and statistics. Although necessary, I was more intrigued by physiological-psychology, anatomy and physiology, and psychometric testing. My theology classes were interesting, but I still remained a protestant. I had one instructor who would often encourage me to become a Catholic, but I felt pretty comfortable as I was.

For one of my final Catholicism classes, we were all part of a student's baptism for his new baby. So as a musician, I volunteered to write a song and sing it during the liturgy. I eventually changed some words and made the song into a wedding song. Because of my metabolic problems, my strength and range of singing was limited, but I could still play the heck out of my twelve-string guitar!

That summer, I endured summer school and tried to enjoy the tremendous Kansas heat and humidity. I had modeled a little at Barton College a couple of years before, so I again had the chance to do a few shows at two of the local clubs. We would wear different themes of clothing and do dance routines for each show. It didn't pay much, but the fringe benefits were nice. Free clothes, eats and maybe a date if I got lucky!

When the fall semester began, I was chumming around with Mick McCallum, a fellow anatomy student. Mick and I had become great friends and spent quite a bit of time together. A nursing student, Mick was also an EMT. He would often tell me stories about helping someone from a car wreck, or finding someone that had been murdered, or committed suicide. Mick lived in the same complex that I did and would periodically come to visit. Once, during an intense three-day study-thon, Mick came up to say hello and hang out. While I studied, he would thumb through my psychology manuals and mutter, "There are no pictures, just words! How can you read this stuff?" I'd laugh and tell him that each page created a picture in my mind.

It was now almost Thanksgiving of 1981, and we could take a break for a couple of days. It was on the eve of Thanksgiving that Mick and I experienced an unusual and sad event. We had a new neighbor downstairs that was going to another private college in town, and he was having a small party. While we were there, we had a drink and met a couple of his friends. The one I remembered in particular was also a psychology major and was about to also finish school. He never said much during our stay, but he seemed to be sociable and in good spirits.

Mick had to go on call at midnight so we all said our farewells early, and I went to bed. The next day, Mick and I got together for dinner at his parents' house and that's when he told me the rest of the story. At 5:00 a.m., they got a call about a person on the outskirts of town that had a stalled or abandoned car. But when they got there, it was worse. A young man had taken his own life with a shotgun in his mouth. Mick said he couldn't recognize the guy until he saw his driver's license. It was the same kid we had met at the party our neighbor had. Good grief! And we never had a clue.

Many times after that event, I tried to reenact my conversation with that kid but it just wouldn't work. I almost felt as though maybe I could have helped him, in some way, but I never really knew what was going on in his head. The holidays are a hard time for lots of people, including myself. I often missed my family and old friends.

With the semester coming to a close, I spent every free moment studying. I was considering medical school but could never afford it. Besides, it didn't offer what I was looking for. Traditional medical training didn't focus on preventive or orthomolecular medicine. They taught the allopathic approach, treating symptoms instead of the *whole* person. It didn't make any sense to me. The human body was the most finely tuned machine in the universe yet it was often treated with less respect than an old used car. I had my eye on a naturopathic college, but without any more V.A. benefits, I wouldn't last a semester. I had to find a job and start all over again.

I'll never forget the day our anatomy and physiology class was supposed to study the chapter on metabolism. When the bell rang, Dr. Zeakes bounced into the room, slid his manuals across his long wooden desk, sat down, and addressed us." Class, I have some good news and some *bad* news today. The good news is, we will *not* be studying the chapter on metabolism. The *bad* news is we don't even study it in medical school." As the class let out a collective sigh of relief, I shook my head in *disbelief*. I was seriously considering medical school just so I could *learn* how to address all of my own physical problems and now I discover there are *no* answers to be found.

When class was over, I stopped Dr. Zeakes in the hall and asked him what I should do about medical school. "Curtis, follow your heart and keep looking for the answers, you will find them, someday, somewhere. Medical school is not the only answer." With that in mind, it didn't take me long to make my decision. I would keep looking for the *truth* after graduation.

The day school ended, I packed my bags and moved to Hoisington, Kansas. My stepbrother Jack lived there and offered to put me up for a while. I had to sell my truck the previous semester, so Mick helped me move. It was a sad evening. When we said goodbye, I felt that our friendship would never be the same.

It was Christmas 1981, and the economy was hurting. With the drop in oil prices, Kansas was hit hard. The lifeblood of the Great Bend area was oil. Without it, the city would slowly die. I thought about working in the oil fields again but soon changed my mind. The hourly wage for a roughneck had dropped from $15 to $5 an hour, hardly enough money to justify risking life and limb in freezing conditions. My father was still a tool pusher for Graves Drilling Company in Kansas and my hat was off to him. He had fought the oil fields for the last thirty years. He was the last of a dying breed of men that was born during the '20s and early '30s in America. Dad helped raise all nine of us kids and we all were thankful for that. He was as tough as they get.

After Christmas, I took a bartending job at a local club. I had served beer during my first couple of years of college but never mixed drinks, so I made a deal with the owner. If I didn't know all the drinks in three days, he could let me go, but if I did, I could stay. After three days, he tested me and I passed. The pay wasn't much, but it was a start.

When Valentine's Day arrived, I brought my guitar in and performed. Afterward, several people asked me to play for private parties and other clubs in town. This, combined with my salary from work, helped me to buy a car. I was driving an old high school buddy's car and wanted to get it back to him.

With the coming of spring, so did the insurance company offers! I guess a college degree pulled them out of the woodwork. I had never sold anything before, but the salary looked good so I accepted. After getting my license, I started to try and sell people life insurance. Talk about stressful! I was trained to listen to people's problems, not try to sell them anything. It took some time, but I gradually reconditioned myself. I was a good actor but this involved a different psychological approach. Dealing with rejection took some time to overcome.

As the spring turned into summer, my health plunged downhill. The added stress of selling made my blood pressure skyrocket. This, combined with several food and environmental allergies, was killing me. I had constant headaches and tons of extra mucus! I also had to change the prescription for my glasses, as my eyes were suddenly getting worse. Each day my blood sugar dropped three or four times causing extreme hunger pains and blurry vision. When this happened, my voice became high pitched, making me feel like I owned a woman's voice! There were times when I felt like life was really not worth living.

With summer turning into fall, I shuddered at the thought of another winter in Kansas. I wanted to move back to California but knew my health would not allow it. My paychecks were slowly increasing, but the quality of my life seemed to be diminishing. I still worked out at the gym periodically, although it would now take days for me to recuperate. I wanted to consult with another doctor but no longer trusted the medical community. Looking back, I should have seen Dr. Eaton again, but my mind was in a fog most of the time which kept me from making even the simplest decisions.

The next six months of 1982 drifted by uneventfully, except for my membership in the "Gunfighters Of The Great Plains." This club put on theatrical "Wild West" gunfights for any special occasion. I loved acting. It was a great way to relax and "cut loose." I was beginning to carry the burdens similar to the corporate businessman.

In March of 1983, I decided to move to Wichita, Kansas, and work for a railroad tie company. They were tearing out a lot of the old railroads in the Midwest and were hiring several laborers. Tired of the insurance industry and wanting to use my hands and muscles again, I jumped at the chance to move and make more money.

When I arrived at the motel room they arranged for me, I unpacked, ate, and got some rest. At 4:00 a.m., the phone rang; it was time to get up! With breakfast hardly swallowed, they shoved us out on the truck and hauled us into the country. Fourteen hours later, with hands bleeding and back bowed, they brought us back. It was slave labor! We weren't paid by the hour, instead it was a salary. They could work us as hard as they wanted to. I had no idea about what I had gotten myself into. This was crazy!

During the next few weeks, I carried so many railroad ties, I counted them in my sleep. The work was grueling and the boss coldhearted. Then, on a hot, muggy Friday afternoon, I had heatstroke. All I could remember was stumbling to the solitary tree for some shade and a cool drink of water. We had run out of water, but the boss wouldn't let us take a break. After another two hours, he finally let us sit down, but it was too late! They said as I stumbled toward the big cottonwood tree, I was actually foaming at the mouth!

That evening, I packed my little MG and swooped out of that joint. I'd get my last check later. My half sister Eraina lived in Wichita, and that's where I was headed.

As summer began, I took various odd jobs to survive. While working the door at a prominent nightclub one evening, I met Rick Freeman. He was a regular every day at happy hour, but this time he took a moment and spoke with me. "You know, there's more to you than meets the eye!" Taken by his statement, I regarded it as a compliment. "Curt, I bet you have a college background, don't you?"

"Well, yes, I've already attended three universities since my service in the Marine Corps. I had even considered medical school but knew that what I needed to learn about rebuilding the body would probably *never* be taught there, at least not anytime in the near future!"

During the next week, Rick and I discussed his background in sales, as well as my short time in insurance. He had several ideas on starting his own business, which definitely aroused my interest. I was anxious to start making more money—especially in any industry that allowed me the flexibility to work for myself!

One week later, Rick managed to get me a job with a communications company selling telephone systems. While we worked together, he was still always talking about new ideas for his own business. With only an eighth-grade education, he was pretty sharp and *extremely* creative. Sometimes he would babble for hours about a "new concept" he had in the retail or advertising realm. Then one day after work, while sipping coffee, he propositioned me.

"Curt, how would you like to be my partner in a new advertising corporation?"

Excited, but a little apprehensive, I nodded and smiled. "Sure, if you really think it will fly." What did I have to lose? The greatest thing about Rick was his ability to convince someone of anything. As we sat and drank coffee, I knew that he was practically broke, but he wore a three-piece suit and drove an older black Lincoln. He was a master of being cool in the eye of any financial storm!

During the next two weeks, we drew up the plans for our company. Our "directory-certificate" book featured merchants throughout the city and was backed by the Chamber of Commerce and the Wichita Convention Bureau. Each merchant would give a discount on items in the store to entice the customer to come in. We would also feature a directory and map of the city, courtesy of the Chamber of Commerce. The book would have over $3,500 in coupons and would sell for ten dollars. That was a lot of discounts in one book. He had a potential investor, although we still didn't have any money to start the business. He wanted to know *all* the details about this new venture.

After three days of meetings, we all agreed upon a $15,000 total investment, dispersed in increments of $5,000. We were finally in business! After opening an account, we set up our office downtown, and shared a secretary with a law firm. Now the fun began.

When the corporate papers were drawn up and the office furnished, we celebrated. We both knew that this project would require at least four or five people, but we were determined to do it ourselves! We had to sell the Chamber and Convention Bureau on our idea first, then put together a facsimile book to sell advertising space to the merchants. Then if that worked, we needed a major nonprofit sponsor to help us market it. Our work was cut out for us!

Once the Chamber and Convention Center came aboard, we began selling ads. Each night, after selling ads all day, I would spend another four to five hours putting the art work together. Careful not to make any mistakes, I would check and double check everything I did. With each dark and bone-chilling day, my health quickly dropped another few notches. Some days, by noon, I would have to rest in the car when we went on sales calls. Rick didn't understand the nature of my health problems, but he was always considerate.

It was on November 5th, 1983 that an uncanny prediction was made by Rick, while we entertained a couple of dates at a local nightclub. Rick had been seeing his girlfriend off and on and convinced her to "set me up" on a blind date with her good friend Cathy. While we were having drinks and watching the band, Rick turned to us both, pointed and made a very strange prediction. "I would venture to wager that you two will be married within *one* year from tonight!" Looking at Rick, then each other, we both let out a very loud but slightly *nervous* laugh. How he ever came up with that vision still haunts me to this day.

When the first part of our investment was spent, we again approached our investor. He reluctantly wrote us a check, curious as to the use of the previous money. After we showed him the books, he began to relax. Good grief, that five grand didn't go very far considering the expenses incurred. In fact, we never even took a salary. That's pretty cheap labor in my books.

The second $5,000 took us through March of 1984. We were almost ready to go to print when the till ran dry again. Although we were running on schedule, the money just didn't seem to go very far.

The morning that Rick called our investor for the final installment, the English butler answered. When Rick hung up the phone, his face was white.

"What's wrong partner? Wasn't he home?"

"He's in the hospital, Curt, he had a heart attack yesterday!" Within ten minutes, we canceled all of our morning appointments and swooped to the hospital. When we entered the room, my heart sank. He looked terrible. Sitting next to the bed, we talked small talk for a few minutes. At times he could hardly speak. I felt so guilty. Here's a man, close to death and we're going to ask him to write us a check. I just couldn't do it. Glancing at Rick, I shook my head. He got the hint. Rick always took over if I couldn't carry the load.

As the words fell from his mouth, I cringed. If he said no, we were finished. Our money was almost gone. Almost at a whisper, he spoke again. Leaning over, I caught his last word. "Checkbook. Get my checkbook from the drawer."

As Rick filled out the check, I began to relax my *death* grip that I had subconsciously placed on my notebook! When he finally signed it, I saw Rick also let out a sigh of relief. We were still in the game!

Of all the people we encountered, our printer was the hardest to work with. He saw the potential of our book and began jacking up the prices! It was typical. Most people want a piece of freshly baked pie! With only a week left before going to print, my health was in shambles. The fifteen-hour days were literally killing me! Each day, after about three hours, I had to stop and rest. After an hour or so of rest, I could then push on a little longer. It finally got to the point that Rick did all of the negotiating. I didn't have enough strength to walk, let alone talk to anyone. It made me so damn angry!

When we were ready to print, we contracted with two sponsors, a country radio station and the Easter Seal Society. We thought this would help us to sell books, but fate doesn't always happen like you would expect. A week after we printed the first thousand books, the Easter Seal office in Wichita was under investigation. Someone was embezzling funds. Great! That was all we needed! They were plastered on the entire first page of our directory, along with twenty billboards throughout the city. We also had a contract to donate three dollars from every book sold. We already had a few private schools selling books, but this news stopped everything. Eight months of work, down the drain. Eight months of our lives, wasted!

When the smoke had cleared and the business was dead, Rick and I sat in our lonely office and sulked. We had tried to sell a few books door to door, but people wouldn't buy. It was finished. Rick talked about performing in a band again and I was considering selling insurance again. We were both in debt and my health was at a standstill! Even Rick looked terrible, although he had the immune system of a dinosaur! He had broken out in hives and was always scratching himself. His bald spot also looked like it had grown considerably.

With the ending of our company, Cathy, now my girlfriend, offered me a place to stay in Winfield, Kansas, less than an hour from Wichita. I had been staying with Rick and his folks, but it was crowded, so I agreed to move. The company car we were renting had to be returned, so now I was also without wheels again. At twenty-nine, I never had lived with a woman before and wasn't sure if it was the right thing to do. Although Cathy insisted on helping me out. We hadn't slept together and I was sure that wouldn't change in the near future, as she was *still* a virgin!

When the company folded, so did I. Here I was broke again and without a job. For the next few weeks, I looked for work but couldn't find anything. The stress of unemployment while staying with Cathy was draining what little life I had left in my body.

One afternoon, after telling her I had to leave, I packed my clothes and went to the backyard. When she caught up with me, she threw all of my clothes on the ground. She wanted me to stay, but I felt so bad I just wanted some peace and quiet. We obviously weren't getting along! We should have parted ways then, but instead we stayed together.

With dismay, I *finally* found a job selling life insurance again. It wasn't much, but at least I had a weekly income, with possible commissions. I also borrowed Grandma's truck until I could afford another car. Since I was working again, Cathy and I seemed to get along better. At least we were beginning to communicate.

As the autumn leaves began to fall, Cathy began hinting around often about getting married. I didn't want to talk about it. I knew we weren't ready for such a commitment, but it was hard to avoid. I already felt a certain amount of obligation because we lived in the same house. Cathy's great-aunt didn't help the situation at all. She also wanted to see her great-niece married before she died, as she was fighting terminal stomach cancer. The tumor in her abdomen was huge and was still growing. Every time we would visit her, she would mention the *M* word. It got to the point that I felt no way out. So finally, Cathy and I decided to tie the knot. In my heart, it didn't feel like a "forever" type of relationship, but I was so tired mentally and physically that I gave up the ghost.

As the November wedding crept closer, I often regretted my decision. Deep down, I felt that it may not last, not for life. We just weren't that compatible. If we could work more on our communication levels it would help, but we were both stubborn and fairly well-educated, a lethal combination. But on the other hand, Cathy's great-aunt was leaving her inheritance almost entirely to Cathy! I had to admit, this could have been a gentle persuader for most men, but I hadn't been raised that way. In fact, I wouldn't want the money and property, even after we were married, it would belong to Cathy. Her aunt owned hundreds of acres of farmland, a beautiful old home full of antiques and tens of thousands of dollars in the bank.

On that cloudy, fall day, on November 3$^{rd}$, 1984, I waited for the wedding march to begin. This was it, no turning back now. Glancing at Mick, I could see the question in his eyes. He knew I wasn't ready for this.

"Curtis, are you sure about this? You can still back out." Nodding, I looked at the floor and prayed for forgiveness.

After a short pre-honeymoon weekend, I threw myself back into my work. It felt good to have an income again. I also was still reading anything I could get my hands on that was health-related. I had just picked up *sugar blues* and was fascinated by the information it revealed.

When Christmas arrived, we took a vacation. Our pre-honeymoon lasted only two days so we tried it again. This time we took a week off and flew to Las Vegas. I had been there once, but Cathy never had. With $1,000 to spend, we enjoyed every minute. I was a seven card stud player and also played the dollar slots. Cathy didn't play but enjoyed watching me play cards.

During my first trip to Vegas back in the Spring of 1983, I definitely had "beginners' luck." After playing seven card stud for about three hours, I was up over $2,000. The chips were stacked around me like a miniature fortress. However, the more free scotch I drank, the less I won. At the end of another three hours, I was back to my original $25. Welcome to Las Vegas, Curtis.

The vacation didn't net us any profits but we had a grand time. Our feet hurt from walking the strip and we hardly ever slept. I could never sleep in Vegas. If I could afford it, I could probably even live there!

After our vacation, I finished reading Dr. Kelley's book, *Metabolic Ecology*, then let Cathy read it. Although she had always poo pooed my never ending search for nutritional answers to all of my metabolic problems, she was convinced that Dr. Kelley had a viable program that I should commit to.

Her sudden attitude change was at first uncanny, but at this point in my life I was ready to do just about anything. It was so relieving to know that there was actually a program such as Dr. Kelley's in existence that could address all of my degenerative conditions.

For three times a week over the past several months, I had almost *religiously* been psyching myself up long enough to go to the gym, run three miles on the treadmill, then pump weights for two hours. This would temporarily stimulate my immune system, as well as increase my appetite and rebalance my blood sugar for a short time, until I collapsed back at the house. It was a vicious cycle.

As I finished my detox, I flipped through Dr. Kelley's book, *Metabolic Ecology*. Almost a year had passed, and I was finally on the road to health. It was almost as if it was planned this way. Whatever the reason, I only knew that each day on this program pushed me closer and closer to a far superior state of health. It also was time to run another metabolic program, as my body chemistry and metabolic type was shifting strongly. As this change was taking place, my body was craving a different variety of foods and supplements.

This new state of mental and physical awareness was so dynamic I felt that perhaps, in time, it could actually affect my entire life and my destiny!

# 5

# MUST I DIE TO GET BETTER?

> *The Angel showed me the river of the water of life, as clear as crystal, flowing from the throne of God and of the Lamb down the middle of the great street of the city. On each side of the river stood the tree of life, bearing twelve crops of fruit, yielding it's fruit every month. And the leaves of the tree are for the healing of the nations.*
>
> —Revelation 22:1

With only two days before Christmas 1985, Cathy and I decided to split up. We had been through counseling with our minister, but it hadn't helped. As I put my books and clothing in the car, it saddened me to think that I may be alone again. I wasn't sure how this would end, anything could happen. I didn't want a divorce, but I did need some time to myself, and so did Cathy. As my health progressed, my personality changed also. I was becoming the complete person I should have been a long time ago. My physiological, psychological, and emotional strengths were all growing at an exponential rate. Cathy could see it, but we never talked about it. Our communication level had dropped dramatically since November.

The apartment I rented was in Arkansas City, a brand-new middle-income housing project. I was one of the first tenants. When I moved in, Cathy came by to see the apartment. After a few minutes of conversation, she hugged me and began to cry.

"Curty, please don't go, come back home with me. Things will work out."

As we embraced, I also began to cry. Although this was only a temporary separation, I felt as though we may never see each other again.

Later that evening, as I unpacked some old books, I started to read through old school yearbooks and newspapers. I had always saved every award or scrap of paper. When I found my old Marine Corps awards, I decided to have them framed. I had received awards for long-distance running, meritorious mast and was promoted several times.

Thumbing through some old newspapers, I noticed an article I had cut out about Dr. Liggett, a well-known neurologist from Great Bend. The article explained an investigation held to determine his guilt or innocence in an arson case. He was accused of torching his home for the insurance money. I recalled attending one of the hearings. I wasn't sure about the verdict, and I didn't much care! He was the doctor that treated me in the spring of 1977. After attending his trial, it reaffirmed my opinion of his medical wisdom. He "dispensed" amphetamines and barbiturates like they were candy. Reliving the time I spent under his care, I caught myself holding a deep resentment inside, an anger that had consumed me for a very long time. Slowly bowing my head, I began to meditate and pray, releasing the anger and pain that had been smoldering for years.

With winter at its worst, I slacked off selling insurance and put most of my time and newfound energy into metabolic typing. I kept in close contact with the institute in Dallas and planned to attend more schooling in February, although my certification as a technician had already gone through.

Up to this point, my body had gone through some deep changes. The first program was designed to push me more alkaline, or parasympathetic. I had just started another program which changed my diet and supplement regime. It was pulling me back toward a more acidic state, although I was still basically on a parasympathetic diet. I knew that the damage my liver had sustained over the years was critical, so I was doing anything I could to rebuild it—carrot juice daily, with organic liver concentrate mixed in, several pancreatic enzymes along with many herbs to help cleanse the liver and blood. Some of the herbs I took were juniper, licorice root, hibiscus, buckthorn and goldenseal.

In late January 1986, I went back to Dallas for more updates on metabolic technology. During the first two days, we reviewed some old work and discussed some new discoveries. Bill Wolcott had been doing some research with oxidation rates and how they were part of the metabolic profile, although Dr. Kelley had initially included this in his original research back in the '60s. Having married Dr. Kelley's ex-wife, I never trusted this Wolcott character. As time passed, it was evident that all of my instincts were right on about Wolcott and his motives.

The second day of the seminar, I met Becky. She had been a technician for the last five years. At thirty-seven, she looked twenty-three! She was beautiful, with baby soft skin and silky black hair. As we got to know each other during the next few days, she shared many of her own personal transformations, both physical and spiritual. She had unleashed, as she once said, the true meaning of the spirit, finding its origin and survival from one person to the next, from century to century. It did make some sense, although my own thoughts and beliefs were based on basic Christian philosophy.

During one of our breaks, I took a moment to chat with Dr. Kelley. During our conversation, I casually mentioned that if I had a million bucks, I could quit my job, finish my book, and open my clinic.

Instead of laughing like I thought he would, he smugly stated, "How about ten million dollars?"

"You're kidding, aren't you, Doc?"

"No, I'm not. I don't know if you can still get into the program, but you can try."

While he explained this unbelievable opportunity, Becky walked by. As the three of us spoke, she gave me more information about this "arbitrage," or international banking project. It seemed too good to be true! For a $4,000 fee, if accepted, I could be eligible to participate in an offshore arbitrage for $10,000,000. It was known as a self-liquidating loan, that in essence, never had to be repaid! Instead, whatever business the money was used for, 50 percent of the profits, for the next thirty years, would be paid back to the bank. It sounded crazy but attractive.

The rest of that day, I daydreamed about all that money. I was doing okay at work, but four grand was quite a chunk of money to dish out at one time. I'd have to think on this for a while.

The last day of the seminar focused on the role of supplements in metabolic therapy and why pancreatic enzymes were mandatory for rebuilding. As we watched an old film, I remembered when I had seen it in college, in my physiological psychology class. It was called the Pottenger cat film. This study was performed on two groups of healthy cats over a period of a few years. One group was fed only regular cat food and raw meat, and the other was fed only cooked meat.

As time progressed, the group fed the cooked foods began to show many signs of metabolic deficiencies. The second and third generations began to manifest different diseases, such as leukemia, bone and vision problems and other forms of cancer. By the fourth generation, they couldn't even reproduce. The results were quite staggering.

When the film ended, we discussed why one group remained healthy, while the other degenerated. The key was *enzymes*. When we cook food, the natural inherent enzymes are changed and destroyed. Without enzymes, we, like the cat, or any other animal, cannot digest proteins, fats, and carbohydrates. The extreme heat in cooking destroys all of the active, life-giving enzymes. Thus enzymes, of all the many supplements Dr. Kelley made, were conceivably the most important.

Enzyme therapy had actually been around since 1888, when the famous Dr. John Beard ran a twenty-year experiment with cancer patients that may have changed the course of medicine. For twenty years, he worked with many forms of cancer patients, giving them liquid pancreatic enzymes via IV. He concluded that cancer was a combination of deficient pancreatic enzymes, combined with a slight hormone imbalance. He also took a group of two hundred people and had them take a pancreatic enzyme cancer test. Once the results were in, he and his colleagues were baffled. Over 70 percent of all the patients had a positive reaction to the test, indicating some form of cancer. Yet after running the traditional tests on the same patients, the results were all negative. Therefore, the enzyme test was considered to be a failure.

But during the next three years, every patient that had been in the test did manifest some form of cancer or relative degenerative condition! Incredible! This test was the best precancer screening test that money could buy, and it was cheap. But what do you think happened to the test? You never hear about it today, unless you talk with a professional that deals with metabolic disorders. It was thrown to the wayside. Instead, we now have chemotherapy, radiation therapy, and all kinds of toxic therapies that not only kill the patient but drain all their money in the process! If that's advancement, then I'd like to live in another century.

When the seminar came to a close, we all said our goodbyes. Becky and I exchanged phone numbers. I wanted to see her again. I was still married, although I didn't know for how long.

Two days later, I got a call at the office from Becky. She wanted to know if I was going to get involved in the arbitrage.

"I'm not sure, four grand is a lot of money."

The longer we talked, the better it sounded. After I hung up, I checked my account. With payday a week away, I might be able to swing it.

The next morning at seven o'clock, the phone rang. It was Cathy. She had filed for a divorce. I was surprised but had sensed that this might happen. She had made her decision, so be it. There was nothing I could do or say to change things now. The time had finally come.

On Friday afternoon, I packed a few items, threw my shaving kit together and swooped to Dallas. I had made the decision to get involved in this arbitrage. In a few hours, I would be giving someone I didn't know $4,000. It was a shaky proposition, but what the heck, it was only money.

After I checked into the Harvey House Hotel in Plano, a suburb of Dallas, I swam a few laps in the indoor pool. The drive in ice and snow had chilled me to the bone and had stressed my entire nervous system. I was going through a "healing" stage and was pretty toxic. My body was taking on a new dimension that felt strange but good. Even my bones seemed to be moving, growing, and becoming stronger.

After dinner, I called Dr. Wilkinson, the man I was to give the money to. He agreed to meet me at the hotel in an hour. When he arrived, he immediately got down to business. When all of the documents were signed, I handed him a cashier's check for four grand. For a moment I hesitated, then released the check. My life was moving along now at warp speed, so I might as well try to enjoy the ride!

The next morning I called Becky and shared what I had done. She was glad to hear from me and wanted to have lunch. I wanted to get back home so I could start getting a passport processed but decided to stick around. She was an awfully beautiful woman and I guess I was almost single.

During lunch we talked about this international banking program and how it worked. To date, there were over four thousand people involved. That was a heck of a lot of money.

After lunch, we went back to my room to get my bags. As we spoke, our auras wove into one another, embracing as though we were actually touching. It was almost hypnotic. Then after she walked me to my car, without any warning, we kissed. It was a short but powerful kiss. A rush of blood forged its way to my fingers and toes as though I had been jolted by lightning. I guess I was single again.

When I arrived back at my apartment on Sunday evening, I decided to do another gallbladder- liver flush. It had been a few months, and I was overdue. Along with the flush, I began to drink some liquid lecithin, as I assumed that it would work well with the extra virgin olive oil. This, combined with the phosphoric acid I was taking to loosen up my gallbladder, caused a severe reaction even before I finished the liver flush. I had assumed that my gallbladder was empty, but I was mistaken. I had only touched the surface!

I started passing large stones again, on the evening before the flush was completed. This time, they were almost all white, and still as big as golf balls. The next morning, after the flush was over and ten to twelve large stones were passed, I passed out. My temperature shot up, and it felt like I was submerged in a deep freezer. During the next two-day period, I was in a complete state of unconsciousness. I truly thought I was going to die.

When I came to, I crawled to the bathroom, then back to the couch. As I drifted between the world of consciousness and darkness, I silently prayed for *death*. With septic shock setting in from the gallbladder, I truly felt that I may not wake to see the morning. But somehow, someway, I awoke a day and a half later hungry and somewhat alert. I drank some carrot juice and crawled back to the couch. As I began to slowly drift back into a deep sleep, I prayed again, but this time for life. But if I lived through this, I wanted two things: the body I had worked hard for years to hopefully achieve, as I was only about 140 pounds, and my voice. I had been singing for a few years but my calcium and metabolic deficiencies, along with hormonal imbalances had limited my vocal strength, tone, and range. If God could somehow work this out then I would *definitely* dedicate my life to Dr. Kelley's incredible science.

Two days later, I called our office to check in and also Dr. Kelley. I explained what I had experienced and referred back to a year earlier when he stated that I may have to "die to get better." He suggested getting blood work done every two weeks and possible antibiotics. But I was stubborn, having taken antibiotics for several years as a kid. I wanted to stick as closely as possible to my metabolic program as I could.

The next week, I went to the hospital and had a blood test done. I wanted to know what had happened at the cellular level. A few days later, I was given the results. Everything looked normal except for an extremely lowered white blood cell count. I was fighting an internal infection so strong that it lowered an entire system! Obviously, the debris in my liver and gallbladder had been released when the gallstones were ejected. Hopefully they were the last. Before I left, the nurse asked me to come back every two weeks and have another blood test. They also wanted to know what was happening with my body.

After the fifth week, I began to regain my strength. The nurses at Winfield Hospital were a bit baffled, amazed at the changes my blood work was displaying every two weeks. My income suffered from this temporary setback, but I had also started advertising my metabolic counseling service. I was receiving client referrals from the institute and was preparing for my first slide presentation in Arkansas City.

During the month I was sick, Becky called often in her efforts to support me as much as possible. I was thankful that we had met.

Cathy and I never spoke again after her last phone call. I signed the documents at her attorney's office, and it was finished. It was both a sad and lonely day. Although we had our differences, we still were a part of each other that would never die.

Three days before my first seminar, Becky came to visit. She had several ideas for speeding up the healing of my liver and wanted to help me with my first presentation. Although I was still weak, I was glad she was there. Her knowledge and years of personal experience on the program could prove to be quite valuable.

During her visit, my health took a quantum leap forward. Her presence boosted my morale along with my spiritual awareness. Many times we sat and talked of this "New Age" philosophy that was currently so popular. I didn't fully understand it but was curious of its origin and how it was practiced. It also dealt with reincarnation, which was another area I had studied very little and was not familiar with.

Becky often spoke of "mediums," "spiritual guides," and karma. She felt that we all have spiritual guides who direct us during our lifetime. Karma is the energy that returns to us in response to things we have done to or for others in our past. Her experiences with a "medium" had revealed her past lives and people she had known centuries ago. I was an open-minded guy, but this was a tad bit over my head. I believed in karma, that was relevant to the Christian faith—as you sow, you shall reap. I supposed "guides" could be compared to angels, but to have lived in other bodies throughout time, that took a small leap of faith. I sometimes felt old, but not that old. Ten thousand years was one heck of a long time!

During her stay, she had me taking more herbs to detoxify my liver. Echinacea, a natural antibiotic, helped me to bring my immune system up, along with a few other homeopathic remedies we found at the health food store. This, combined with some stretching exercises she taught me, helped me to jump start my body to another level. It was amazing to experience the effects of so many different supplements, herbs, homeopathic tinctures, and methods of detoxification.

After my first seminar, I began working with my first client. He had an undifferentiated carcinoma on the occipital lobe, or in English, a brain tumor on the back of the head. At sixty, he was still functioning well, in fact, he was stronger at the time than I was. Both he and his wife had grown up with Dr. Kelley during their grade school years. After coming to our seminar, they had decided to try the program.

When his results came back, he suddenly changed his mind. But the longer we talked, the closer I came to understanding why he was apprehensive. Throughout the session, his wife kept interrupting. She had a very "toxic" personality herself combined with an extremely acidic or hyper blood chemistry. The bottom line was, he wanted to proceed, but she wouldn't let him.

"I just don't know if I can cook and prepare all those foods for him. I cooked for forty years and now I deserve a rest! Besides, insurance doesn't cover all those supplements yet, and we can't afford any more bills!"

As I listened to her make decisions for her poor husband, I began to realize what Dr. Kelley had taught us in school. The fact that once someone began a metabolic program, it was *crucial* that their significant other support their decision. Otherwise, the client would be caught in the middle of a "tug of war" between the program and their unbelieving partner.

A week after I left their home, I gave him a call. His wife answered and gave me an overview of his condition. He had gone back to his doctor and started more cobalt treatments. Now, bedridden, he was unable to function. That was our last conversation. I never knew his final fate until a few months later, he never made it.

When Becky went back home, the apartment just didn't feel the same. It felt as though I had been visited for a short time by a leftover flower child of the sixties. Although we had different spiritual attitudes and beliefs, we still "connected" as human beings.

As spring turned into summer, the year 1986 marked the beginning of a mission I would begin that would become lifelong! I had started writing my book and was anticipating quitting the insurance business. I wanted to open a clinic and help the world to rebuild itself.

As my energy and mind were increasing and expanding, I began reading for several hours a day after work at the agency was finished. The more I learned about insurance companies and the banking system, the less I respected the country we had evolved to. It seemed our government, since the early part of the 20$^{th}$ century had been misleading the American public. If that was true, then history could possibly repeat itself again and America could once again relive the days of civil disobedience.

I never followed the political realm, but I knew that the health care industry would go through some dramatic changes during the next few decades. If my assumptions were correct, the pharmaceutical and medical industry would love to completely control the nutritional supplement realm. They may be poo-pooing us now but in a few years they will publicly turn completely around and support this growing phenomena! When millions of people in America want something, they eventually will get it!

As I browsed through some literature from the American Cancer Society, I found a brochure that caught my eye. It depicted the seven supposedly "warning" signs of cancer and then made a bold-faced statement that I knew would someday be a slap in their bureaucratic face! It said, they *knew* within a shadow of a doubt, that diet and nutrition had no relationship to any type or form of cancer! Humbug! The Institute had data dating back fifty years that made this statement obsolete!

Then out of the blue on Saturday, at six in the morning, I received a phone call. Richard L. Jones was dead of heart failure. The man who put this huge arbitrage together was dead. After I let out a nervous breath of air, I asked about the status of the arbitrage.

"Curtis, as far as we know, it's still on. Richard had an alter ego that was to take over if something like this happened."

Hanging up the phone, I saw my $4,000 flying out the window. I couldn't see how this opportunity could proceed without Richard. He was the key that could unlock the invisible door to the international banking world. Unfortunately, we all knew he wouldn't live much longer. He had been poisoned a year earlier!

Becky called the next day, very upset about Richard's death. This could abort the dreams we all had for that money, but the only thing we could do was wait. I already had my passport and was ready to leave at a moment's notice. Waiting was the hardest part.

With the arrival of summer, I began to work on a golden suntan. With my liver and other systems functioning at such a high level, my skin turned much darker in half the time it normally took. One afternoon, I woke up after two hours of sleeping in the sun. As I went into the house, Theresa, who I was dating at the time, stopped by to say hello.

When she came in, I told her it was time to conduct an experiment. Curious, she followed me into the bathroom. Grabbing a bottle of pure aloe vera gel, I began to apply it to my stomach. Within a few minutes, my skin turned about five shades darker than before. Obviously, my melanocyte reproduction was accelerated tremendously! Theresa was dumbfounded! I was even a little astounded myself, but I had a feeling it would happen. All of my metabolic systems were functioning at least ten times their old capacity. I only wished that I had videotaped it. This needed to be documented!

Throughout that summer, my strength came back and my white blood cell count began to normalize. I was still having a blood test every few weeks, which had all of the lab techs and nurses at the Winfield Hospital asking me tons of questions.

After fifteen years of being clogged up, my liver was very sensitive. Although it seemed to be functioning at a much higher capacity, it was almost like having an open wound at times. Whenever I would cheat on my metabolic program and start eating the foods that caused candida albicans overgrowth, my liver would almost shut down. This internal fungus-parasite could travel via the mucus membranes, the lymphatic system and could even change its form and infiltrate the blood stream.

Because it could grow exponentially, it could invade weaker internal organs and systems almost overnight. If left untreated, it could be life threatening.

I had stopped using dairy products, except for yogurt, although it was even difficult to digest. I was still expelling tons of milk-based debris from my colon and upper G.I. tract. I couldn't believe that this small body actually still had so much accumulated metabolic junk in it! To keep the yeast overgrowth at a standstill, I combined a variety of supplements: garlic, caprylic acid, Pau d'Arco, acidophilus and thirty-five percent food grade hydrogen peroxide, taken both orally and in my detox coffee.

I also restricted my diet, eating nothing that included yeast, including bread and mushrooms. I also refrained from alcohol, sugar, fruit, vinegar, and monosodium glutamate (MSG) which all immediately stimulated yeast overgrowth at a spectacular rate. If I did happen to have a sudden strong surge of this overgrowth, I could detoxify and virtually expel most of this internal pest.

Before I quit the insurance company, I took out a large life insurance policy. Because of its size, I had to take a routine physical, which was scheduled with a prominent young intern in Winfield from an entire family of doctors. I didn't know much about him, besides what my wife had told me. She wasn't very fond of the elder doctor because he had supposedly tried to perform brain surgery. There's nothing wrong with that, unless you're only a general practitioner, which is what he was.

During my examination, the doctor checked me over pretty thoroughly. My liver was sore, but when he palpated it, he couldn't feel anything unusual. If he knew, I'd probably be a candidate for a liver transplant. That's all I needed.

As the exam continued, he noticed a slight heart murmur which wasn't news to me since it had been there from birth. Most doctors didn't even notice it and if they did, would comment on it and continue. They knew it was nothing to worry about, but this guy spoke to me with great concern.

"Curtis, we need to run a test on your heart and see what turns up. You may need surgery. I'm not sure, but it's important to find out what's wrong. Before you leave, schedule a time with the receptionist to come back and run a battery of tests."

"Sure, doc, whatever you think."

When he left the room, I shook my head. I didn't want to believe that he saw a price tag on my head, or another surgery for credit toward his schooling. Maybe he was just concerned. So instead of scheduling another appointment, I just walked out, waving goodbye to the cute little redheaded secretary!

When the policy was issued, it was standard. I never paid the clinic another visit. My heart was in better shape now than a decade before.

During my next visit to Dr. B's chiropractic office, he took X-rays of my back. The results were remarkable. The calcium deposits in my lumbar spine and hands were breaking down and almost completely gone in some areas! A year before, the vertebrae were almost connected by these deposits. The excess calcium had broken down and been redistributed. I couldn't believe it.

My adrenals were also much stronger. My lumbar spine still needed adjusting occasionally, because of my fall in gymnastics during my senior year of high school. The ligaments had been severely stretched, but now the elasticity was coming back. Even the pain was gone. For the first time in over a decade, I was walking upright and without any pain.

After leaving his office, I drove to my dentist for a routine cleaning and checkup. About a year earlier, I had surgery at his colleague's office for receding gums. It was at the same time I had started Dr. Kelley's program. I had received a skin graft from the roof of my mouth for my left canine. The right one was also receding so the dentist rescheduled me to come back in a few months. I told him that Dr. Kelley suggested in two months' time it would rebuild itself, but he just laughed. Then when I went back, he smugly stated that the graft was now unnecessary. That's when I laughed and thanked him for not having to slice me up anymore!

Now that I no longer worked for the insurance company, I had much more time for research. I was fascinated by metabolic therapy and was hungry for any new information I could learn that was related. While reviewing one of my manuals from school in Dallas, I was taken back by the staggering statistics on water. One in four of every city in the United States depended on drinking water that failed to meet the government's health and safety standards. Also, certain authorities had reported a forty percent chance that the next glass of water you drink will have passed through someone's toilet, a sewer or an industrial conduit filled with wastes, poisons, lethal forms of bacteria and viruses. I began to feel sick. I had been drinking that crap for thirty years. There was also a forty percent probability that the water we drink in our homes, at work, or in a restaurant could cause polio, infectious hepatitis, typhoid, dysentery, cholera, anthrax, tetanus, tuberculosis, salmonellosis, round worms or flukes. This wasn't just an opinion, it was a documented fact! We have to reuse most of our water, no matter how polluted and disease-bearing it is. The federal report showed that some cities were reusing water as much as *five* times by "recycling" this liquid trash which teems with germs, acids, dirt, human excrement, and other toxic elements.

Reading further, I came across some very old facts about the use of chlorine to "purify" water. It seemed that experimental use of chlorine began in the late 1890s, and was highly accepted by the 1920s. Then after years of investigation and testing, a direct correlation was found between the amount of chlorine ingested and the speed and degree of development of arteriosclerosis. A direct causal relationship supported the strong condemnation of a chemical almost everyone in America considers perfectly safe!

Dr. Harry Johnson had also done some interesting research for several years on our water problem. He found that chlorine completely destroys vitamin E. Also, the research on fluorine was astounding. It indicated beyond a shadow of a doubt, that fluoridation of water and food is extremely harmful and at times, fatal! Homeopathic physicians have found that fluoride in doses of one part per million (the amount commonly used by dentists) is a harmful dose of medication and when continued, acts as a poison with serious physical and psychological effects. Fluoride is one of the major causes of obesity, interfering with the function of the thyroid gland and all the enzyme systems of the body. For a moment I stopped reading. I thought back to July 1973 and San Diego, California, where I went through basic training for the Marine Corps. During our initial medical exams, which were done by the Navy, I was forced to swallow a mouthful of fluoride after having my teeth cleaned. Thinking of it disgusted me. There was no way to find out how that had affected me. That was thirteen years ago.

Continuing to read, I felt a tinge of anger. Fluoride was also a contributing cause of abnormally tall growth among young people and of abnormally broad butts among women. In reality, there is no unprejudiced scientific evidence that fluoride is helpful in cavity prevention. Magnesium, not fluoride, reduces cavities by strengthening tooth enamel and protecting it from decay.

Here is a quote from Congressman Jim Wright:

"Pollution from ordinary sewage and related organic substances is perhaps the worst with which we have to contend. There are fifty-nine million Americans living in approximately two thousand cities who use sewer systems which are either partly or totally inadequate in their treatment of human wastes, before those wastes are dumped into rivers and streams. Among these are some of our largest cities. We have never attacked this, one of our most primitive problems of civilization, with sufficient boldness and forethought."

He hit the nail on the head. Reading further, I discovered another horror story. A chicken-treating plant located on Gravois Creek near St. Louis unloads the effluvia of its kill into the Mississippi. The river actually runs red with blood! Chicken entrails and packing-house wastes are so thick on the water that the paddle wheels of steamboats are fouled with them. Chicken blood and guts cannot be absorbed by the normal flow of a clean river, much less in the already filthy Mississippi.

The Missouri River has been known as the "Big Bloody" for years. Today, a canoe can hardly cut a path through some of its stretches. Slaughterhouses in Omaha, St. Joseph, and Kansas City extrude viscera and fats in such quantities that they create huge grease balls, matrixed with animal hair which are often mistaken for people capsized from a canoe. The Connecticut River has also become a filthy conduit. A sampling of its waters revealed the bacteria of typhoid, paratyphoid, cholera, salmonellosis, tuberculosis, anthrax, tetanus and all the known viruses, including polio, as well as tape, round, hook and pin worms and blood flukes.

Clean water standards are determined by a coliform count. The coliform is a rod-shaped bacterium typically found in human waste. The maximum coliform count usually tolerable for swimming is 1,000 per 100 millimeters of water. The count on the Connecticut reached a peak of 947,000 per 100 millimeters at Chicopee, Massachusetts!

One cup of water taken at random from the Connecticut River, near Hartford, was found to contain twenty-six different infectious bacteria which are transmitted through human wastes. An obvious threat to our national health was being created. Almost all synthetic organic chemicals such as pesticides, agricultural chemicals, synthetic rubbers, synthetic detergents, dyes, etc. are insoluble in water. Some can thoroughly foul the purification processors so as to make them minimally effective for treating other forms of pollution.

With our technology, we still treat our sewage far less scientifically than do reputedly backward coolies in the rice paddies of the orient! After centuries of progress, we still make open latrines of rivers from which others must draw their drinking water. Thank God I had discovered Dr. Kelley and his ecological approach to life. It was late, but I was already on the road to a new life.

Even though distilled water was only one aspect of our program, it was irreplaceable. The human body is over eighty percent water and can't synthesize the proper nutrients if its element of transference is polluted. Purified water *must* be ingested to initiate the total rebuilding process. It is common sense to start rebuilding at the fluid levels of every tissue you have. You have to walk before you can run!

Many pseudo-authorities feel that distilled water draws minerals from the body. Actually, they are correct, but they fail to mention that the minerals removed are destructive inorganic minerals that cause inflammation of the kidneys, thickened joints, painful nerves, weakened arteries, valvular diseases of the heart, apoplexy, rheumatism, and circulation disorders. Distilled water never removes organic minerals needed by the body.

(Although during the '80s through the turn of the 20th century reverse osmosis water was also deemed to be a good way to purify drinking water, but science began to realize its negative health effects. By taking *all* of the minerals out of the water, both large and trace over a long period of time, it was realized that R.O. water actually *chelated* or pulled many minerals out of the body. I will elaborate more on this later.)

When I looked at my watch, it was 7:00 a.m. If I found something that aroused my interest, I'd stay up all night reading it. My brain felt like it had ten times the learning capacity in comparison to my days in college. This was another great side effect of this nutritional program!

It had been over seven months since my last program, and I was anxious to reevaluate. This was to be done at least once every six to eight months during the first two to three years of this therapy. Because of the nature of any type of degenerative disease, the body will be seriously depleted of even the basic essential elements. This factor will determine the length of time it will take to rebuild, along with the various phases one will relive metabolically as he journey's back up the spiral of health. Genetics also play a strong role in the rebuilding process. Just like our fingerprints, our cell prints are unique and individualized, with no two people exactly alike.

I was surprised when I received the results of my metabolic survey. The extensive computer printout indicated that I was starting to pull strongly toward the parasympathetic mode again, with my blood chemistry becoming more alkaline. I had progressed from the bottom of the metabolic schematic as a type three to a type five. Hopefully within the next year, I would climb to a type eight, although I had a suspicion that my *true* genetic type was type five. I knew that my body had been barely hanging on for years, so I didn't get my hopes up thinking that someday I would be a type ten.

On Dr. Kelley's metabolic type chart, the following sequences were presented: "Numbers three, nine, eight, and ten are the balanced types, with three at the bottom indicating disease and ten at the top, very close to perfect health. One and four indicate an acidic blood chemistry, which is linked to sympathetic dominance, with number one the most out of balance. Numbers five and two are the alkaline types with number two the most out of balance. Six and seven fall a little outside of the spectrum with six as an acidic type and seven as a more alkaline type. The numbers eleven and twelve are just a little beneath ten and slightly acidic or alkaline."

Striking a balance between sympathetic and parasympathetic isn't the only desirable aspect of the program. It is very important to maintain a strong metabolism capable of efficiently using raw materials. Now that I had passed type three myself, I felt that each stage would bring me closer to a strong body, free of disease and toxins. (Keep in mind that since Dr. Kelley's original theory of metabolic types in the 1960s, his research has evolved considerably. More information in respect to this will be revealed later in my story!)

Imagine pouring water on a sponge that has lain in the desert for twenty years without rain. It quickly becomes dry again. The human body operates likewise. After being starved for several years, it immediately absorbs what it needs until it can finally reach a saturation point. This will take time depending upon the level of degeneration that has taken place.

I had progressed from assimilating only ten percent of my foods to over seventy percent, which made a tremendous difference in my energy levels. I was thankful for the institute and the Council on Nutritional Research which was founded in 1968 and had contributed to and approved the institute's research and development of the metabolic types.

As I skimmed over some more of Dr. Kelley's research, I ran across the historical development of all the metabolic types. It was astonishing:

The semitropical area where God originally placed man on earth supplied the fruits, nuts, seeds, and vegetables necessary to support man's original metabolism, type one. As some people left that area, they began adding other foods to their diet such as goat's milk. Those who remained in the original area were still type one metabolizers but those altering their diets eventually became a different type. Greece and Northern Italy supported a different climate so the people no longer had the same foods available all year round. They learned to cultivate grains and added them to their diet. The children who adapted to the addition of grain were strong enough to survive. In turn, their children adapted even more to the dietary changes. These people eventually became type four metabolizers.

As civilization moved into colder climates, people depended more on grains and stored foods as well as the meat of small animals to survive. Thus, type five metabolizers emerged. During these difficult periods of history, people born with other genetotrophic types, such as three, six and seven, could not survive and usually died at an early age. Civilization expanded to inhabit northern regions which caused people to depend upon larger animals like bear and deer to survive. Children who could not adapt to this dietary change didn't survive but those who did were quite strong and did well on the heavy purine foods. They became type two metabolizers.

Similarly, this adaptation took place among people from the eastern areas of India, China, and many of the Pacific Islands. Children born in these areas had to become type four metabolizers or remain type one because of the food available in these areas. Many religious sects forbade the eating of all animal products so people born in these societies that were parasympathetic types two, five, and seven would not survive. A good example is Guam where almost the entire population is diabetic and free diabetic clinics are provided throughout the island. Genetically, these people are parasympathetic that have been pushed physiologically to the sympathetic mode and, therefore, an increased tendency for diabetes.

From this synopsis of metabolic history, a true metabolic type apparently cannot change in one generation. In fact, it takes at least eight generations to effect any significant changes. Each person is born with a certain true or "genetic" metabolic type. Ignoring these biological guidelines will eventually create metabolic problems within the individual. This can be seen with people who base their diet on a particular philosophy or religion rather than the needs of their bodies. Learning to recognize our metabolic type and living in agreement with it is important because no matter how hard an individual tries, he cannot make a change in this genetically programmed fact. Everyone is aware that America is considered the melting pot of the world. This also is true in regard to the metabolic types. All types of people of different nationalities, cultures and religions have intermarried until there are almost no "pure" metabolic types left. There is such a mixture of these genetic elements that it has been difficult to develop metabolic classifications. Until the 1900s, the ethnic and cultural groups in our society were fairly stable and pure. Their metabolic patterns were constant throughout one's lifetime. By the early 1940s, however, the mixing of genetic backgrounds was so complex that very few, if any, metabolic patterns were of a pure type. This then caused percentage mixtures of metabolic types. By 1950, medical science had achieved low infant mortality rates but high incidences of the defective metabolic types three, six, and seven resulted. Throughout the 1960s, the stress of modern lifestyles began to cause severe exhaustion of most genetic metabolic types. For example, a person with a strong genetic sympathetic nervous system dominance has excellent functioning of the brain, pineal, anterior pituitary, parathyroid, thyroid, and adrenal medulla glands. He also has a strong heart, bones, muscles, connective tissue, kidneys, gonads, and uterus or prostate gland. Eventually, the stresses of modern living exhaust these glands and organs causing the person to feel bad. His lifestyle pushes the sympathetic glands to the point of total exhaustion. Now only his weaker parasympathetic nervous system glands are maintaining life. He becomes lethargic and depressed and starts going from doctor to doctor. Unable to find answers, he again tries to maintain his lifestyle, causing exhaustion of his parasympathetic glandular system. When this happens, he flips metabolic types completely to a type six, then a type seven. With still more exhaustion, he finally flips to type three. His system is so out of balance that he is not capable of coping with everyday routines.

Another example would be the parasympathetic dominant like myself. He is a happy, calm, "nothing makes me mad" type of individual. He is slow but powerful with a lot of reserve strength. While trying to keep a rapid pace, he exhausts his parasympathetic system. This flips him to a sympathetic dominant mode and he becomes irritable, high strung, and has insomnia. His personality does a complete reversal so he pushes himself harder, putting extreme pressure on the weaker sympathetic system until it also collapses. This flips him to a type seven, then a type six. Finally, he falls to a type three just as I was when I began metabolic therapy after ten years of searching. His health is now in deep trouble and adequate changes *must* be made immediately!

Another factor entered the picture in the late 1960s and early 1970s. Agribusiness has been responsible for the production of the food consumed by our nation and people have become more interested in taste and eye-appealing features than intrinsic nutritional factors. Our foods have been hybridized and chemicalized far beyond normal. As a result, starvation and insidious poisoning are two additional major stresses on our metabolic processes. From the mid-1960s, we have been afflicted with *religious business* and cultisms. Our churches have done the same as agribusiness, except on a spiritual level. They have devitalized our spiritual food supply and allowed people to be deceitfully poisoned by the many religious doctrines infiltrating our society such as close-mindedness, abstinence from "everything" including good sound nutrition and self-awareness combined with a hardening of the spirit or inner self. We now have the additional stresses of spiritual insecurity and mental confusion to complicate the individual metabolic difficulties. Combined with governmental, legal, economic and other stressors, this contributes greatly to an unhealthy environment.

People needed to be rebuilt spiritually, structurally, nutritionally, physically, mentally, and emotionally. The mere treatment of a certain condition, instead of rebuilding the whole person, is no longer acceptable. The time for metabolic typing was *long* overdue!

Closing my manual, I again envisioned our program someday becoming a household word. Maybe that day was closer at hand than I had anticipated.

With fall of 1986 approaching, I couldn't believe how time had flown by so quickly. During the last year and a half I had evolved from a sickly, low self-esteemed, negative wanderer, to a vibrant, healthier, optimistic, energetic, highly self-esteemed winner. The winner had always been inside me but was unable to come out. Actually he was *too sick* to win anything! It wasn't until I properly nourished him that he became alive again. It was a simple transformation. Because of my biochemical inadequacies, my mind was also incapable of functioning anywhere near its capacity. Although I mentally set goals and objectives, they could never be met, at least not by the body I was attached to. Then a strange thing happened. I finally began to feed my body and mind the right raw ingredients. This, with the proper detoxification process, reversed the deterioration of cellular life and revitalized the machine. Now it was functioning again, in fact I had to monitor myself so I wouldn't short-circuit! My adrenals and liver still had months if not years of rebuilding to do.

There was only one word for all of the incredible changes I had already experienced—metamorphosis. I was undergoing a complete change internally and externally. I was a bit taller, my joints were beginning to open and function again. Almost all of the gray was gone from my hair, and it was thicker and much healthier. My muscles were beginning to take on a new dimension, like those of a teenager. I had started to work out a little but only twice per week. My protein metabolism was still not at 100 percent and wouldn't be for some time still.

My liver, gallbladder, pancreas and adrenal glands had been repairing for the past eighteen months and now other organs and systems were rebuilding. My eyes were shiny and full of life again and my voice was deeper than it had ever been. I almost felt like a teenager going through puberty again. Even my face was changing dramatically. I could see my cheek bones again! After a decade of fluid retention in my face, it was finally starting to look and feel normal again. Also, I hadn't given it much thought, but I no longer had to soak my feet in hot water on winter nights before going to bed. My diabetes was gone and my circulatory system was working for the first time in fifteen years! Even my bladder, kidneys, and colon were working marvelously for the first time since I was a little kid.

I had wised up to the massive amounts of steroids pumped into commercial beef and poultry. This, combined with heavy doses of antibiotics, was tainting much of the meat that everyone eats on a daily basis. This contributed to the sensitivities among people for these products. Looking back at my adolescence, I remembered being given massive doses of antibiotics for strep throat and poison ivy for years. I probably had very few *friendly bacteria* left in my digestive system. I was taking acidophilus bacteria, caprylic acid and garlic daily but still had severe problems with yeast overgrowth. Until my liver was healed, this malady would be one of my greatest enemies internally!

Another side effect of the program was the fact that I didn't have to wear my glasses all of the time. My vision was gradually getting better, but an astigmatism in my left eye did require glasses at times when I would read for an extended amount of time.

One afternoon, after reviewing Dr. Kelley's latest book, *Dr. Kelley's Answer to Cancer*, I scanned his own seven warning signs of cancer which are a little different from those compiled by the American Cancer Society and the orthodox medical community.

1. gas on the stomach or bowel
2. sudden weakness of the eyes
3. tired feeling most of the time
4. muscle weakness and cramps—first in the back, then in chest
5. extreme mental depression
6. sudden change in hair texture or color
7. development of various hernias (only in slow growing tumors)

Thinking back, I had suffered all these signs except for number seven. Although I did have hemorrhoids many times, they were now completely gone. I also had discovered two benign tumors during the first six months on the program, one on my left leg and another just inside my anal sphincter, the size of a BB. Today they were both gone, broken down by the enzymes I had been taking.

Reading further, I reviewed the seven *traditional* warning signs for cancer:

1. any sore that does not heal
2. a lump or thickening in breast or elsewhere
3. unusual bleeding or discharge

4. any change in a wart or mole
5. indigestion or difficulty in swallowing
6. hoarseness or cough
7. any change in normal bowel movement

At best, clinical judgment is inadequate because by the time a tumor is discovered, it is many months old. Even under favorable conditions, the accepted methods of clinical judgment and biopsy are not adequate. This is not specifically the fault of the doctor; he is doing the best he can. His education and knowledge is lacking in this area. When some "accepted" drug company or promoter tells him of a better method of cancer diagnosis, he will be the first to accept because he knows as well as you do that the cancer diagnosis and treatment system is lacking.

In actuality, metabolic research has concluded that cancer is caused by the changing of an ectopic germ cell into an ectopic trophoblast cell. Any excess of female sex hormones can bring about this change.

This contradicts the general assumption that cancer is caused primarily by viruses, X-rays, smoking, chemicals, trauma, sunlight, and so forth. Sometimes these can be contributing elements but the biggest single cause is the upset of the delicate balance between male and female hormones. When this takes place, the balance of pancreatic enzymes is also disrupted. This deficiency must be attacked by reestablishing adequate enzyme levels to break down the existing tumor. This, along with nutritional therapy, rebuilds the entire individual.

Closing the book, I contemplated the changes I had experienced. I hadn't given it much thought but I hadn't even caught a cold since my first day on this program. That was a record in itself for me! The one time that I did feel the flu coming on, I did my detox which completely cleared it from my body. We not only had the most practical, inexpensive, purest form of cancer therapy in the world, but also a weapon against the viral and bacterial world. No wonder the medical community was trying to hush us up. We could put a serious dent in their trillion-dollar business!

Three weeks later, after a conversation with Dr. Kelley, I thought that my world had ended. Dr. Kelley was closing the doors to the

International Health Institute. He could no longer afford to keep the computer system operating. IHI was a nonprofit organization, existing solely for the benefit of science and now it was going to vanish.

But there also was another factor involved which Dr. Kelley revealed to me later on. There was quite a bit of espionage going on within the institute that many people were not aware of. As I read the newsletter in disbelief, I lowered my head and wept, not only for myself, but for the thousands of people who desperately needed our help but would never receive it. Slowly lifting my head from my hands, I prayed for an answer—any type of answer to this sudden dilemma. The pending arbitrage could possibly help to reopen the institute's doors but may not happen for months—even years.

With the institute closed, I had but one choice for myself, find a job. My savings was almost gone and could not count on my counseling service, at least not until the smoke cleared and we knew what was going to happen.

For the next two weeks, I searched through the classified ads of the newspaper. It was a frustrating process. Each day as I passed over the many listings of insurance positions, I contemplated calling them but couldn't. I promised myself that those days were over. I just wasn't comfortable with all the knowledge I had about the insurance realm as a whole.

Finally, an interesting ad caught my eye: "Airline school seeks qualified counselor for admissions position. No limit to earnings, must be sharp and aggressive." Jotting down their address, I made a mental note to stop by their office Monday afternoon. I usually called first but I wanted to check this company out. I didn't want to get involved with a shady business.

The next day I strolled casually into the airline school office. A cocky, young, sympathetic-dominant lady named Cindy greeted me. After I explained my curiosity, she handed me an employment application. A bit hesitant, I filled it out. The vibes she sent out were a little strange because of either the stress of her job or her lack of sincerity. She seemed honest but incredibly intense.

After being hired and a week of "military training," I began to travel the state and enroll high school seniors in this school that was based in Miami, Florida. With the Winter of 1986 approaching, I decided to move back to Wichita, Kansas, which was where our regional office was. During the next few months I started to build up my savings again and my body was taking on yet another metabolic dimension. I did have a setback the first few weeks after moving back to Wichita, which was probably linked to the chemicals that were constantly in the air and water. Boeing, Cessna, Beech, and Learjet all had manufacturing plants there and on the edge of town was another toxic chemical plant called "Vulcan" that had been picketed many times over the years. On certain days, after shaving in the morning, I would go outside and my face would actually tingle and burn.

I wasn't quite positive, but it felt as though my polycythemia was affected by the change in air quality when moving to Wichita. After giving whole blood again at the Red Cross, I could actually breathe better and my energy levels increased considerably. I was sure that it would probably take many years to overcome this malady.

With the passing of Christmas, I began to receive calls from our state coordinator on the pending arbitrage. We all were anxious for this transaction to take place and were preparing to travel overseas at a moment's notice. The fact that Richard was dead had not affected the outcome of this huge event.

As January 1987 approached, I decided to quit my job and focus on the arbitrage. The income was nice but the school had not disclosed all of the costs involved to any of the students I had already enrolled. Although they considered it trivial, it was enough information for me to terminate. With my innate sense of business ethics, I should have been a private investigator! Little did I know that someday in the future, my thoughts would become a reality!

# 6

# PLEASE, DOCTORS, ONLY ONE DIAGNOSIS!

*But God chose the foolish things of the world to shame the wise; God chose the weak things of the world to shame the strong.*

—1 Corinthians 1:27

*But he said to me, "My grace is sufficient for you, for my power is made perfect in weakness." Therefore I will boast all the more gladly about my weaknesses, so that Christ's power may rest on me.*

—2 Corinthians 12:9

Now that 1986 had passed, I waited closely by the telephone. Rumor was the arbitrage was again close at hand. I had my doubts, but still anxiously awaited the moment. Too much was invested to just forget about it.

As I prepared for my detox, I read the daily paper. The AIDS scare was now a daily topic for the media. It was a lethal virus to contract, but it didn't have to be fatal. I knew of a few cases that were on our program and in complete remission. AIDS centered on the immune system. The entire metabolic regime was designed to *initially rebuild* one's immune system!

During one of our classes at the International Health Institute, during the fall of 1985, Dr. Kelley shared the story of one AIDS patient that he had helped. It was in the early part of 1983 and Dr. Good of Sloan Kettering in New York City had a patient that was considered terminal! At the time, Dr. Kelley had been talking with Dr. Good about metabolic therapy and incorporating it into their hospitals AIDS therapy. Intrigued, Dr. Good referred this patient to Dr. Kelley who immediately started the patient on a full supplement, diet, and detoxification protocol, leaving nothing to chance!

After about six weeks, Dr. Good had his staff run a routine blood profile to determine the status of this patient. But when the results came back, he was *confused*! The blood panel indicated that many levels were beginning to normalize, which in his mind was *not* possible! Not happy with the results, he again had another blood test done. But *again*, the same results were obtained. At this point he got so upset, he decided to *oversee* this last blood profile. When he again received the results, he shared them with Dr. Kelley, shaking his head in disbelief.

With a huge grin on his face, Dr. Kelley told us that at that point in time, Dr. Good did *not* want Dr. Kelley to monkey around with any more of their AIDS patients! Obviously, there could *never* be a connection between AIDS and the *possibility* of rebuilding the human immune system especially with concentrated nutrition, combined with detoxification tools that cleanse the liver, kidneys, lymphatic system, etc. How *dare* Dr. Kelley even *consider* this factor!

As I began to start my detox, I meditated back in time again, something I had made quite a habit of since starting this program. I couldn't help it. When my body would begin to release all of those funky toxins, my mind would kick into overdrive and vividly stimulate my long-term memory. It was my personal escape that I looked forward to so much. Besides, this procedure was rebuilding my body and life!

Drifting back in time, I remembered my return home from the Marine Corps and my first civilian job. It felt strange not being a military policeman anymore. I had considered police work but wanted to use my hands for a change. It was mid-November 1975, and I was back in Great Bend, Kansas, the town I had spent my teenage years growing up in.

I landed a job at the only health club in town, as a weight lifting instructor, lifeguard and supervisor of the indoor pool. The pay was minimal, but I enjoyed working with people and being in charge of the pool. It gave me a sense of authority I had learned to accept and demonstrate in the military. It would take some time and reconditioning to change this learned behavior! The civilian world operated a little less intensely than the Marine Corps, which was something I had temporarily forgotten.

Since my bodybuilding kick in early 1974, my health had deteriorated and I suspected that the massive amounts of *milk-based* powdered protein I had taken were a major part of the problem. I assumed that my body would eventually rebalance itself if given the correct combination of raw materials, so I still worked out vigorously each day, trying to increase my endurance and muscle mass. Although each workout was of high intensity, I still couldn't make any gains. I felt as though I was running on an eternal treadmill.

One night just before closing, I had a scary experience. After a hard workout and shower, my head began to pound and my face turned beet red. I was under some stress from work but didn't think it was enough to cause high blood pressure! When my boss saw me he suggested I head for the emergency room up the street at Central Kansas Medical Center. When I arrived, the nurse took one look at me and called for the attending physician. When he took my blood pressure, it was sky high, 215/115. His only solution was to get some rest along with the Valium he gave me. I didn't know much about drugs at the time, but I was willing to try anything before I actually exploded!

After a few months at the spa, I became restless. The only excitement I liked was at the local club on weekends. Dancing and music helped me to let loose and forget about my physical problems. One quiet weekday evening at the club, I sat at the bar while the owner spun the records. As I watched him awkwardly try to find the right music to play, I got an idea. Why not be a disc jockey? I loved music and knew almost every song on the charts. It could also broaden my personality. I needed to loosen up some. Without hesitating, I walked toward the booth, watching the owner sip beer from an incredibly huge glass mug.

"Clark, how would you like to have a new DJ?" Blinking at me, he frowned.

"Like who?"

"Why me, of course." As he scratched his head, I waited for a response.

"Well, I do need a part-timer. Have you got any experience?"

"No, but if you let me audition, I can learn. I already know a lot about music."

From that time on, I was hooked on being a DJ. I knew that with some experience, I could shape my voice into the exact style I wanted. This then marked the beginning of "Curtis Raye"—my *new* stage name. My middle name was Robert, so it wasn't too far off.

I became a permanent fixture on Wednesdays, Fridays and Saturdays at Eleanor Rigby's. What better way to earn twenty bucks than by spinning records. It almost made me feel guilty, getting paid for doing something I enjoyed, plus all the *free* beer I could drink, which was quite a loss to the bar!

When spring arrived, I made a trip to my dentist. I had always tried to keep my teeth in working condition. The thought of false teeth made me very conscious about good oral hygiene. My father had to get false teeth in his early twenties while in the Navy, but I wasn't planning on following his footsteps.

After X-rays were taken, Dr. Mingenback recommended the removal of all my wisdom teeth. All four of them were deeply impacted and crowding both my upper and lower jaw. If they weren't removed soon, my entire mouth would be a mess. Being a recent veteran, I scheduled surgery at the V.A. hospital in Wichita, Kansas. The price was right—it was *free*! I had already been there once, as a follow-up to all the tests I had before I was discharged, but they still couldn't find the origin of all my mysterious symptoms. The gastric problems, high blood pressure, hypoglycemia and other symptoms basically confused most of the doctors who examined me.

It was raining the afternoon I checked into the hospital. The trees had begun to turn green and flowers were blooming. Walking through the halls toward my room, I sensed a feeling of desperation. I began to look at the men in their rooms as I slowly glided by. There were some without arms or legs and a few on life support machines, entangled with tubes and wiring. I was stunned. Were these men still here because of the war? And which war? Many of them were at least seventy years old or more. It greatly saddened me.

I surveyed my room as I entered. There were twelve beds, half of them full of old, old men. I definitely was the youngest patient in the entire hospital. After undressing, I sat on my bed and read a book. When the nurse came around with pitchers of water, she bypassed my tray. Curious, I questioned her as she scurried toward the door.

"You've got two feet, don't you?" she replied. "Get your own water!" Flipping her hair off her shoulder, she jaunted out of the room. So much for room service.

When I awoke from surgery the next morning, my mouth felt like a chipmunk's. Touching the protruding skin, I noticed the lack of ice packs. Had they forgotten? Lifting my hand into the air, I waved it, hoping someone would notice. Finally, a hefty black nurse stood over me, glaring down in my face.

Trying to speak, I mumbled the words, "Ice, Ice! Need ice!" She finally got the message. They had forgotten the ice. By now the swelling had reached its maximum!

Throughout the next two days, I was still treated like I was able to fend for myself. Once, when I had to urinate, *desperately* I rang my buzzer. Nothing happened. Finally, I waved my arms to some people visiting an old veteran to my left. An older lady noticed and rang for help. Twenty minutes later, the nurse waddled in. Then, after she finally gave me the "vase" I had no privacy. She wouldn't even pull the curtain. At that point I didn't much care. Another minute would have been too late!

Later that same day, I asked for more gauze as my gums were still bleeding heavily. When the nurse brought the gauze, she threw it on my tray, still in the sterile wrapper. This was getting a little ridiculous. Sure, I was young, but I didn't deserve this kind of treatment. Before my stay, I thought V.A. hospitals were pretty decent. Now I had second thoughts. The surgery had been successful, but the care afterward was rather poor. They needed to give their nurses a course in public relations and basic human respect!

It was another week before my dismissal from the "Happy Hilton." During those few days of recovery, I became acquainted with some of the patients. Many had been coming for treatment since their discharge, some for over thirty years. One gentleman who was shot in the leg in Korea, had treatment twice a year. It was sad to think that one bullet could affect a person all his life. It wasn't fair. War wasn't fair. It was crazy. It reminded me of my uncle Richard who fought in the Korean conflict. Although he was stabbed in the back, he made it home. Uncle Richard was one hell of a tough old cat! Once, after a hot poker game in St. Louis, a sore loser shot him at point-blank with a .38 caliber pistol. Even though he was shot four times (twice through his left arm and twice in the chest, piercing the edge of his heart), he still survived. I could still remember the night he was shot. We were watching TV on a Saturday night at Grandma's and I was about eight or nine. Around 10:30, the phone rang and Grandma answered it. When she hung up, her face was white and void of expression. Someone had called and told her that Richard had been shot and was dead. It wasn't until the next day that the hospital called and explained that he was still alive. Amazing, even the criminals of yesteryear had such a conscience as to call the family of a loved one after he had supposedly been "offed."

As my memory focused on Uncle Richard, I recalled another incident that had taken place not long after he was shot. It was a rainy summer day, and he was visiting us on a Sunday afternoon. I was sitting in the recliner reading comic books, while he and my grandparents were sitting talking at the kitchen table. During the onset of a sudden thunderstorm, lightning struck our TV antenna. The TV was off but it was still plugged in. In one short second, I heard a tremendous *crack*, then felt and *saw* the blue lightning bolt pass inches away from my body. "Son of a bitch," he exclaimed, as the smoke began to clear. In that split second, I witnessed my uncle surviving another one of his nine lives! The thunderbolt had struck the metal-riveted chair he was sitting on and had thrown him completely off. As he sat on the floor in disbelief, I could still smell the electricity that hung silently in the air, along with burnt hair and flesh! Any other person would probably have been killed, but not Uncle Richard. Again he had cheated the grim reaper.

After my dismissal from the V.A. hospital, I walked around for two weeks with fat cheeks. It put a kink in my announcing ability for a short period, but I didn't mind. It was a necessary operation and would save my teeth in the many years to come.

As summer approached, I often visited my biological mother in Larned, Kansas, about twenty minutes from Great Bend. I enjoyed going to church and eating her home-cooked meals. Mom and I were just beginning to get to know one another. We hadn't really talked much until I was seventeen. She had been through many changes in her life, but her faith in God brought her a new inner strength. Her husband, Dale, was a good man except when he hit the bottle. Their marriage had been on the rocks for quite a while.

One Sunday at her Pentecostal church, I had an experience that etched itself into my memory. It was shortly after my baptism. The service was held at the old Girl Scout camp west of town. During the sermon, the minister's wife began to speak, then sing in tongues, which I had never witnessed before. Her voice began to take on different tones as it flowed into a strange but familiar melody. Gradually, the entire congregation was singing in this foreign language. Young and old they sang, all a little off-key. Feeling uneasy, I wasn't sure of what to do. I wanted to sing but didn't know how to begin. I could only watch and listen.

Then as if by a magical transformation within a split second, every voice was singing in harmony. I opened my eyes and listened carefully to make sure I wasn't dreaming. A mysterious spirit moved through the entire congregation, leaving me breathless. I had heard many tales of the Pentecostal faith, but never actually witnessed such an event. For the first time since my enlightenment from the spiritual world, I felt the omnipotent power of God.

For the rest of that summer, I played a lot and worked a little. My DJ job at the club brought in enough money to pay the bills and then some, since I was used to living on very little. Looking back, I see why my health took a nosedive that year. That was before I read labels on food products from the grocery store. Each time my brother Jack and I went grocery shopping, as we were sharing an apartment together, we bought everything we liked. The two of us wolfed down a gallon of milk and a large package of Oreo cookies at least once a week. That, combined with many other unhealthy eating and drinking habits, surely contributed to a gradual degeneration of my already imbalanced body. I didn't have anyone to blame for that except myself.

In September of 1976, I enrolled at Barton County Junior College in Great Bend, Kansas. I took some communication and radio classes but didn't have a goal in mind except getting an associate's degree. I knew that without more of a formal education, I'd never get very far financially. My thirst for truth and knowledge had been smoldering since high school. Now that my rebellious years were over, it was time to take a serious look at my life. I wanted to make a difference in this world, not only for myself, but for future generations. I had a statement and contribution to this life which I was *compelled* to follow through with! So a college education was just the vehicle I needed to mount, in order to reach that innate destination.

During that first semester, I began to shed the tough Marine Corps shell that I had accumulated during my short but intense enlistment. Once one becomes a military policeman in the Marine Corps, the persona is hard to shake. It follows you around long after the job is finished.

After our closing performance of *Strange Bedfellows*, the first play I was casted in that year, my advisor congratulated me. "Curtis, I saw something in you tonight that needs to be expressed, a part of you that has never come forward until now. You need to do something with that talent." Surprised and flattered, I thanked him as I hurried toward the dressing room. Removing my stage makeup, I remembered what my high school counselor said when I was home on leave to speak to the senior English classes, "Curtis, you have a gift, a talent that you should refine and share." He saw the same quality in me as my college advisor. This was something I could never have grasped alone. It was this friendly and sincere advice to which I later gave credit for my performing and public speaking abilities.

The power of a belief in something or someone can move mountains. The belief these two men had in me helped me to move several mountains in my lifetime. For this I will always be thankful.

With Thanksgiving 1976 near, I looked forward to my visit to the famous Hertzler diagnostic hospital in Halstead, Kansas. I wanted to get to the bottom of my health problems. My blood sugar was going crazy along with my blood pressure. My stomach was upset all the time, and I had grown tired of drinking Mylantin, which I started a year before leaving the Marines.

After checking in at the clinic, I was given a pleasant room with my own TV, quite a change from the V.A. hospital. For the next three days, I was given a multitude of tests including upper and lower gastrointestinal, gallbladder X-rays, glucose tolerance, blood pressure, blood profile, EKG and EEG tests. Finally, the head physician called me into his office. As he thumbed through my results, his face took on a blank expression, as if he was a bit confused. He then gave me the rundown on my diagnosis.

"Curtis, everything looks fairly normal, except for one area. Your tests have indicated you have pheochromocytoma, but it's not quite pathological yet. Until it is, there's not much that can be done to treat it."

"Doctor, what is pheo…chro…?"

"Pheochromocytoma, and it's basically a lesion or tumor on the adrenal medulla, which is not yet *malignant*."

"Isn't there anything I can do for it?"

"No, but I do recommend that you try some biofeedback and get some counseling from a psychologist to control the high blood pressure. That's about all you can do to prevent this from happening. Chemotherapy at this point would be too invasive and could cause *much* more harm than good."

Nodding, I shuffled to the door. After all those tests, I still feel like crap and now this cat tells me it's probably my nerves! And if it isn't, there still isn't a thing I can do to prevent this disease from taking over my body. Something's not right, not at all. Either he was as much in the dark as I was, or I was nuts. At times I felt a little crazy, but no one feels sane *all* the time. No one except maybe *God*!

A week after my stay at the clinic, I decided to find a good psychologist for some biofeedback. What did I have to lose? After finding a fairly well-known shrink, I made a phone call. "Mr. Rosenberg will see you on the second at 3:00 p.m. Please be on time!"

On December 2nd, 1976, I walked into his office at exactly three o'clock. Twenty minutes into our discussion, he flat out told me I was defensive. Of course I was defensive. So what else was new? Who wouldn't be after what I was going through. During the remaining few minutes of our session, he talked about the benefits of biofeedback. It seemed like a helpful tool although it couldn't cure any type of physiological problem. Although I was a willing subject, deep down I *knew* that all of my problems were of an organic nature.

For the next several weeks I tried the biofeedback. It did help me to relax and concentrate more but that was it. It didn't much change the way I felt physically. The headaches, blurry vision, chronic fatigue and indigestion persisted. At that point I was ready to throw in the towel. I just wanted to be *normal*, to feel like a human being again.

With second semester starting, I was anxious about which classes I should take. I wanted to sing in the choir but had forgotten how to read music. Jane, a girl I was dating at the time, encouraged me to take the class. She also got me to enroll in voice lessons, a class I never would have taken without her gentle push. She could see much deeper into my creative mind than I could. After enrolling in both, I discovered the challenge was exactly what I was looking for.

For the next four months, I spent all of my time and energy working out, announcing at the campus radio station, studying and singing. I had dreamed of singing again since the seventh grade. That was the last time I had sang in any school choir. I had completely given up on the idea of singing because of what my stepmother had done to me at our Christmas concert. A month before the concert, our choir teacher told us that the boys had to wear a white shirt with a black tie. After explaining this to Wanda, she just nodded her head and said she would "think about it."

When the week came of the concert, I still bugged her about the shirt and tie but to no avail. We often went to the Salvation Army to get most of our clothes, but she would *not* budge that week! The night of the school concert, I had to show up without a white shirt and tie. Although I told the teacher I had forgotten, I think she knew that there was a deeper problem. That one incident had left an emotional scar that would literally last a lifetime.

That semester passed too quickly. Before I was ready, spring had begun. Because of my busy school schedule, I even managed to put my physical distress to the side. I was still seeing the therapist, but it proved to be of minimal value. In fact, by April of 1977, he suggested I see a neurologist who might be able to help me. He agreed that there were some physiological causes of all the symptoms I had been living with. Frustrated with what little progress we had made, I was willing to meet with Dr. Byron Liggett.

A younger physician, Dr. Liggett had a certain class about himself and his clinic. Sitting in his office, I noticed that all his clients that day were my age or younger. This was interesting. During my initial examination, I explained all my long-term symptoms and the biofeedback I had been taking. After the exam, he wrote out a prescription and gave me some pills.

"Curtis, take these for a few days and then come back. We'll see how you feel then."

For the next several weeks, I was zinged out. I started on Valium, then graduated to Thorazine, Stelazine, Compazine and SK Pramime. Once, after complaining about a sudden case of acne, he even prescribed some antibiotics. When he eventually noticed that the drugs were only masking some of the symptoms, he decided to run more tests. This made me breathe a lot easier. All those drugs were making me function like a zombie!

It was during my testing at Central Kansas Medical Center in Great Bend that I experienced a slight *blunder* made by the attending nurse. One morning during a soft tissue X-ray, I had a sudden reaction to the intravenous liquid iodine. That wasn't so bad, except there was no one around to treat it. When the nurse did finally stroll back into the room, her jaw dropped. Before I could even react, she was gone again. As the minutes ticked by, my impatience grew. I knew that something was wrong but wasn't about to panic. I could feel that my lip was swelling and assumed that it was some type of allergic reaction to the drug.

After what seemed to be an eternity, she returned with a doctor who immediately gave me a shot to counteract the reaction. As he asked me several questions about my medical history, I interrupted him to ask for an explanation of my current condition. His only reply was that I had a *routine* reaction to the iodine. He then handed me some pills to take until my lip went back to its normal size. For some reason, I still felt in the dark.

The next afternoon while talking to a visitor, I had another reaction, unrelated to the iodine. It took place about twenty minutes after I was given Thorazine. While we were talking, my tongue began to feel like a piece of limp rubber. I couldn't even talk. As my friend panicked, I tried to be cool. We called for help, and she told the nurse what was happening. She seemed to know what to do, although I was leery of any new tricks. When she returned with more pills, I reluctantly swallowed them. After that I refused to take any more of the drugs Dr. Liggett had prescribed.

The morning before my departure, Dr. Liggett sat down and gave me his evaluation. "Curtis, first of all, I cannot be held responsible for what happened in the X-ray lab. There should have been a trained physician or nurse with you at all times. A few inches lower and that iodine could have taken your life, by cutting off your air supply! You were very lucky. Secondly, after reviewing your test results, I can find no indications of *severe* disease except for a very high red blood cell count which indicates polycythemia, which is causing your high blood pressure. I suggest that you get off the health food kick and eat normally like everyone else. You will *have* to start giving whole blood every few months to try and normalize this condition, for the rest of your life. As far as your current medication is concerned, you may have to also rely upon it for the rest of your life. That's up to you!"

After he finished, I sat nodding my head. One thing I had learned after talking with so many doctors was to always agree, they liked that.

As I walked toward my car, I tilted my head back, inhaling the soothing sunshine. It seemed the closer I got to the root of my problems, the further away the doctors tried to take me. Opening the car door I remembered my internal strength, despite all the turmoil and useless searching I had suffered. I would never give up until I found the answers. This wasn't just a seek and find paradox, it was a search for a resting place, a destiny.

A week after my departure from Dr. Liggett and his advice, I made an appointment with my girlfriend's family doctor, Dr. Unrein. During our first few minutes together, I pulled out my bag of drugs, curious to see how he would respond. Taking a step back, he gasped, as he grabbed all of my drugs from my hand!

"Good grief, you've been taking *all* of these?"

"Yes, sir, one type of pill progressed to another, for the past several weeks!" As he examined each bottle more closely, he had me sit down, as he formulated some words of wisdom which I appreciated, but at the same time confused me.

"Curtis, it's up to you, but my professional advice would be to stop taking all of these drugs and take a healthy approach toward your unique situation. Try to eat correctly and don't stress yourself with all of these drugs. You're too young to have high blood pressure and everything else that's indicated on your chart. Obviously, your body chemistry has been extremely 'hyper,' which is why your doctor has prescribed all of the drugs you have been taking."

Nodding my head, I agreed with Dr. Unrein but had to also stop for a moment and ask myself and him one extremely important question.

"Which doctor was correct? Did I really need to take all of these crazy drugs for the rest of my life or should I trash them and try to start over?" Dr. Liggett was a very prominent and respected physician as also was Dr. Unrein. Following my gut instincts, I tried to imagine what Grandma Kuhn would have done.

With that final thought, I glanced toward the trash can. Letting out a sigh of relief, I tossed my bag full of drugs, even the antibiotics. With my health and ultimately my life at stake, I chose to listen to this wise doctor's advice. A decision that proved to *greatly* increase the length of my life and health.

At semester's end, my health seemed to be somewhat better. Getting off the drugs was the smartest choice I had ever made. I just couldn't visualize myself walking around in a daze all my life. I had too many things to do.

The following summer was a busy one. I landed a full-time job at the city park taking care of the grounds and worked three nights a week as a disc jockey at the local disco. I also was enrolled as a full-time student at the college again. It was a hectic schedule but working outside seemed to give me the extra energy to take on several projects at the same time.

During the last week of summer, the circus came to the Britt Spaugh park there in Great Bend. After watching them perform for two days, I approached the family that made up the trapeze act. I had thought about joining the circus even in high school when I was on the gymnastics team. After meeting with them and sharing my experience on the high bar and rings, they agreed to let me come with them when they left Great Bend. They gave me twenty-four hours to decide if this was what I really wanted to do. Until I was an accomplished trapeze artist, I would be a basic grounds person that would help everyone to set up and tear down at each performance sight.

For the next day, I dreamed of what it would be like to actually live and perform with the circus. It was exciting but also made me think about my quest for knowledge and my college education. I couldn't just give up my thirst for this, especially my own health problems. I needed to someday find the answers to all of my physiological imbalances.

That next afternoon, I met with the senior trapeze artist and told him of my decision. I eagerly wanted to join their group but knew that my heart was set on finishing my education. As we shook hands, I knew that had I went with them, it would have been a wonderful and fulfilling experience.

As summer ended, so did my plans for returning to Barton County College. I was impressed with the music and drama divisions at Fort Hays State College in Hays, Kansas, and had decided to attend there. They were well known for their exceptionally strong fine arts department.

A friend from high school lived in Hays and agreed to have me for a roommate. It was very convenient. With his goofy schedule at Halliburton, we rarely saw each other. I was up every day at 6:30 a.m. and didn't get home till after 10:00 p.m. I not only had a full schedule but was continuity director of the radio station and read the news on Thursdays for the campus TV station. Besides performing in several plays, I also took voice lessons and managed to work out at the gym two hours every day. Three nights a week, I was the DJ at a local club. That semester was the busiest one I ever had.

Jane also was attending Fort Hays that semester, although we had broken up right after we enrolled. She had started dating a very popular varsity football player, while I began to enjoy the wide selection of females this larger campus provided. Being in theater, music, and a *popular* disc jockey *definitely* boosted my ego, as well as allowed me to date a few different young ladies. I had no intentions of getting too involved, as my busy schedule with school and work kept me continuously occupied.

With the first semester almost over, I decided to move back to Great Bend during Christmas and finish the year at Barton County College. I really liked Fort Hays, but the tuition was cheaper and I could receive my associate's degree in May. That diploma meant a heck of a lot to me! It was the first step toward my bachelor's degree and if I could afford it, a master's. Fort Hays was a good school, but I realized I had to follow my priorities.

I spent Christmas with my family and friends. With three weeks to loaf in between semesters, I made the best of it. With hair past my shoulders and a beer in hand, I resumed my high school "party animal" days. I thought I needed the release. My health was getting worse, so I tried to mask the pain with alcohol. It seemed that the outdoor activity in the summer made me feel much stronger, but the winter months were always gloomy and depressing.

A few days into my vacation, I had to regroup. The alcohol and bad eating habits already had formed a cloud over my senses. As old symptoms manifested again, I vowed to take better care of my body. I had enough to deal with without adding fuel to the fire.

After school started again, I began to study the effects of vitamins and minerals on diseases and athletes. I had tried a few different types, but only for a short time and was unfamiliar with the healing properties of food and supplementation. The more I studied, the hungrier I became for information, which led me to the health food store. I gradually began to select supplements I thought could reverse the problems I was plagued with. As I experimented, my energy levels began to increase dramatically, but only to a certain point after which they would fall again, bringing me back to my starting point. Something internally was definitely functioning inadequately. If I could find that piece to the puzzle, it would surely open the gate to my internal junkyard! I just hoped that the junk could still be straightened out and possibly disposed of after it was found.

It was in January of 1978 that I decided to fight one last time in the Kansas-Oklahoma Golden Gloves Championship. I had fought a few other times in high school and wanted to try again. At twenty three, I was still in pretty good shape despite my nagging metabolic imbalances. I relied upon my brain to push my body over that pain threshold. The Marine Corps could be thanked for that.

With a full schedule and a part-time radio job, I trained whenever possible. Weighing in at 151 pounds, I wanted to drop to welterweight or less, which meant a lot of roadwork and physical conditioning. Each day after running five miles, I would jump rope, shadow box and lift weights. I only sparred on weekends when I could visit my old trainer who lived about sixty miles away. Bill would do his best to kill me with hours of sparring, heavy bag and road work. He showed no mercy.

By late February, I was ready. At 141 pounds, I was six pounds under welterweight. I felt good except for a handicap of hypoglycemia and stomachaches which I would mentally ignore.

The night of my fight, Ed Sander, a high school buddy who also worked at the college radio station, volunteered to tape the fight. I agreed that it was a good idea, considering I didn't lose! The thought of losing on the radio was not very appealing.

Four hours before the fight, we weighed in. At 140 pounds, I was only one pound over for the 139-pound division, so I decided to jumped rope and spit for forty-five minutes to drop another pound. At 139 pounds and five foot nine, I was pretty lean and mean. The kid I fought was about three inches shorter and a natural 139 pounder. We were fighting in the open class, indicating he also had fought a few times, although he was only eighteen.

As the bell rang, I shuffled toward the middle. When we met, I sensed his uneasiness. I was obviously stronger with a much better reach. The only way he could hurt me was to work inside. Throwing a jab and a right cross, I stunned him but a flurry of punches came at me when he regained himself. This kid was fast, real fast. I knew he couldn't hurt me, but he was scoring more points than I was. Then with a double-body hook, I knocked his mouthpiece out. He was hurt. Taking a ten-count, he resumed his stance. A southpaw, he always led with his right. I hated that. It made me move in the wrong direction. As the round neared the end, I caught him in the midsection with a jab thrown from a crouched position. Again his mouthpiece came out. He was winded. Ding! The round was over.

The next two rounds were close, but I lost the fight. Of the three rounds, I won the first, lost the second and barely lost the third. The judges scored it a split decision. As I left the ring, I made the decision that this was my last fight as an amateur. Unless I could ever overcome my metabolic problems, I knew that my overall potential as a fighter would forever be handicapped. Besides, I wasn't going to spend thousands of dollars on my brain just to have it punched out from some clown in a boxing ring.

The day I graduated from Barton College was long awaited. I still struggled with a career choice but was proud of this first phase being completed. That summer, I took a job with Halliburton, an oil field service company. I worked on oil rigs and learned to drive an 18-wheeler dry cement truck. The work was hard, but the pay was excellent. We were on call twenty-four hours and were guaranteed at least a sixty hour workweek, although most weeks we worked eighty hours or more.

By the end of the summer, I could carry two 110-pound pipe connections up to the drilling floor. There was no doubt about it, I was strong. Not as strong as my father once was, but close. I could remember Dad doing one-arm pull-ups without using his other arm for balance. He was tougher than an old boot. He was part of the last generation in middle America that was still considered "salt of the earth" type of men.

With fall gradually revealing itself, the midwestern terrain began to take on a very wide spectrum of vivid colors, reminding me that I should once again resume my scholastic pursuit. I was considering going to a private college in the near future but wasn't sure of which one I should apply to. Bethany college in Lindsburg, Kansas, was a very astute protestant college and Marymount College in Salina, Kansas, was one of the most prominent Catholic schools in the Midwest.

Before I could make a decision upon the school I should pursue, the time to enroll had come and gone. Actually, I was a bit relieved, as it gave me more time to consider what specific line of study I should immerse myself into.

By late September, I also was offered another job in Great Bend, with the Kansas Natural Gas Pipe Line Company. They needed another microwave tower inspector to replace one that had gone back to college. Comparing the rate of pay, steady daylight hours and chance to travel out of state each week with room and board covered, I jumped at the opportunity. I had grown tired of the twenty-four-hour call and grueling work of the oil field industry.

Traveling weekly up and down the pipeline from Northern Nebraska through Southern Oklahoma was a nice change from the Kansas oil field profession. I began to look forward to my daily challenges of climbing microwave towers, that at times were several hundred feet high. Inspecting the towers, lights, lines, coaxial cables, and tensions inspired an innate need to challenge both my body and brain with equal stimuli. This, combined with the daily travel from one city to the next, also kept me from getting too bored with the work in general.

Staying in motels all week long, I was compelled to start playing my twelve-string guitar again, although I was still a strict amateur, knowing only a few chords. I had never attempted to write any songs, although the idea was beginning to consume me each evening, after having dinner at the local café.

One foggy, moonlit, fall evening, as I strummed away, words began to come from nowhere. Grabbing a pen and piece of paper, I wrote them down. For the next two hours I worked on my first composition. That evening marked the beginning of an inspiration that slowly evolved into a lifelong pursuit—a search for the ultimate expression, combining words and emotions with music.

As fall slowly evolved into winter, I began to hunger for the thrill of college life and the pursuit of knowledge. My work was definitely challenging and paid the bills but could never replace this fire deep inside my body, mind, and soul. In December, I quit and enrolled in more classes at Barton County College. My search for a career was still driving me to finish school. Curious, I enrolled in general psychology, a class I had bypassed the last two years. After my second week of class, I realized that this was my calling. The study of human behavior fascinated me to no end. I was so relieved to finally declare a major that would help me to better understand myself. I had *no* idea that this was the beginning of a scholastic transformation that would become the focus of my life as time progressed.

It was now January of 1979. I was just getting back into the swing of school, when I began to notice that my vision was strangely changing. A little disturbing, I reluctantly made an appointment with an optometrist. My left eye had begun to blur after a few hours of reading. I didn't like the thought of wearing glasses but was ready for whatever the doctor was about to discover. After my visit, my first prescription for glasses was ordered. The right eye was perfect but the left eye was functioning at 20/30 capacity with a few degrees of astigmatism. Something told me that the vision and physiology of the rest of my body were closely connected. Although I didn't have a clue to follow, other than I knew that my health was gradually slipping away from me and I was unable to stop it. With my vision beginning to spiral downward, I dreaded the thought of other physical conditions manifesting themselves.

That same week, I was offered a job at Larned State Hospital at the Youth Rehab Center. It was perfect timing. This could serve as an internship for my psychology class. As I began to work on third shift, I would often visit several of the other wards on the hospital grounds. It often disturbed and depressed me because I had been unaware of the many types of organic and functional problems many people had. At that point, I made a decision. If I did eventually begin to counsel others, I would only work with those who were capable of recovery. Otherwise, I couldn't do my work justice. I had to see progress. It was what I was made of. Working with severe genetic disorders such as organic brain syndrome along with several others was definitely out of my league.

As my time at the hospital passed, I began to notice several types of nutritional deficiencies among the patients. Almost every patient that I saw on the other wards seemed to suffer from some form of malnourishment. It was at this point that I became keenly aware of the connection between nutrition and the brains development. It seemed only logical that if the biochemistry of the brain were rebalanced, the body would respond accordingly. With this theory in mind, I began to address my own physical conditions. Surely they could be reversed if my blood chemistry and organ integrity were reestablished. The human body functioned as a single unit with trillions of cells and components contained within itself. The unit could only work at its best level if all the parts were functioning properly. When one malfunctioned, the machine lost a certain amount of energy like a car with a fouled spark plug.

As spring of 1979 approached, I began to toss around the idea of moving to Los Angeles. I needed a change. Kansas was a good place to grow up but I wanted to expand my consciousness. I dreamed of attempting an acting and singing career in Hollywood. I at least had to try. Whether I succeeded or not wasn't that important. Some stars weren't discovered for years!

As I finished my detoxification, the phone rang, shifting my attention back to the present. It was my friend Tony. It was Saturday night, and he had a blind date for me. I wasn't too hip on blind dates but then again I was an eligible bachelor. What the heck. The last blind date I had was my ex-wife!

As I dressed, I thought about the changes I had experienced during the last twenty-one months. It all seemed so close to being impossible. If I hadn't lived it, I wouldn't believe it. The ability of the body to rejuvenate itself was astonishing. I whistled as I imagined future transformations I would likely experience. Lord only knew when I would finally reach a plateau, although deep inside, I wanted the metamorphosis to last *forever*!

# 7

# FROM THE COUNTRY TO CITY AND HEALTHY TO SICKLY

> *Be happy, young man, while you are young, and let your heart give you joy in the days of your youth. Follow the ways of your heart and whatever your eyes see but know that for all these things God will bring you to judgment.*
>
> —Ecclesiastes 11:9

The next afternoon, Grandma Kuhn called. It had been a while since I had visited her and I could feel that she was lonely. Living alone in Reece was a choice she had made after Grandpa died. She vowed never to sell her home and property. It held too many precious memories. I agreed that she deserved her small haven in a world of transition and turmoil. I only wished that I could somehow convince her to hire someone to stay with her, to keep her company, cook, and clean. Grandma couldn't use her left arm or leg very well because of her stroke back in the sixties. This, combined with her gallbladder surgery last summer, had left her much weaker than she had ever been.

As we talked, I mentioned a surprise that I had for her. If everything turned out well with the arbitrage, I planned to send her to Hot Springs, Arkansas, for eight weeks to rehabilitate after my return from Central America. However, that still was far from becoming a reality. With a year already gone, I had lost most of my initial enthrallment and faith. I wouldn't believe it was happening until I had a plane ticket in my hand. To live with this surrealistic dream of wealth would surely kill me, especially if I dwelt on it daily. I had to be honest with myself. Still, I wanted the best for Grandma. Without her loving-kindness and care, my childhood wouldn't have been worth remembering. It was hard to imagine spending the first twelve years of my life with my father and stepmother, Wanda. I loved my father, but Wanda and I never quite saw eye-to-eye. She had disliked me from the start, at least that's what I thought! It wasn't until I was in the Marine Corps that I finally learned of her animosity for me. She wanted to exchange a deep-seated anger she kindled for my father, a personal type of revenge.

Supposedly, Dad had mistreated her oldest son when they were first married. When her oldest son Rodney was a teenager, he was "hell on wheels" when it came to the family car. He got caught "drag racing," so Dad grounded him from the car. In retaliation, I suffered her negativity from the age of seven to eighteen. I could still vividly remember the night she made me wash my socks in the toilet because of "stinky" feet. This happened in second grade, when I spent a short time living with them. Those traumatic events were hard to forget, but time can heal most wounds. Over the years, I had forgiven her. In fact, looking back, those were the years that I truly became a fighter. In a way, she had psychologically prepared me for my future journey into the world of holistic medicine and metabolic therapy.

As we finished our conversation, I promised to visit Grandma soon. Hanging up the phone, I spent a few minutes thinking back on my childhood, relishing the years spent in Reece. Every kid should experience such a lifestyle. They had no idea of what they were missing.

With childhood visions in my head, I searched for my photo albums. Photos always brought back good memories. I was also a camera buff as a kid, taking pictures of everyone and anything worth remembering. It helped me to express myself.

Flipping through a photo album, I came across a picture of myself standing next to Grandpa. I was three years old. The catfish hanging next to me was almost twice as long as I was, a good forty-pounder. Grandpa always caught huge catfish. He was a professional fisherman. As I stared at the photograph, I began to recall some of my first experiences as a child. Living in the country was so peaceful and tranquil, it sometimes felt like time stood still. The only recognizable sign of the passing day was when the sun slowly set, casting brilliant rays of color across the face of the Flint Hills. Their serenity spoke louder than words could ever portray.

I remembered the time my father gave me my first bicycle. It had training wheels, at least for the first day. Once they were discarded, I knew that in no time I could possibly *fly*! I always wanted to do things without any help, a trait inherited from Dad. He was as self-sufficient as any human being could be, a mark of his strong German heritage.

At five, I was quite healthy, despite a long bout of asthma shortly after birth. A condition which I eventually outgrew. Looking back, I could understand it's origin. When a child suffers stress early in life, its body reacts purely from a survival instinct. Subjected to the turmoil between Mom and Dad, my body spoke for me and asthma became my method of communication. A psychophysiological dysfunction such as this is often the result of a deeply rooted trauma experienced early in life. Children sense much more from their surroundings than their parents give them credit for.

With the care that my grandmother gave me, I soon overcame this problem. I also was not breastfed for very long, which helped contribute to my milk intolerance early in life. Baby formulas on the market today have fewer nutrients than dog and cat food. Soy milk, the basic ingredient in many of the formulas today, is a very difficult protein to assimilate, especially for a newborn child. Why man still tries to outdo mother nature is beyond my comprehension. Breast milk has only been around for tens of thousands of years and it's worked wonderfully.

Another physical defect I overcame from birth was a serpentine leg. As I began to walk, Grandma noticed that my right leg was shorter than my left and that my foot wasn't straight. Instead, it pointed outward. Our doctor suggested wearing braces, but Grandma didn't think that was necessary. She felt that I could learn to walk without a brace if I worked at it, and she was right. I can vaguely remember her helping me to walk, encouraging me to do it on my own. By the time I was a little over a year old, I could walk and run like any other child. Evidently, my problems had been caused by some type of calcium deficiency, another indication of milk intolerance. It wasn't until many years later, that Grandma told me about my father's rare bone afflictions that led them to pull all of his teeth during his time in the Navy. This genetic predisposition also could very well have set the stage for my polycythemia condition.

It was at the beginning of second grade that my father married Wanda. She had four children from her previous marriage that I hadn't met yet. When she asked me to come stay with them in Great Bend, I wanted to, but deep inside I felt that something was wrong. She was very friendly but it didn't seem real, like she was saying things to make me feel good.

A month after I moved in with them, they separated. She took everyone except me, leaving Dad and I alone in that huge two-story old farmhouse in Heizer, Kansas. His strange hours in the oil field complicated things even more. Within a week, I was staying with a classmate's family. For the next three months, I had no idea what was going to happen. I felt like I was becoming an orphan. Thank God I enjoyed going to school and learning. It made living with the neighbors a bit more bearable. They were *definitely* a very unusual family.

After Christmas, Dad came and took me back to stay with them. He and Wanda were together again and Randy had been born, another addition to our growing family. Now there were six of us, with three more coming over the next three years. By the end of the school year, I was pleading with Wanda to send me back to Grandma's. I missed my old style of life considerably. Not really that concerned, she agreed to have my mother come get me for the summer. Reluctantly, I looked forward to staying with Mom, since it was that much closer to Grandma's.

The day Mom came to pick me up, I remembered something Wanda had said a few weeks earlier. "I'll dance on the roof, the day you leave, Butch!" As Mom and I stepped onto the Greyhound bus, I turned to Wanda and gave her a puzzled look. "Aren't you gonna dance on the roof, Wanda, before we leave?"

As time momentarily stood still, Wanda gave me the *strangest* look, as if I had actually said something *stupid*! Had I? Children do have a knack for naive honesty. Shaking her head in disbelief, my mother said something rather foul under her breath as she tightened her grip on my little hand and almost *lifted* me off the ground, as we boarded the smelly, tightly packed bus!

That summer, I spent my days at the public pool with my half sister Eraina and my nights at the skating rink. I was a pretty darn good roller skater. We rarely saw Mom all summer. She spent her days working and her nights out dancing with Dale, her husband, so Eraina and I took care of ourselves. This created a streak of independence that remained dominant the rest of my life. Behavior learned at a young age is etched strongly into a child's blood, like a drawing in wet cement. It can last a lifetime.

At the end of summer, Mom called Grandma and had her take me home. School was starting again and I had reminded Mom of it on a daily basis. She sensed the bond that had grown between Grandma and me. It was like mother and child. Grandma was the only stable person I could cling to in life.

The day I left, Eraina was sick with the chicken pox, which she had contracted from me. Saying my farewells, I was off once again to my own little paradise. Even the thought of going home again gave me a surge of energy.

The next three years were spent growing, studying, and fishing. In the fall, Grandpa and I went night fishing on weekends at Fall River and Otter Creek. He never failed to bring home a stringer full of huge catfish.

From the ages of five to twelve, I couldn't remember ever catching a cold or the flu. Also, I didn't miss one day of school. I had certificates of perfect attendance for every year except second grade. Although I didn't miss any school days that year because of illness, I do remember a gradual weakening of my immune system, which was related to my change in diet and the stress of living with another family. Luckily, I regained my strength not long after I moved back to Reece.

Each year on the farm, I entered the 4-H Club. The projects I undertook always included photography and woodworking. I enjoyed working with my hands and capturing creative moments on film. I also raised rabbits but never entered them in any contests.

They were a small part of our barnyard family which also included geese, pheasants, ducks, chickens, dogs, cats and a goat. We no longer had any livestock, since Grandpa moved from their very old farm house on the hill, outside of Reece. He worked for the railroad and wasn't home enough to properly care for a big farm like he did back in the forties.

The garden was filled with every vegetable you could imagine, even grapes and peanuts. We were almost entirely self-sustained. The fruit trees we planted wouldn't bear for years, but that didn't change the amount of care they needed. Every week in the summer, we spent hours carrying water from the well, hoping that none would perish. The summers were unbearably hot at times, causing the grass to turn brown. Until the rains came, we were all temperamental, even the animals.

I was in the fifth grade when Grandma had her stroke. While she was in the hospital, I stayed at a friend's place down the road. I wasn't aware of what happened, only that "she was sick" and wouldn't be home for a while. Because of this sudden catastrophe, I was again urged to stay with Dad and Wanda. When Grandma arrived from the hospital, she walked with a limp and couldn't use her left arm. It made me cry. The day I left, I promised to come visit her as often as possible. I wasn't sure how I'd get there, but somehow I would. My will was very strong, another trait she had passed on to me.

It took time, but I gradually adjusted to the move. One incident that stuck out in my mind, happened two days after moving back to

Great Bend. Before going to bed, I gulped down a large glass of milk. Within twenty minutes, I ran into the front room, complaining about an itching rash all over my body. The rash dissipated but the memory didn't. That first allergic reaction to milk began an intolerance that lasted for the next twenty years.

From sixth grade through junior high school, my scholastic abilities began to decline. I had dropped from an A and B student to an average student due to several metabolic changes which took place after my move. My diet was fair but lacked the fresh foods farm life had offered. I also began to catch colds, had several bouts with the flu, tonsillitis, and strep throat. Athletically, I still was a superb runner, a feat I had mastered because of my leg problems from birth.

During the first half of my seventh grade year, we lived right across the street from a family-owned doughnut shop. Each morning, my stepbrother Jack and I would walk past the doughnut shop and take in the wonderful aroma of fresh doughnuts as they came out of the oven. With thirty-five cents in our pockets, for a hot lunch at school, we *dreamed* about going into the shop each and every morning. Finally, after a week of constant discipline, we broke down. I'll never forget the taste of fresh cream-filled long johns, glazed doughnuts and cinnamon rolls! It was truly *heaven*!. This, combined with a large coke, or an occasional carton of milk, gave us both a sugar high that was probably equivalent to some of the most powerful drugs available at the time!

But this did create a most unwanted dilemma when it came to lunch time. With only ten to fifteen cents left over from my morning splurge, I could no longer afford lunch! So what was the alternative? Ice Cream bars! For a nickel each, I could eat from three to four each and every day that I had already spent the bulk of my lunch money on my mouthwatering breakfast. Obviously, these unsavory eating habits formed a metabolic *weak* link that would eventually lead to all of my incredibly *strange* health conditions over the next few years!

During my freshman year at Roosevelt Junior High School, I took a driver's education class, which lasted all year. I was excited about the prospect of obtaining a driver's license, although I *already* had experienced driving a car without the permission of my parents! One night, in the late summer, before school started that year, my friends and I were bored and were walking the streets all over town. When we stumbled across a used car lot, Mark and Jay decided to look inside a few cars, hoping to find the keys. After a few minutes of nervous searching, *bingo*, we struck pay dirt!

Jay found the keys, which were stuffed neatly in the glove box.

After a few minutes of debate, we decided to *borrow* this car. For the next couple of hours, we drove all over the outskirts of town, relishing this chance to drive a car! Finally, after they both finished their turns driving, it was my turn. Although it was an automatic, it still was a pretty scary event! For the next half hour, I drove down several country roads, *enthralled* by this chance to actually drive a car.

Then just as the sun began to peer across the clear eastern horizon, I hit something. At ninety-plus miles per hour, I didn't even have time to react! Pumping the brakes, I backed up, expecting the worst! As the dust began to settle, we all got out. Half afraid to see what I hit, I squinted as I slowly walked toward the now red-and-gray animal. It was a jackrabbit! Wiping my brow, I let out a huge breath of uneasy air. As we all piled back into the car, we laughed a little uneasily, agreeing that it was time to take the car back. When we parked it back in the same spot we found it and placed the keys back in the glove box, we all agreed that we *probably* should not *tell* anyone about this. Although it was a bit thrilling, we also agreed that we should *never* ever attempt this fiasco again! At thirteen years old, the last thing any of us wanted to be known for was *grand theft auto*! Even though the keys were available, it surely didn't give us the right to borrow the car. Thank the Lord we didn't get caught.

With only a few days of summer left that year, I was anxious to start school again. It was Labor Day weekend and the last day for the municipal swimming pool to be open. Jay and I decided to go for a swim, although the water was already getting a bit nippy as the weather was indicating an early fall.

The pool was not very busy at all, as the clouds were rolling in and a few raindrops began to chill all of the kids and what few adults were there. As I climbed back up the ladder from the deep end, after diving off the high diving board, Jay pointed at Tony and Jimmy, two identical twins, who were just coming in from the dressing rooms. It had only been a few days earlier that rumor was they both wanted to kick our butts! We had been out late one summer night, climbing from rooftop to rooftop on many of the larger business buildings downtown. Their cousin Roger, while riding his bicycle, claimed that we had thrown eggs at him. Actually, we had just thrown a few sticks that were stuck in the gutters of a store.

Sensing a bad feeling from the twins, we both agreed to cut our swimming day short and get dressed. Neither one of us had ever been in a fight before, so we were not prepared to tangle with these dudes. They were *supposedly* the toughest kids in Great Bend, at least in junior high school! In fact, rumor was, they had kicked the crap out of several kids in high school!

But as fate would have it, while we were getting dressed, Jimmy began yelling and punching Jay! Even though he was still dressing! I was sure that Tony was also going to challenge me, but instead he just stood there and smirked. As I watched in disbelief, I was completely helpless and frozen with fear!

As fast as it began, the ordeal was over! Both brothers gave me a mean look as they scurried out the door, although they didn't lay a hand on me. Once they were gone, I tried to console Jay, as he wiped the blood from his face, holding back the tears. With the twins already out of the building, I took a deep breath thinking that I had been spared a beating! But as soon as we stepped upon the grass outside the pool, I was immediately confronted by Steve, the older brother of the cousin that sold us out!

Trying to step past him, I tripped, as he stuck out his foot and pushed me to the ground. I got up quickly but was not sure what was about to take place. Then as he began to yell at me with a barrage of questions about his brother, he punched me in the jaw, chipping a tooth in the process! Dazed, I could see stars, as he again threw a couple of wild punches, knocking me to the ground.

But before I could get to my feet, George Morrison, another kid from our class, stepped up and challenged Steve. "Think you're pretty tough, picking on a smaller kid, don't you?" Backing up a few steps, Steve definitely looked a bit *frightened*! As I rose to my feet, George challenged Steve, pointing toward a spot concealed from the upcoming fight. As they began to walk toward a grove of trees about fifty feet away, the crowd that was gathering shuffled with them. The kinetic electricity of this fight began to collect exponentially!

With the crowd forming a circle, they squared off. Steve looked pretty scrappy, but George was a few inches taller, about thirty pounds heavier and a *self-confidence* I could only *dream* of ever achieving!

For the next several minutes, I witnessed a fight that *changed* the course of my life! As George literally *punched* the life out of this kid, I began to experience the euphoria of another human being standing up for me! I don't think Steve even got one punch in on George. By the time it was all over, he also made Steve *apologize* to me, in front of the entire crowd!

That night, I spent at Jay's house. As we relived the events of that day, we vowed *never* to get beat up again! When school began, we started to study karate and judo books, but I was still fascinated by George's boxing technique. So each night after school, I would visit the public library, spending hours studying the history of boxing and the techniques of many famous fighters throughout the twentieth century!

I spent my entire ninth grade and sophomore years, entrenched at the public library, studying, learning, and memorizing every aspect of this sport. With the recreation center right next door, I also started to work on the heavy bag, the speed bag, jumping rope and shadow boxing. By the beginning of my sophomore year, I was ready, both mentally and physically for the next guy who wanted to bully me!

It wasn't long before my unique scholastic approach to fighting was challenged! During my second week of my sophomore year, a kid tripped me at the top of the third floor stairs on my way to first-period class. I was going to dismiss it as an accident, until he punched me in the back and challenged me to a fight after school. "You think you're pretty tough, don't you, Kuhn, learning how to fight at the library and the recreation center? I'll kick your ass tonight at the back of the Sinclair gas station on Washington!"

Nodding my head in agreement, I scurried to my class, a little bewildered about what just happened. Guess I was already starting to get a *reputation*, although I had yet to be in a scuffle!

By the time the three o'clock bell rang, it seemed the entire school knew about our upcoming fight. All of my friends were quizzing me about it, as we walked toward the gas station. When we finally arrived, there were already dozens of kids there! Even my brother showed up.

When Jerry finally appeared, I was ready. With several kids forming a circle around us, I made the mistake of taking my T-shirt off by pulling it over my head. As soon as I could not see, he sucker punched me, throwing a few jabs at my stomach and face. When I finally discarded my shirt, I squared off, throwing several well-placed jabs, knocking him off balance and to the ground. This kid outweighed me by fifty pounds but was shorter and really slow moving. He got back up, but I again threw several jabs and crosses in a flurry! This time, as he fell, I kicked him in the ribs on the way down. As he lay on the ground, I could see that his nose was bleeding profusely and probably broken, as were possibly a rib or two! For several minutes he lay there, as I circled around him, telling him to get back up and finish what he had started. I was truly, mad as hell. The adrenalin was pumping, as the vivid memory of getting beat up the first time played itself over and over in my mind.

That fight began my journey into the world of boxing and of course, street fighting. Although I was never very big, I always held my own when someone would pick a fight with me. During the rest of high school, I defended myself on a few occasions, utilizing the basic principles I had taught myself at the *library*. Then during my senior year, I started training for the Golden Gloves with a heavyweight coach and also was approached by several other students that wanted me to start coaching a new boxing team myself. The coaching aspect was good for me, helping me to discover leadership qualities that otherwise may never have been discovered.

A week before I graduated from my sophomore year, I caught my first case of poison ivy. I had gone handfishing at the Cheyenne Bottoms spillway and somehow rubbed against it. As a kid, I was always around it but was never affected. Since my immune system was weaker,

I was evidently susceptible, but I didn't discover it until my long wait at the bus station in Wichita. I was on my way to Reece, visiting my grandparents for the summer. As I sat on the old wooden bench, I kept scratching the back of my right leg. The itching was driving me crazy. This, combined with a nasty cough, made me extremely uncomfortable. The cough was a product of too much swimming in freezing water, but I hadn't yet determined the source of the itching.

When I finally arrived at Grandma's, I was exhausted and famished. Her first comment was that I "looked like heck!" She immediately fixed some hot soup and sent me to bed.

I spent the next two months practically bedridden. The poison ivy spread all over my body and my cough turned out to be whooping cough. It was one hell of a bad summer. Every time I ate a meal, I would cough and throw it all back up. This, along with the running sores on my skinny legs from the poison ivy, drained all my energy, reducing me to a skinny "bag of bones." There were even a few times that Grandma became a bit concerned, but she took care of me herself. We could have gone to the doctor, but I trusted Grandma's herbal potions and home remedies. Thank goodness for grandmothers. I didn't know then that I would have my share of antibiotics and steroids later on in life. She prolonged the wait.

By summer's end, my cough was minimal and the poison ivy had vanished, leaving deep scar tissue up and down both legs. There were times when the itching became so extreme that I would scratch up and down my legs with a needle, then pour hydrogen peroxide on it. I was probably lucky to be alive. It was hard to forget the endless nights I endured tossing and turning, burning up with fever and waking up drenched in sweat from terrible toxic nightmares! My toxin levels must have been incredibly high.

The day I returned to Great Bend, I called up two of my best friends, Jay and Kurt. They were anxious to tell me something, so we met at the city park. As we walked through the park, they tried to explain the "rest of the story" during an excursion they had on the Fourth of July. They had driven to Reece in Jay's parent's car, drinking beer all the way. By the time they had found me in Eureka, they were loaded to the point of no return. I had asked them to stay the night at my grandparents', but they insisted on going back to Great Bend. Their folks had no idea that they were two-hundred miles from home, instead of the local drive-in movie. They never made it back to Great Bend that night. A few miles west of El Dorado, Kurt fell asleep and rolled the car.

For some reason, we never saw the news report on television, although Grandma always kept up on the local news. They were both truly lucky to still be alive. The thing that probably saved them was the fact that they were drunk and passed out. They were so relaxed, their bodies bounced around like silly putty as the car rolled over six times. For battle scars, Kurt owned caps on all of his upper and lower front teeth, while Jay still was recovering from a few broken bones. They had *definitely* used up another one of their nine lives!

With school starting again, I pondered the idea of trying out for the football team, but after running on the track team my sophomore year, I decided to take a break. I could think of better things to do besides getting beat up every night after school. That was my brother's calling. Jack was a first string pulling guard and had been since his sophomore year. Personally, I felt safer in a street fight. At least you knew when someone was going to hit you.

My high school years were far more memorable than junior high. At least I could finally buy my own school clothes. The clothes we all wore from the Salvation Army worked but weren't quite in the style of the times. I was never that picky, but it was a good feeling to actually work and buy my own clothes, it made me feel productive.

I was thankful at fifteen to be past the babysitting years. It had been fun for my brother and I, but it cut into my social life too much. We had both taken care of our six younger brothers and sisters since I was twelve. We would always turn our babysitting sessions into miniature basketball and football games.

On weekends, I worked for a local farmer that I had started working for during the summer before my sophomore year. I also washed dishes during the week at a Chinese restaurant, as well as keeping score with my brother on Friday nights at the local bowling alley during tournaments.

My junior year passed without many highlights except the junior class play. I "lived" for each rehearsal, as I was casted as the *lead* character in the classic play, *Up the Down Staircase*. The theater held me captive each time I stepped on her stage. For the first time in my life, I felt as though I had found a truly pure format to ultimately express myself.

It was in the spring of 1971 that I again got entangled with the dreaded poison ivy. Within a week's time, it had spread to my bloodstream and caused my lymph system to swell and pulsate. The red dye in the colored socks I had worn seeped into the running sores that had developed on my ankle. I soon had a fever and was unable to eat, drink, or even urinate. The lymph glands in my groin area were so swollen, it affected my ability to release even small amounts of urine and the open sores on my ankles were *oozing* a clear green fluid. I felt like I was going to die. Even Jack thought so. That Friday evening, when he flipped on our bedroom light switch, he gasped and turned it back off. He said he couldn't handle seeing me so sick and thought our room had an aura of death about it. After he left, he persuaded Wanda to call our doctor. Things may possibly have been worse than I thought.

The next morning, she called Dr. Beahm, but he was on vacation, so we got to see Dr. Shivel. After I explained my symptoms to him over the phone, a long pause followed. Then after a slight stutter, he gave me a diagnosis of my condition. It didn't seem to make any difference that I had already said it was poison ivy. Instead, he said that I had a "venereal disease," possibly syphilis. Unable to say a word, I held the phone as if it were contaminated. I couldn't believe my ears. Wanda was listening from another extension and began to cuss me out. "I told you not to fool around with those girls. Now you're in trouble!" As I collected myself, Dr. Shivel asked me to come in immediately. Trying to explain what the real problem was wouldn't work. He was positive that I was infected with this dreaded disease, probably a subliminal Freudian problem he was struggling with. I knew I was a victim of poison ivy, not a Saturday night fling, I was still a *virgin*!

After waiting in his lobby for an hour, we finally were shuttled into his dinky office. As he checked me over, I felt another wave of nausea hit me. I had puked twice the night before and felt my stomach looking for another place to exit its meager contents. Before I could answer his next question, it spewed out! Jumping for the sink, I managed to miss completely, puking all over the shiny tiled floor! Leaning over his sink, I could feel my forehead beading up a fine sweat, as my knees knocked. I could barely hold myself up. Offering no help, he called for the nurse to "clean this mess up!" Stumbling back to the exam table, I resumed the question-answer exchange.

Finally, halfheartedly, he announced his diagnosis. "It's the rarest case of poison ivy I've ever seen." Relieved, I swallowed hard, wanting to punch him in the nose for his earlier judgment. He could at least attempt an apology but he didn't. He was a doctor. God and doctors didn't have to apologize. That was an unwritten law.

During the rest of that weekend, I took the prescription I was given but felt worse instead of better. By five o'clock Monday morning, my fever was back and climbing. Reluctantly, Wanda agreed to admit me to the Central Kansas Medical Center under Dr. Beahm's care. I must have looked pretty bad to warrant that.

The last thing I remembered was passing out in the emergency room. When I woke up, two days later, I was in my own room with the door closed, a private nurse and IVs in each arm. After coming to, I questioned her about my condition, but her only comment was that the medicine I was taking had caused a severe allergic reaction. For four more days I recuperated, enjoying my unexpected vacation. I loved the attention. All my friends visited, which made me feel more alive than any medication I was given. I was quite starved for affection.

The day I was dismissed, I made an effort to thank Dr. Beahm and all the staff on my floor. They had made this unpleasant ordeal much easier to cope with. But when I left, I was still in the dark about this poison ivy stuff. I just couldn't believe that a simple rash could destroy the body so quickly. It was really spooky!

It wasn't until six years later that I learned the truth about my stay in the hospital. While attending Barton College, I gave whole blood to the Red Cross every few months. One afternoon, I ran into one of the nurses that had private duty in my room during my stay. As we talked, she chuckled and introduced me as "Ole Poison Ivy" to a fellow nursing student. Laughing myself, I faintly overheard her speaking softly to her student, as they walked away.

"You know, we almost lost that boy. He's lucky to be alive." In disbelief, I quickly turned my head, not believing what I had just heard! "You are kidding, aren't you?" Surprised that I overheard her statement, she quickly turned around and responded.

"No, I'm not. We almost did lose you, Curtis. Your heart actually *stopped* for over twenty seconds when we hit you with the IV antibiotics! It was something that we *never* expected to happen. But by the time we were about to use the paddles, it again started on its own. It was one of the strangest reactions I have ever seen during my career as a nurse!

For the rest of that day, I relived that week spent in the hospital. I had no recall of my first two days there. Many people who had died or been close to death had some type of experience to recall, but I remembered none. My mind drew only a blank slate. I wanted to remember something, anything, but it was no use. That time was gone forever. I could only be thankful for another chance at life. There must be a reason for me to keep hanging around. My time for death had been interrupted, perhaps as a lesson to help me in my search for the answer to all my metabolic questions.

A year after graduating from high school, I enlisted in the Marine Corps. I was going to join the Navy and work on a nuclear submarine, but before signing the final paperwork, I turned and asked the recruiter one *important* question. "What is the *greatest* challenge you can give me in the Navy? Especially in boot camp?" Scratching his head, he again stated that I would be working on a *nuclear* submarine, which was considered an extraordinary job.

"No, I mean physical challenge. Is there any?"

"Honestly, if you *really* want the ultimate physical challenge, especially in boot camp, you need to see the guy down the hall." As he pointed toward the *Marine* recruiters office, I got the picture. Thanking him, I shook his hand and walked down the long corridor, into the Marine recruiters office. After watching a short but dynamic film, I spent the next two days pondering this opportunity. I also spoke with my father, who had been a Navy man, as well as my high school principal, an ex-Marine.

Both my father and principal thought that it would be a very good career choice, especially because I was not ready to further my scholastic pursuit. By the time I made it back to the recruiters office, I was 90 percent sure about this career move. I only had two questions for him to answer for me. Firstly, could I possibly have a chance to be chosen for the Marine Corps boxing team and secondly, was there any type of program that I could sign up for that would give me just enough active duty time to decide if I wanted to make this a career?

"I'm glad you asked, Curtis. We currently have a two-year active duty program that can allow you to serve for just two years active, then four years 'inactive' as a reservists. The only catch is that there is a 95 percent chance that you *will* go to Vietnam, right after boot camp and combat training school."

"Wooo! So how do I qualify to *not* go to Vietnam?"

"You have to be in the top 10 percent of your class!" Scratching my head, I thought for a moment, then asked him about the chance of qualifying for the boxing team. "Curtis, once you arrive at your first duty station, the rest is up to you. Depending where you are stationed, you can always request within your command for the chance to join this elite boxing program."

Sitting there in silence for several minutes, I pondered this incredible challenge! Yes, it was risky, especially the Vietnam part. But I needed this. I really wasn't ready for college and needed something or someone to help push me along this path in my life! Maybe I would have to go to Vietnam, but I would give it my best and try to excel throughout boot camp and combat training school.

Finally I stood up, shook his hand and agreed to take on this challenge! They also had a delay entry program, so I didn't have to leave for boot camp until July 17th. With four months to basically goof off, I decided to start running and lifting weights every day. But by the second day of running through the park, I quit half way through and decided to go have a few beers. Big mistake! I never worked out again until that first day of boot camp, in San Diego at MCRD.

On July 17th 1973, I prepared to board my first plane flight to San Diego and begin an entirely new phase in my life. As I sat patiently, chatting with my girlfriend, Kala, I stopped for a moment, looked up at the clouds and said a silent prayer. But not just *any* prayer. I didn't want to just be another Marine, like so many other tens of thousands before me. I prayed for God to use this new vocation to not only shape my life but also my *destiny*! I needed a *new* purpose in my life, one that would somehow, someway make a difference to all of mankind!

As I finished this unusual prayer, I shook my head a little and smiled to myself. I rarely ever prayed, unless I saw *trouble* coming my way. Even then, my spiritual life was pretty much stunted! My grandma sent me to church every Sunday as a little boy, but that came to a halt when I moved to Great Bend at age twelve. After that, I rarely pursued the spiritual aspect of my life during my teenage years.

The rest of that day was truly a blur. My first plane ride with free drinks all the way to San Diego. Then suddenly, the reality of boot camp! Once we were shuttled from the airport to MCRD, several drill instructors surrounded us, yelling instructions from *every* direction. With a warm evening summer breeze, gently blowing my shoulder length hair and the smell of the ocean, I knew that my life was about to change forever!

Standing on a set of yellow footprints, we all stood at attention, waiting for the next set of commands to be screamed out of some drill instructor's big mouth! "All right, scumbags, line up for haircuts!" Instinctively, we shuffled toward the front of the barbershop trying not to trip over one another.

Up to this point, I still had a bit of an attitude as did a few of the other guys I had met on the plane. But when a burly, 300-pound Mexican barber grabbed me and tossed me in the chair, I was beginning to feel that this was getting pretty serious! As he began to shave my head, I tried to hold back a huge grin, as I watched the guy next to me going bald in a matter of seconds!

There was a huge mirror behind me with my back to it, but I forgot that there also was a real small one directly in front of me. Catching my cocky grin, the barber grabbed all of my hair with his right hand as he snatched a straight edge razor off the counter. "You little son of a bitch, do you think this is funny?"

As his hot breath and words hit my face, I could feel the cool edge of the razor against my neck, as it began to cut into my skin. "I'll cut your damn throat, you punk kid!"

For a moment time stood still until I found the courage to spit out my answer to his question. "No, sir, I do not, sir!" From that moment forward, every minute of every day was more serious than I could have ever imagined!

After several weeks of boot camp, I finally wrote a letter to dad stating how I felt about his marriage and Wanda. I guess I had to release the anger inside that I had for her, although she did have many qualities that I liked. Dad hadn't taken a vacation for over twelve years. That's one heck of a long time. I just wanted him to take a break and take out a little time for himself. I rarely ever saw Dad smile. He was working himself slowly to death. As I finished writing that letter, I hoped that I would someday get to know my father and somehow forgive my stepmother, as well as be forgiven by her. I was no angel as a kid. My lack of communication with my parents had created a need deep inside me to rebel and be noticed. Perhaps this was one reason why I yearned to express myself. It supplied the reinforcement that I hadn't received at home, the psychological stimulus that many children lacked in their upbringing.

Although my tour of duty in the Marines was fairly short, a two-year active enlistment, it was a tremendous turning point in my life. The year 1973 marked the only year that an experimental two-year program was offered, which basically meant that unless I excelled in boot camp and combat training school, I would be going to Vietnam. There were *no* guarantees!

When I graduated from boot camp, instead of being lean and mean, I was just lean and weak. All of my buddies had dropped pounds and bulked up, but I was scrawny and tired. Thank God I had ten days leave to rest and repair before five weeks of combat training school. Combat training school was tough, but as the *only* squad leader in our entire company, without a stripe, I was *compelled* to graduate with *honors*. I did contract poison oak the week before graduation, but nothing could have stopped me from being in that ceremony! I got my first stripe and with honors! Besides the fact that I also got my choice of duty stations.

Because I was in a serious relationship back home, I decided to take military police duty on a Naval Air station in Brunswick, Maine, guarding nuclear weapons and the perimeter of the base. It was beautiful country, but I missed home terribly. During the first few months, I practically drank myself to death on my days off.

I'll never forget one terribly cold night in February of 1974, while out drinking with my friends. I passed out in a snowdrift after chugging several bottles of beer and a few tequila shots! I had called home to talk with Kala earlier and somehow it ended up in a petty disagreement. So instead of trying to settle it verbally, I submerged myself in alcohol! It was fifty below zero with the windchill, and I had wandered into a snowbank. After barfing on myself and coming too, a couple of my buddies finally found me. As I began to sober up, I started to slowly realize how stupid I was acting.

Then later on that weekend, when I was talking with Sergeant Baker, First Sergeant O'Malley appeared in the squad bay. "PFC Kuhn, did I hear you correctly? Did you call Sergeant Baker by his first name?" Caught completely off guard, I answered him honestly.

"Yes, Sir Top, we are good friends." As the First Sergeant stumbled, I could see that he was *wasted drunk*!

"Son, you *never* address anyone who outranks you by their first name! Where are you headed?"

"It's my weekend off, Top, so I was on my way to the enlisted men's club."

As Top glared at me, he began to look me over, shaking his head. "Boy, you are starting to look *fat*! You better forget the club and go run a few miles! We don't need another *scumbag* Marine in this outfit!" With that said, he turned toward the door and stumbled down the hallway.

For a moment, I felt like I had literally been slapped! But he was correct! I was drinking on every day off and eating way too much food at the chow hall! I had been starved for the past several years and couldn't help myself when it was time to eat! I had never been exposed to so much good food and desserts in my entire *life*!

So that day, I took inventory and began a workout routine that pushed my body to incredible limits over the next decade.

Although my chance to get on the Marine Corps boxing team was stifled, as there was no boxing on this base, I decided to start a bodybuilding program.

As I closed my photo album, I focused back on the present and pushed my old family and military memories to the back of my mind. I couldn't change the past, but I did have control over the present and future. Hopefully, I would not make the same mistakes in the future. Life is far too short to be lived with regrets.

# 8

# $10 MILLION ONLY A PHONE CALL AWAY

> *Cast but a glance at riches, and they are gone, for they will surely sprout wings and fly off to the sky like an eagle.*
>
> —Proverbs 23:5

Now that Christmas was over and I wasn't working, I spent most of my days studying and anticipating that one phone call that could possibly…change my life!

Then on January 3rd 1987, I received a call from Riley, the state coordinator for Kansas. A meeting was scheduled for those people from Kansas to attend.

On that night, they told us everything which had transpired since Richard's recent death. We were given handouts to review which read like a murder mystery. After Richard Jones's death, his wife tried to run his business affairs along with the money we had given him, close to ten million dollars. However, the executor of his estate found documentation stating that she had no legal access to run his business affairs or tend to his remaining funds. This was a privilege that automatically transferred to Richard's "alter ego" after his death. But because he did not make himself known, the money had been sitting in limbo. So our money had once again changed hands, this time to the federal government. I would probably never see my $4,000 again.

Even though they had close to ten million dollars of our money, the arbitrage was still in motion. The collateral base had been set in mid-July of 1986 which is the most crucial aspect of such a huge transaction. All we could do now was wait. After a year of this, my patience was thinning, as were my hopes of this event actually taking place.

That money could help tens of thousands of people and allow the institute to reopen its doors. I couldn't accept the possibility that metabolic typing could not transcend with the holistic movement because of inadequate finances. I just couldn't envision a world without metabolic therapy. It was truly "Medicine's Missing Link."

As the seminar came to a close, I took one last look at the crowd of people I was sitting among. To some, $4,000 was a week's wages, but to many others, a life savings. For myself, it was close to my life savings. I never was that good at putting money back for the future. As I walked toward the exit, Riley caught my attention.

"Curtis, all we can do now is wait and pray."

Nodding, I agreed as we walked through the dimly lit corridor. If anything did happen, Riley would be the first person in Kansas to find out. As in the past, I would make it a point to stay in close contact with him. I didn't want to miss the boat when it sailed! This was one trip that could change my entire life and thousands of others.

Throughout the month of January, I stayed close to the phone and waited. As January faded into February, the arbitrage became an obsession to myself and many others I had gotten to know during the last year. With my mind and body functioning at such a high capacity, my sixth sense had begun to work overtime. It seemed that every time I stopped to visit Riley, the California office would call. It got to the point that as soon as I showed up, Riley would sit by the phone in anticipation. One Saturday morning after dancing all night, I answered the phone to hear Riley asking me about my "vibes" concerning the arbitrage. At 6:00 a.m., I wasn't awake enough to tune in to any kind of supernatural "vibes." This ESP stuff was beginning to bother me a little. At times, the feelings were so strong, I couldn't erase them from my mind. It was an uncanny gift.

The next afternoon I packed a few boxes of books and clothing to take over to Grandma's house. With the offshore event so close at hand, I wanted to travel as lightly as possible. I knew that once that transaction had been made, I wouldn't come back to the states for a while. Central America seemed like a nice place to start when traveling around the world.

As we ate dinner, Grandma told me several times to be careful in Central America. I knew they were having political problems, but where we were going the area was relatively safe, at least for now. After several trips upstairs to pack books and clothes away, I began to rummage through my old toys and clothing. Grandma had a house full of old relics that were probably quite valuable.

As we sat and talked about my childhood, Grandma mentioned Cathy again, wondering how she was doing. I hadn't seen her since our divorce, so I had nothing to report.

"You know that her aunt Mary was very wealthy and had promised to give most of it to Cathy."

"Yeah, I know, Grandma, but that couldn't justify staying with her. We could never be best friends, and that's what I really wanted from our relationship."

"Well, maybe so, but all that money would have been nice!"

As I sat with my chin in my hand, I tried to imagine Cathy and I together again, but it didn't work. We were better off this way. The money would have been nice, but it wouldn't have been fair. She deserved someone who could give her what she wanted, something I wasn't quite ready for yet.

Driving back through Wichita, I could see the huge cross high above Wesley Hospital. Gazing at it reminded me of the gradual change medicine had been moving through the last several years. Orthodox medicine seemed in some ways to no longer be a science. But rather was more concerned about monopolizing the degenerative disease market. It was beginning to try and make up for the aspect of nutritional science that was *not* being taught in medical school. The treatment of all degenerative diseases was exclusively left up to this establishment. Now emergency medical care, that was a different story. My hat was off to the fine surgeons in this country along with EMS specialists. They were saving lives and doing a great service for the nation. My best friend Mick, who was now a nurse, was a great EMT all through the eighties. Mick saved more lives than I bet *he* could even remember.

As I crossed over Highway 54, I focused on metabolic typing and Dr. Kelley. It had been two months since any newsletters had been sent and I was anxious to know what was taking place. Lanny Smith had mentioned metabolic typing restructuring under the name of Healthexcel. That meant I could reestablish my counseling service and continue my own research. I was anxious for all of this to happen. It would be a tremendous loss to humanity if metabolic typing died. But at the same time, I was a bit skeptical, as Dr. Kelley would no longer be with us. How could that even be possible? How could this science keep evolving, without the man who brought it into existence? I guess I soon would learn the answer to that million dollar question!

For the next few days, I began a tissue cleansing program designed by Dr. Bernard Jensen. After making the decision to begin this cleansing regime, I was amazed by the results. After the third day, I began to loosen up and pass strands of black-green mucus that had been inside my small and large intestine for years. This regime was not a fast, but instead combined supplements, fiber, and bentonite to help remove metabolic waste that had built up on the walls of the upper and lower intestinal tract. I didn't eat any solid foods except for potato soup each evening before bed.

On the fourth day I became quite weak, as my liver still had much repair to do, so I stopped the cleanse and started eating again. After it was all over, I was still freaked out by the amount of metabolic junk I had passed from my body. My diseased liver had caused years of digestive stress which in turn slowed down my organs of detoxification. I must have passed a few pounds of that "intergalactic" space goo during those four days! But I did feel squeaky clean inside and out, my mind was crystal clear, my sinuses were open and my energy levels were good, despite the temporary weakness that I had experienced.

As the weekend approached, I made arrangements to visit Jennifer in Salina, Kansas. We had been dating since January and I enjoyed her company. It was on this particular visit that I again encountered a strange situation, a habit I seemed to be forming. Because of the weather, I decided to spend the evening in Salina.

Jennifer was house and babysitting for some friends who were away for the weekend. That evening after she went to bed upstairs, I finally made it down to the basement. After what seemed an hour or so, I was awakened by a blast of heat across my face and an eerie image gliding through the doorway. Half asleep, I convinced myself it was a dream and lay down again, hoping to fall asleep, but for fifteen minutes I could have sworn someone was standing close by watching me. Several times I scanned the room but there wasn't a soul to be seen. It gave me the willies.

After explaining the encounter to Jennifer the next day, she looked at me with wide-opened eyes.

"Curtis, are you sure about what you saw and felt last night?"

"Positively, but why does that matter? There aren't ghosts here, are there?"

Nodding her head slowly, she told me a strange story that left me vibrating to the bone. A short time ago, the lady of the house had a similar experience. While everyone was gone one evening, she heard screaming from the basement, followed by a noisy struggle. Not having her TV on, she panicked. Running downstairs, she expected to find someone in the basement, perhaps a burglar. Instead, she found the curtain had been torn from the west window and the rod was bent in half. With no one else in the house and the window closed and locked, there was only one answer. She had spooks! There was an energy force present that could not be explained.

Then she told me the rest of the strange story. A few years earlier, a murder had taken place in this house, in the basement! It was a domestic fight that had taken place between husband and wife, leaving the woman deceased. Could it be possible that there was still an energy force present that could not be seen? I wondered. Whatever the reason, this force was so strong that the family had the house "exorcised" after the curtain incident. To this day, I still think about that night, the mystery of it gave me a stronger grip on the reality of God and the hereafter.

The day after my arrival back in Wichita, while thumbing through the classifieds, I came across a peculiar ad: "Need professional singers and performers for Las Vegas show. Only serious minded need apply!" After I called the number listed, I was granted an interview at a local hotel the next day. Showing up a few minutes early, I took one last sound check with my guitar. With twelve strings, it didn't take much of a temperature change to pull it off-key. After I was interviewed and played a couple of original numbers, the short fellah behind the fat cigar shook my hand and offered me a job.

"The only stipulation is that you move to Vegas, son. Can ya do that?" Scratching my head, I searched for an answer. If the arbitrage did come through it wouldn't matter where I was, as long as I could get to the airport and take off.

"Can you give me twenty-four hours to think it over?"

"One day, that's all I can wait. Then I'm gone. If you can't make up your mind by then, we'll have to use somebody else for the spot you would be given."

All night I searched my soul trying to decide on what to do. As the twenty-four hours flew by, I inspected my finances and made a decision. I'll sell all of my furniture and move to Vegas. What did I have to lose? Immediately I called Frank, the short guy with the big cigar, and told him my plans. He was glad I accepted the offer, gave me a week to move and agreed to reimburse my travel expenses. It wasn't much, but it would help. The next day I signed the contract, sold all of my worldly goods and packed my clothes.

The 1200-mile drive to Las Vegas was tiring but fun. It was March of 1987, and although it was still very cold in Kansas, it was already over eighty-five degrees in Vegas. When I arrived, I called Frank and rented a room for a few days. The city was already a zoo as it was convention time. After a couple of days of petty gambling and sightseeing, I began to sense a phoniness about Frank and his talent agency. Having booked all of his acts, he told me to wait for an opening—just for a few more days longer. With my funds dwindling, I didn't have much time to spend waiting for a job. Frank did reimburse me for the move but he still couldn't honor his part of the contract. I hadn't moved to Vegas for the fun of it, I wanted to perform. I had played the night clubs in Kansas right out of college and loved to entertain. As my health gradually began to backslide, I had to do something. I had ran out of supplements and could feel that my body was still far from being totally rebuilt. My timing had actually been rather poor. Las Vegas was a bad place to be weak! It could easily drain all of your existing energy. I finally decided to wait no longer. It was time to go home.

I started my journey back to Kansas at 3:00 a.m., when the traffic was slow and the weather cool. The temperature in Vegas had been in the upper 80s and it was only March! But by the time I reached Flagstaff, Arizona, it was snowing. Within twenty minutes, cars were sliding off the interstate all around me. I thanked God that my car had front-wheel drive, it again would save my neck!

I searched for an exit, then panicked as the car in front of me spun into the ditch. I wanted to stop and help but couldn't. If I stopped, I'd never gain enough momentum to get up the next hill. Finally, an exit came into view. As I drove down the barely visible ramp, I could make out a small hotel a half mile up the road. I prayed that my little Dodge Colt would make it!

Pulling into the hotel parking lot, I heaved a huge sigh, as I released the tension of the past two hours. Freeing my hands from the steering wheel, I opened the door and stepped into a foot of freshly fallen snow. As I glanced back in the direction of the interstate, I was amazed. Visibility was now only about twenty feet and as the sky darkened everything was completely blanketed in white! I was truly very *lucky* to still be in one piece and alive!

For the next three days, I hibernated in my room, catching up on the latest news and TV shows. As I watched a Barbara Streisand special, I picked up the phone and called Darcel, a girl I had met just before leaving Kansas. Surprised to hear my voice, she couldn't believe that I was returning. I couldn't believe it either, but it felt like the right thing to do. Obviously I wasn't quite ready for Vegas yet and vice versa.

Evidently, I still had work to do back home. I then called Riley and told him my plans. Everything was still on hold, but the arbitrage would definitely take place he said. We just didn't know when.

The next day, I cleaned off my snowbound car and again took off for home. I had no idea what I would do for work, but it didn't matter. The Vegas dream was already out of my mind. There would someday be another chance with another agent, hopefully one that cared more about his handpicked talent! Frank, that son-of-a-buck, never did fulfill his end of the contract. I would be back someday, somehow and when I did, I would be ready!

When I arrived in Wichita, I called my half sister Angie. She said I could stay on the couch until I could afford another place of my own. With only a few dollars left, I immediately started looking for another job. I didn't want to go back into sales, but it offered the best wages. A few days later, I landed a job with a marketing company, selling books to retail dealers. The pay wasn't great, and I began to notice that my energy levels were dropping dramatically. The stress of the Vegas move, lack of supplements, and the move back to Kansas had really taken its toll on my body. I had to order more supplements as soon as I could afford it.

As Darcel and I became closer, she often spoke of her grandfather's practice in Inman, Kansas. He was a homeopathic chiropractor and had the amazing ability to hold his hands a few inches from your body and determine what organs and systems were weak or diseased. This was an art I had vaguely heard of but had never before seen practiced. So one Sunday, at a family reunion with Darcel's family, I asked Dr. Knackstedt to check me over. As he scanned my liver, he said that "much healing had taken place there." Then scanning my upper back, he stated that my "adrenal glands were on fire." He was correct on both organs. My adrenals were very weak again from lack of nutrition, stress, and being overworked, and my liver had been through some incredible rebuilding during the past two years. It was amazing to watch Doc check me out. Whenever his hand waved across an area of the body that was dysfunctioning, his head would jerk to the left, as though his body was a conduit tapped into my own electrical and biochemical field.

On the next weekend, we paid a visit to Doc's office at the end of the day. As I studied the various homeopathic remedies he used, I noticed that he also had a patent and built his own colonic board. I had never taken a colonic before but knew that it was a tremendous cleanser of the large intestine. Doc had patients that came not only from other parts of the country but from around the world for this type of therapy.

The next day, I experienced my first colonic and was *shocked* by the results. When the nurse came back into my room, she looked at the debris in the large clear plastic flow tube and gasped! "My Lord, it's almost like *baby poo!*" As I leaned over to see what she was talking about, I knew *immediately* what it was.

Partially digested *dairy* products over my lifetime! Even though I had been doing the detox now, for over two years, my body still was holding on to much of this debris.

With spring turning to summer, I resumed my research, both for myself and the new Healthexcel program. The Healthexcel Research Institute had its computer online and was beginning to process new programs on clients across the country. This new "Healthexcel System of Metabolic Typing" was different from Dr. Kelley's original system of Metabolic Typing. It used the autonomic nervous system as a basis for typing, but also incorporated the endocrine and oxidative systems. Now instead of twelve metabolic types there were seventy-two. Although I was anxious to resume studying and working with clients again, I also was reluctant, as Dr. Kelley was no longer with us and his original concept of metabolic typing had been altered. Dr. Kelley had taught us specifically that the autonomic nervous system was the *master* control system that also was in charge of the endocrine and oxidation systems. Time would tell if this new system would be as effective as Dr. Kelley's original work.

Among the new literature I received was the composition of new elements being introduced to nutrition. Coenzyme Q-10 and germanium were two elements highly praised for their effect on heart, gum disease, and oxidation rates. For the last decade, researchers had been testing coenzyme Q-10 on humans, amazed at its regeneration power. Because of my constant battle with candida, I still was looking for the right combination of elements that would counter its savage growth spurts. To keep it in check, I was using dioxychlor, caprylic acid, biotin, garlic, and acidophilus. Hydrogen peroxide 35 percent food grade also helped to destroy it, although the side effects were pretty rough pulling the blood chemistry very acidic.

It was now midsummer of 1987. I was starting to do seminars again and was working a lot on my book. I wanted to finish by 1989 and try to self-publish before the summer of 1989. My counseling service was picking up slightly although I had to maintain part-time work to keep the bills paid. As 1987 faded into 1988, my body again was transforming and changing at many different levels. It seemed that most of 1987 was a year of setbacks both financially and metabolically. But with the spring of 1988 in the air, I began another program on myself and was getting stronger with time. After reviewing my program results, I decided to have a few mercury fillings removed and replaced with composites, as the hair analysis still indicated high tissue levels of mercury.

Each day again was bringing a new and dramatic change to my entire being. Now that my liver, pancreas, adrenals, and other internal organs and cells were rebuilding, my muscles and bones were growing and actually expanding! I began to feel a little *strange* at times! I now was approaching 180 pounds of solid bone and muscle. No more chicken legs, and I even had a rounder butt! I wasn't working out yet, just doing stretcher exercises daily and walking and sometimes jogging three times a week. Several of my friends were beginning to notice the dramatic changes I was going through and would often quiz me about this dynamic program.

As I finished reading the last chapter of Dirk Benedict's autobiography, *Kamikaze Cowboy*, I sensed a similarity in our writing styles. He overcame prostate cancer utilizing a *macrobiotic* diet, which was vegetarian, but without the help of nutritional supplements and pancreatic enzymes.

With the clock striking 2:00 a.m., I caught myself dozing off with his book falling in my lap. During the last two weeks, my mind had been preoccupied with thoughts of Grandma Kuhn, who was walking a thin line between life and death at the Eureka Hospital. Her heart just couldn't take it much longer. After eighty-three years, its circadian rhythm was about to complete its full cycle. I had visited her but couldn't bear to watch her as life slowly crept from her once vibrant body.

Grandma was tough, but I knew that would be our last moment together on the physical plane. When our hands finally parted, I could feel her life force sliding away. As her eyes closed, I said a prayer and walked out into the corridor. The time was soon to come, a day I prayed would never arrive. My grandma would leave me all alone in this world, a world that sometimes felt rather alien to my way of thinking and living.

As I opened my eyes to find my glasses, the French doors to the bedroom suddenly opened, as though someone were on the other side. Startled, I got up to close the front door and any open windows, presuming the wind was blowing the bedroom doors open. But as I turned to close it, I was taken by surprise. It was already closed, as were *all* of the windows also! There wasn't *any* type of draft in the apartment. How could the doors have opened by themselves? As I settled in to finish the book, the French doors opened again! Shutting them once more, I felt a shiver through the length of my spine. Something unusual was happening here, but I couldn't put my finger on it. Then just before 3:20 a.m., it happened again. I had just turned out the light and an eerie blue beam melted its way across the living room floor, creeping across the paned glass of both French doors. I was pretty spooked. It was time for bed. As I drifted to sleep, I remembered Grandma and saw myself growing up in Reece again, feeling all of the love, security, and joy my grandparents had given me.

Before leaving early that morning, I called the hospital to check on Grandma's condition. When the nurse paged my father, I knew something was wrong. The next few words gripped me with a heaviness I had experienced only once before.

"Butch, Grandma died early this morning, but she went peacefully." After our short conversation, I began to sob, regretting that I hadn't a chance to fulfill my promise to her. Then as I relived my life on the farm, I remembered the times I had slept with Grandma when I was only a couple of years old. Grandpa was always gone all week working on the railroad, so I would stay in her room to make sure she was okay. Several times each night, I would wake up and check to see if she was still breathing. I was always afraid that Grandma would die and I would have to take care of myself. At the time, I guess she was the only person who seemed to really care about my well-being.

Now that day had arrived, and although I was prepared for it, I still felt like that little boy who had suddenly lost the most important person in his life, the lady who had instilled all of his hopes and dreams, his grandma.

# 9

# FROM CLINIC TO BRANSON AND THEN VEGAS!

*Search me, O God, and know my heart; test me and know my anxious thoughts. See if there is any offensive way in me and lead me in the way of the everlasting.*

—Psalm 139:23–24

For the next few months, I concentrated on finishing my book and continued to take part-time work of any kind, to support myself. I was also working for a company doing singing telegrams whenever they had a job for me. My years of music theater and radio work, helped me to transform into the different characters I portrayed as well as create a few new ones. I had ran back into my old partner from the advertising agency, Rick Freeman, who convinced the owners to hire me.

In August of 1988, while visiting a few old high school friends back in Great Bend, Kansas, I ran into Don Zimmerman, or Big Z as he was better known as. He had just came back from Washington State after the death of his brother. Z had been living in Salem, Oregon, since

1979, the year I had moved to Los Angeles. Since then he had gotten married, divorced, and had two children. As we sat and talked about "old times," he told me how his brother had died. He had fallen off a four wheeler and broken his neck, which also caused him to slip into a coma. After a few days in the hospital, he was declared "brain dead," although his body was still kept alive by machines. Ironically, just a few months prior to the accident, Z and his brother had agreed that if either one were to ever be on a machine, the other would have the plug pulled. But after discussing this with his family and the Doctor, the Doctor wanted the body to be kept alive for several days until they could find the correct match for all of the organ donations. He had specified this on the back of his driver's license.

With his brother's children and the rest of the extended family in the room, Z spoke to his brother's wife, as well as his parents, about pulling the plug. Once they all agreed to this, Z ushered everyone out of the room. He wanted a little privacy with his brother, even though he was in a coma.

As Z sat down next to his comatose brother, he held his hand, and asked him to squeeze his finger, if he wanted the plug pulled. For a split second, Z said he could feel his brothers hand move, but that wasn't all. Within the next few minutes, he said his brother's body actually sat up and black projectile vomit came out of his mouth. He still was not conscious, but that was a pretty clear indication that he understood what Z was saying. At this point, Z went to the head physician and urged him to cut the machines off, as his brothers children were watching their father's body slowly drift away before their very eyes! But he adamantly refused, stating that they must keep the body alive, for other recipients of all his internal organs. That's when Z said enough is enough! At six feet four inches tall and 425 pounds, most people with any sense listened when Z was upset. As he backed the Doctor out into the hallway next to the fifth story stairwell, he asked him if his brother's *children* would get any of the money for all of the organs that would be donated and transplanted. Shaking his head, the Doctor stared at the floor as Z suggested that if they would not turn off the machines, he would personally *carry* his brother to the newspaper and share his story with them! Not wanting the bad publicity, the Doctor agreed to pull the plug immediately.

As Z finished his emotional story, I began to explain my own story about metabolic therapy. The last time we had been together in the spring of 1979, I had diabetes, polycythemia and was sick most of the time. Looking at my body, he was amazed that I looked so young and much healthier than back in '79. I also had added about forty pounds of bone and muscle to my lean frame during the past year! As I looked at his body, I was also amazed and a little freaked out! In 1979, Z was a lean, mean, 265 pounds on a six foot, four inch frame. But now he was over 420 pounds and was bald. We definitely had to get him on a program someday soon. As we finished our conversation, I agreed to drive up to Oregon before the winter came, so I could meet his family and take in the great northwestern scenery.

As November arrived, I packed some clothes and made my way to Salem, Oregon. The trip was going great, until I was about ten miles out of Rock Springs, Wyoming. That's when my timing chain broke on my old Mercedes. Luckily, I hitched a ride into town and had my car towed to a local garage. He had to order the parts, as most of the valves were bent, so I jumped on a bus to finish my journey.

When I arrived at the bus station in Salem, I called Z and got something to eat. It was a Friday night, about midnight, and the place was pretty busy. Suddenly, I spotted Z at the back of the bus station. With sweat pants, a ripped T-shirt and an Australian outback hat on, he looked like the leader of a "soldier of fortune" army! The first words out of his mouth scared about half of the meandering crowd. "Hey, is this the only bus station in town?" As the lady he spoke to shook her head and scurried away, I waved my hands, laughed a little and shouted, "Don't hurt anybody, Z, I'm right here!" Z had a presence that was a bit overwhelming if you didn't know him. I enjoyed working him in public, I guess it was the actor in me.

For the next month, I got to see Oregon and Washington, a most beautiful place to be. I loved jogging in the rain and the smell of all the wilderness that surrounded me. Then a week before I went back to Kansas, I tried an experiment out on Z. As we watched TV one afternoon, I asked him to change the channel. He didn't have a remote, so he had to get off the couch and manually turn the knob.

After several minutes of channel turning, we finally agreed upon a station. Once he had positioned himself back on the broken down couch again, I started the questions. "Z, it sounds like you just ran around the block, do you have any heart problems or high blood pressure?"

"What, who, not me," he stated as he gulped in more air and his face turned flush.

"Come on, Z, you just turned the channel and it winded you! Look at your couch it's practically broken down! We need to talk about you doing a program and add some years back to your life!"

After a few more minutes of self-realization, we both agreed that he had to take control of his body and life again. Although he only ate one meal a day, he still was gaining weight all of the time. That was because his body was not breaking down several elements and was storing it for a later time to be utilized. He was living on adrenalin, just as I had been before doing my first metabolic program.

When it was time to go back to Kansas, Z was also going, so he drove me to Rock Springs to pick up my car. I then followed him to his sister's house in Northwest Kansas and then went back to Wichita.

By February of 1989, I was almost ready to self-publish my autobiography. I also had been negotiating with a homeopathic physician to open my office in his clinic. Dr. Beyrle was a great guy and was the first holistic doctor willing to give me a helping hand with my business.

Then early one cold and stormy morning, I received a phone call from my half sister Theresa. Brian, my stepbrother, was dead. He had been working on a girlfriend's microwave oven and was accidentally electrocuted. It hadn't been plugged in, but had an element that was still active, which he must have touched. Once he had been shocked, he fell on the gas floor furnace. They didn't find him for a couple of days.

After I had regained some composure, I offered to sing at his funeral. Brian and I had become close in 1982, the year I had graduated from Marymount College, and he had been discharged from the Air Force. Brian was always a wiz kid with electronics from a very young age. When he was just six, he fixed my transistor radio and other appliances in our home. While in the Air Force, he had extensive microwave training and could practically build any type of microwave contraption.

The day of the funeral was again cold, dark, and stormy. As I sang "Amazing Grace," I began to recall Brian as a little boy. He was always so shy and introverted. I was thankful that we had gotten to know one another back in '82. As the service closed, I sang one more song I had written back in the fall of 1978. It was the first song I had ever written on my twelve-string guitar called "Follow."

Midway through the song, I suddenly realized that it was written when I too was involved with microwave technology. For a short time that fall, I had climbed microwave towers for the Kansas Natural Gas Company. The irony of this was too much for me to take. Singing the last verse, I began to weep, trying to hold back the tears but failing to do so.

When spring arrived, I moved into Dr. Beyrle's clinic. It was called the "Kansas Clinic of Traditional Medicine," although it wasn't traditional in the way one would expect. In actuality, homeopathic medicine is much older than modern allopathic medicine, making it truly the first "traditional" approach to medicine.

The first week in his clinic, I also had my first run of books printed. *Metabolic Metamorphosis* was now a reality. I had hired an editor before going to print and designed the cover myself, although the artist at the printing company drew the final graphics. During that first week in the clinic, I would put a new book in the reception area in the morning, but at the end of the day, it would be gone. By Wednesday I was concerned, so I asked the receptionist if she had sold any of my books. Shaking her head, she had no idea where my books were going. I lost four books that week, but during the following two weeks I also solved the puzzle. Four of Dr. Beyrle's patients had taken my new book home to read, two brought it back and the other two brought me back the money. I guess my story was pretty interesting, people were already starting to shoplift it. Ha!

It was May of 1989 and I was starting to do book signings at local health food stores and health fairs. I'll never forget the day I was doing a book signing at one of the health food stores in Wichita and an old friend came in. As our eyes met, he looked me up and down, as if he had just seen a ghost. Don Pizinger and I hadn't seen each other since Christmas of 1985, my first year on the program. Even then he was amazed that I looked so much healthier and different. After some small talk and signing his book, he asked me to step outside for a moment.

As soon as we walked out the door he turned around and blurted out an unusual question. "So how long have you been taking steroids, Curtis? Even your bones are bigger! *My god man*, you look great!" Laughing, I just shook my head and told him the truth, I was still on my metabolic program. In fact, I didn't even work out with weights yet, I just ran periodically and did stretcher exercises. But Don was dumbfounded. He could not accept the fact that nutrition could cause such incredible growth, as I was now five feet ten inches tall and weighed a comfortable 200 pounds. Quite a switch from five feet nine inches and 150 pounds!

The rest of the evening, as we ate dinner, he questioned me about metabolic science and everything I did. Don was a very sharp guy, with a couple of different master's degrees. He also at one time was the youngest admiral in the Navy. I guess it was difficult for that left side of his brain to accept the reality of my personal transformation. But as the next few years unfolded, *many* people I knew well were actually *astounded* by my dramatic change of appearance and demeanor.

It was during another book signing at a local health fair that I met Valerie. With long dark flowing hair, dark eyes, and skin like alabaster, she almost hypnotized me. She also was pregnant at the time, which gave her a certain dynamic glow to her entire being. We became close friends, as the summer turned into fall. Although she was fifteen years younger than me, the age difference never came between us. She looked so young, but at times seemed so much older, possibly because she also was partially raised by her grandparents. She also was a great cook and showed me how to make dishes such as basmati rice, lentils and other Middle Eastern dishes.

During that first year in the clinic, I ran several programs on clients with various metabolic disorders, such as prostate cancer, bone cancer, liver dysfunction, allergies, lupus, bodybuilders, diabetes, AIDS, and other metabolic disorders. I also ran a program on Big Z, which helped him to control his blood pressure while dropping over 150 pounds. But the greatest result was his energy levels. He no longer lived on the couch! In fact, he was running around like a kid again.

When Z first began his program, he gave me a frantic call from Oregon. "Curtis, what's up? Man, I don't think this program is working. I felt great for the first seven or eight days, but now I'm draggin'!" As I began to ask him some questions, the answer to his complaints became obvious.

"So how is your detoxification coming along?" Waiting for his reply, I smiled as Z stammered with his answer.

"What detoxification, you mean that coffee enema thing, dude, I can't be doin' that!" After several minutes of gentle but *educational* persuasion, Z finally agreed to attempt this *scary* procedure. I laughed out loud as I hung up the phone. Not just at Z's brawny approach to this method of cleansing the entire body, but ultimately at myself. I too had been very reluctant to introduce something so seemingly foreign to my one and only *body*. Looking back, I guess it was kind of a strange and unusual experience, like having sex for the first time, or having a *rectal* exam by someone you didn't even know. But after the first few times, it became as simple and easy as eating, taking a shower or any other daily activity. In fact, it became much more important, as it was the final step to the entire *rebuilding* process!

People in America, as well as the *world* in general, still have a slight problem with touching themselves, especially if they have to admit it! I mean let's face it, how many people would openly admit that they have even *once* masturbated in their lifetime? Would you? Obviously, detoxification is just as intimate and personal as that. This is the main reason that so many metabolic patients are reserved about their individual program. It is the most personal and gratifying program existing on our planet today!

An hour after my candid conversation with Z, the phone rang again.

"Curtis, you were right, I haven't had this type of mental clarity in years, and I'm hungrier than hell! My headache is completely gone and my joints don't hurt anymore. You were right!"

Of course I wanted to tell him so, but I tried to remain as professional as possible. Ha! It was always gratifying to help another fellow human being toward the *metabolic truth*. Lord knows how many millions of souls are still searching to no avail.

My book was selling well in the local bookstores, but I was anxious to market it via the national talk show circuit. Because I had self-published, it was rather difficult to break into the national bookstore industry. Then in the spring of 1991, a year after I moved out of the clinic, I began to market my book on radio talk shows across the country. Without enough money to properly advertise my counseling service, I couldn't afford to keep my office open.

Just as I began the talk show circuit, Michael Landon was diagnosed with liver and pancreatic cancer. He was being treated with experimental hormone therapy and chemotherapy but was also on a metabolic program designed by Dr. Nicholas Gonzalez. I had studied under Dr. Kelley at the same time that Dr. Gonzalez was doing research at the International Health Institute. His clinic was in New York City, but his program was not exactly the same as Healthexcel's or Dr. Kelley's.

I contacted Michael Landon's agents, Harry and Pam Flynn and sent them a copy of my book for Michael to read. We also talked about doing a movie of my story, and they gave me the names of a few studios to submit my screenplay to. They tried to get the book to Michael, but he was hard to get close to during the last few weeks of his life. One evening, not long before he died, I saw him being interviewed on the Johnny Carson show. As they talked, Johnny was actually *amazed* that Michael looked so good, although his doctors still said that he wouldn't make it. Agreeing, Michael said that he felt pretty strong when he drank his carrot juice, took his supplements, and did his detoxification. But when he was given the chemotherapy and hormone therapy, it knocked him back down again. It saddened me to know that if only he would stick to the natural therapy, he could possibly make it. It was a great loss to the entertainment world and all of America when he passed on.

One evening, after finishing a radio interview in Texas, Dr. Schultz called. After a few minutes of small talk, he made an extraordinary statement. "Curtis Raye, guess what? You are about to write Governor Joan Finney's theme song for her antidrug campaign." Laughing, I asked him to continue. "You also will be receiving the 'I Believe I Can Achieve' award for overcoming liver cancer!" Laughing again, but with some concern, I again asked him to tell me more. "The lyrics for the song can be used from her campaign as the first female governor of Kansas. She asked everyone to 'Join Hands' with her. She talked about old hands and young hands, strong hands and weak hands, black hands and white hands. You get the picture don't ya?"

"Sure, but you are kidding aren't you? I mean come on, the governor? I've met her, but me get an award, how do I rate?"

"You're a humanitarian and the governor likes you. You also can sing the song after you receive the award in a couple of weeks at the state capital!"

"A couple of weeks, that's not much time!"

"Well you can start writing it now, and I will call you back in an hour or so to see how you're doing. And by the way, you know Barry Sanders, don't you? The Heisman trophy winner back in 1988 that plays for the Detroit Lions? His mother and all of his sisters will be your choir, they are the choir for the Paradise Baptist Church here in North Wichita."

After I hung up the phone, I was still in shock. Me writing a song for the governor and singing it for a few thousand people at the state capital? And what about that award? She was also giving it to a few other select people such as Miss USA, a Kansas University girls basketball team that was undefeated, and two other elite groups.

When the day came to accept my award and sing "Join Hands," I was ready. The fact that Whitney Houston had just performed in the same auditorium, gave me goose bumps. The ceremony was to start at noon on Monday, as all of the schools were being dismissed to participate, so I got there early to rehearse my song. We had spent a week in the recording studio with the choir, laying down the tracks for the background tape. Mrs. Sanders and her daughters were great people to work with.

At eleven thirty on Monday, after waiting three hours backstage to rehearse my song, the soundman finally gave me the cordless mic! With my face flushed with anger, I blurted out, "I never even got to test my vocals on this system!" Looking at me halfhearted, he asked. "You are a professional, are you not?"

"Of course I am!" I stammered.

"Then I'm sure you will do fine." As he walked off the back of the stage. Just as I was about to utter a few choice words, Dr. Schultz patted me on the back. As I turned around, he grimaced at my red face.

"Curtis, what's up? Woo, this is *definitely* no time for high blood pressure!" As I explained the incident, he assured me that I was a professional and that everything would come together.

When it was my turn to accept the award, everyone else had already received theirs, so it gave me the chance to end the ceremony with my song. Then halfway through my acceptance speech, the same soundman *clown* started the background music. Instinctively I raised my hand and stated, "Please stop the music, again, please stop the music!" At that point, he finally got the message, I still had important things to say. When I finally finished my speech, I walked to the center of the stage, turned on my cordless mic and motioned for the soundman to start my tape.

Afterward, I signed a few autographs, shook many hands and thanked Dr. Schultz for putting me in the right place at the right time. Obviously timing was critical in most aspects of life. Then just as I finished signing an autograph, someone yanked the cordless mic from my left hand. Turning quickly around, I saw the same sound guy that had originally given me the mic, right before our ceremony. His face was beet red as he broke through the waiting crowd. He *definitely* was still angry about me taking control, when it came time to sing the governor's song. *Karma* is at times a wonderful thing!

The award from the governor was a life-changing experience, but three months later, another incredible event took place. The birth of my son Ciarston Riece Kuhn. Valerie and I had been seeing each other off and on for the past two years and the unexpected had taken place. Although we never even lived together, she still wanted to keep him. I did not want to see another child born into this world without both parents, so I agreed to be part of his life, although we had no plans of *ever* even living together.

The night of July 24th 1991, which was also my father's birth date, Valerie stopped by my apartment, complaining of unusual pains, that quickly turned into *labor* pains. When her water broke, I called the midwife stressing the urgency for her to get there *now*!

When she arrived with her assistant, he was ready to greet the world. As I sat on the edge of the bed, Valerie almost ripped my arms off as she pushed and pulled simultaneously! When he finally emerged, the soft music and candlelight seemed to be a warm welcome for his sudden transition. Once he was detached and cleaned up, he stretched out on the bed and fell asleep, with only a couple of whimpers, as he greeted the new world.

For the next year, I ran a few more programs and worked at part-time jobs. Then in the fall of 1992, just before moving to Branson, Missouri, I stumbled into a friend I had worked with during my time with the airline school. Being a strong Amway member, he invited me to a meeting. I agreed to go, although I never much agreed upon the philosophy of multilevel marketing.

After the meeting was over, we stood out in the hall of the century II building in downtown Wichita. As Randy introduced me to a few of his friends, I saw a couple approaching that he had introduced me to back in 1986. As he began to reintroduce us, a strange and bewildered look came across both of their faces. Repeating my name again, Randy emphasized the time and date that we had met back in the fall of 1986. Then as the lady's jaw dropped, she lit up and looked me up and down several times. Her husband also began to remember our first meeting. For the next ten minutes, they quizzed me on how I could possibly have changed so much physically during the last six years. It was rather funny to watch the expression on someone's face change that hadn't seen me for a few years.

A few weeks before I moved to Branson, Missouri, Valerie asked me to speak at one of her computer vo-tech classes about the science of metabolic typing. When the evening arrived, I anxiously told my own personal story and talked about the mechanics of metabolic therapy. For the first hour, the class was rather lethargic and the instructor kept interrupting me or upstaging me would be more like it! Finally, just as I was ready to throw in the towel, during the question and answer phases, one student asked me a strange question. "Wait a minute, are you from Great Bend, Kansas?"

"Yes," I answered, sounding startled. As she looked around the classroom, the next words out of her mouth even surprised me.

"He's right, he was sick way back in high school, my older brother was in his class. You were in the class of '72 weren't you, Curtis?"

"Yes, I was. What class were you in?" As she rattled off the year she graduated, her name and her brother's name, I remembered him well. We had been in vocational agriculture together. It truly was a small world! For the next two hours, the room suddenly came alive as students began to bombard me with tons of questions. Apparently, I now was "believable."

After I finished that evening, I thought back to a few months earlier when I had attended my twenty-year class reunion. Many of my old friends were pretty amazed at the changes I had been through since high school, but a couple of them were skeptical. After talking with them for a short time, I learned the reason why. They were both working in the allopathic medical field. One even commented that all chiropractors were "quacks." When he made that foolish statement, I simply made my exit. I didn't have time for small minds and foolish ideas.

By Thanksgiving of 1992, the snow was falling and I was on my way to Branson, Missouri. My old friend and partner Rick Freeman, was living and performing there, trying to get us a theater to put our own show in. We stayed at Rock-A-Way Beach, just a few miles North of Branson. Rick was performing at a small theater in town and also at the "Bob Evans" restaurant. We began negotiating with a few investors, trying to get a commitment to back a theater we wanted to lease, but it never materialized. I also was negotiating with a chiropractor that had recently moved there from California. He was semi-retiring from his position as the sports Doctor for the San Diego Chargers. My goal was to open my metabolic clinic again in his office and utilize my show *Metabolic Metamorphosis*. This unique show would tell my story by utilizing my own original music, pop music, a slide presentation, special effects, and dramatic storytelling.

We also had written a comedy show that was called the *Welcome to Branson Show*, which was to be the only free show in Branson. Our characters, the "Dueling Nerds of Branson" were both created when we performed singing telegrams back in Wichita. To test our idea, we got in character a few times, walked up and down the strip and performed at a few clubs and theaters. The crowd response was always great.

During one of my meetings with the chiropractor, he suggested that I get a full spinal X-ray. Since it had been a few years, I agreed to let him do it. But the next time we met, he asked me a strange question. "Curtis, when did you break your neck?" Startled, I took a deep breath and sighed.

"Why would you say that, Doc?" As he pointed to the top of my spine in the X-ray, I could see a small line that went completely across the C-1 spine.

"It looks as though there was a hairline fracture to this area about twenty or so years ago."

"Well, in the spring of 1972, I fell off the high bar in gymnastics and landed on the left frontal area of my head on the floor. Then two days later, I wrecked my motorcycle after flying off a twenty-five-foot embankment. The bike fell directly on my back. I had X-rays again, but the doctor never did notice this!"

"You were a fraction of an inch away from being a quadriplegic young man. You should be thankful for a strong genetic background. That metabolic foundation *probably* saved your life!"

By the end of March 1993, I had been in Branson five months and we still didn't have a theater secured. Doc and I had agreed to work together, but our theater was to be the main marketing tool for my business. Branson was a very small town that could not survive without the tourist industry, so we had to cater to this particular market. I had a silent partner in Kansas City, but we had spent most of the money he had set aside for this Branson venture. If nothing came together within the next few weeks, Rick and I had agreed that I would go back to Kansas and regroup. Rick, on the other hand, was going to stay in Branson. His love for country music, his girlfriend, and the area, was too strong to fight. I also loved the countryside but my taste in music was more within the realm of gospel, blues, folk, and jazz.

The week before I moved back to Wichita, I met Tammi. Rick and I met a group of investors at the home show in Springfield and dressed up in our characters to illustrate the jest of our comedy routine. As I passed by her interior design booth in my "Jimmy Raye" character, she gave me a peculiar stare. Swayed by her tall stature and dark eyes, I told Rick that I was going to swing back around and try to talk with her. When we finally met, I knew that I wanted to get to know this young lady better.

When the show finished, Rick had secured two investors that were ready to move on our project. The following Monday, we met Tammi in Branson and took her to the theater we were to lease. She measured the stage area for curtains and gave us quotes on tables and furniture. John Davidson, the famous singer and actor was rehearsing there at the time, so we had to work around his crew.

Then after three more days of intense negotiating, the bomb was dropped. The investors liked our ideas, but still were not ready to commit. They wanted the security of knowing that our theater would always be full, something that would be hard to put on paper. They also were concerned that the *Crook and Chase Television Show* was going to be filmed out of our theater.

By April of 1993, we were almost broke again and the investors were still not ready to deal, so I decided to go back to Kansas. For the next few months, I stayed with my nephew Cody and worked on my thesis for my doctorate degree. I knew that it would take a few more years of experience on Dr. Kelley's program, as well as observation of many future clients, but I was anxious to share his science with the world.

In November of 1993, I again flew to Germany and met with Horst Christian Link, the trade ambassador. Chris and I had met when my clinic was in Kansas. We had flown the first time to Germany in the spring of 1992, right after my twenty-year class reunion. Chris had purchased a consulting firm in Heidelberg, and I owned ten percent of its total market value. Our plan was to purchase a license to market franchises in Europe of my metabolic clinic and eventually go on the stock market. We met with a few physicians and were pleased with their response to the science of metabolic typing. Although I knew that I had the cart before the horse, I was anticipating working with Dr. Kelley again, after putting together some kind of deal with our German franchise.

Chris Link had been the trade ambassador to Germany for the past forty years. His main business thrust was to find new American business ventures to establish in Germany and other countries in Europe. I enjoyed Germany and was impressed with the people. They were quite friendly and hospitable. Both of my grandparents on my father's side were from Germany, so I spent some time looking up the name "Kuhn."

When I returned from Europe, I decided to run an ad in the paper for a partner to open my clinic. Las Vegas was growing tremendously fast, so this was to be the place I would relocate to. The night before I received my first response on the ad, I had a peculiar dream. It was set in the country, within an old abandoned farmhouse during the dead of winter. As I walked into the front door of the house, I suddenly ran into an old friend from my past, Tom Vanaman. I had known Tom since my grade school years.

He and his brother Wayne always played sandlot football with us after school. I couldn't remember anything else that happened during the dream except for the fact that Tom had spoken to me. That in itself wasn't unusual, except for the fact that Tom stuttered! In fact, Tom was the only friend I ever had that stuttered.

When I awoke the next morning, I was actually laughing in my sleep. My conversation with Tom had brought back many joyful memories from my childhood past. As the day progressed, I would often relive the intense dream of the night before. That evening, when I got home, my nephew Cody had left a message that someone had called about my ad in the paper. The gentleman had left a number and wanted more information about my venture. Finally, after making a few other calls, I returned the call to the potential partner. After speaking to his wife, she summoned him to the phone. As we began to talk, an immediate rapport was established. Then after only a minute or so, it happened. He began to stutter. At first I would try to finish his sentence, but then I had another image of the dream I lived the night before. When our conversation was finished, I hung up the phone and shook my head. Could that dream somehow have been an indication that this person would answer my ad? If so, this truly would turn out to be an uncanny experience.

During the next few days, I met with the gentleman and we finalized a partnership agreement. Then another opportunity knocked at my door. At least it seemed to be an opportunity. An investment group in Dallas, Texas, was advertising venture capital for new companies across the country. After calling the number in the ad, I received literature explaining how their program worked. They would evaluate my business plan, determine if it was a viable project, then find a bank that would loan me the capital. Once the bank was located, a letter of credit was created that basically guaranteed the loan would be made to myself and my business project. But there was a catch, it would cost me to get that letter of credit. The price—$4,000.

During the next two weeks, I sent my business plan to Dallas and spoke with the owner of the firm several times. Finally, he called and congratulated me. It seemed that my project to open a metabolic clinic had been approved for funding. All I had to do was send him a $4,000 cashier's check and my letter of credit would immediately be shipped overnight. Then all I had to do was contact the bank and fill out the paperwork for the $300,000 loan.

The next morning, I called Chris Link in California and Big Z in Oregon. After explaining the loan program and the up-front money, they both encouraged me *not* to send this guy any money. But after so many years of pursuing this business goal, I was still willing to take another calculated risk. That same day I went to the bank, got a cashier's check for four grand and strolled to the post office. As I stood in line waiting to send it off I silently prayed, "Lord, if there is any way that you can show me that this is a mistake, please make it so." That was on a Thursday afternoon. The next day, I called the firm in Dallas after lunch to confirm they had received the check. They still hadn't. By 4:00 p.m., they still hadn't received anything, so I called the post office. By four thirty, they were convinced that it somehow had been stolen. That's when I called the bank and had them stop payment on the cashier's check. It possibly was already cashed, but no one knew for sure.

Finally, at three o'clock Monday afternoon, I received a call from Dallas. The check had just arrived. So much for overnight mail! For the next few minutes, we shared some small talk, then he asked me if I could release the stop payment on this check. At first I hesitated, remembering the small prayer I had said before sending it on Thursday. Had this truly been a sign? In my heart, I felt that it was, but my mind and humanness for the moment overruled! "Sure, I'll call the bank right now and have it reversed."

"You won't regret this Curtis, you have made a wise decision."

The next week I received a letter of credit from some bank in Northern California. I called them a few times but could never reach anyone, only an answering machine. Frustrated, I called Dallas but began to get the run-around from them also. Panicking, I called the securities division for Kansas. Once I had explained my story, they informed me that this had happened to several dozen other people across the nation. Hanging my head in disbelief, I thought back to that moment in the post office. If only I would have listened to my heart.

Once this "letter of credit" fiasco had taken place, it again reminded me of the "arbitrage" that we all were *still* waiting on to take place. After so many years passing, I was pretty sure that my money for that project had also grown wings and disappeared forever!

Shortly after this financial woe, I ran into a client that I hadn't seen for over a year. Greg was recovering from a severe liver disease that had almost taken his life. When we met in 1991, he was completely jaundiced and told me that his Doctor said there was nothing more that he could do for him. He basically was just waiting to die. He was given another sixty or so days to live. Greg at the time had no appetite, was very alkaline and seemed to be a slow oxidizer, which didn't help matters any. He had lost the will to live but was still looking for anything to reverse his disease!

As I stepped out of my car, this vibrant young fella with a huge grin, waved at me from across the parking lot at the health food store. Squinting at the sun, I had to take a second look to see if my vision wasn't tricking me!

"Curt, how are you doin' man, it's good to see you again." Stunned, I wasn't sure of what to say next.

"Greg, I almost didn't recognize you, you look bigger and you're actually smiling."

"Curt, I'm still on your metabolic program, and my entire body is rebuilding."

Looking him up and down I could see that he was putting weight on that frail frame, his complexion was great and it looked like his bone structure was actually changing and growing. Greg was thirty when he started a program and had been suffering from alcohol poisoning for at least ten years. Now that his liver was functioning semi-normally again, he had an entirely new outlook on life. But I did warn him not to get too comfortable with his newly regenerated liver, as a few bottles of booze could bring him back down to earth real fast. A lesson I had to learn the hard way myself. I was also a bit surprised, as the Healthexcel program I was running on other clients wasn't nearly as effective, but Greg was adding several other elements to his original program.

After we spent some time at the health food store, Greg suggested having some lunch and a drink at a local pub. I was a bit hesitant at first but agreed to meet him at his place and drive us both to a bar up the street from where he lived. It had been a while since I had even thought about taking a drink and assumed that he would not over indulge.

After lunch, he ordered a pitcher of beer and another after we finished it. Greg was still talking a hundred miles an hour, excited to share his newfound health experience with me. It seemed that his oxidation rates had completely flipped restoring his *fast* oxidation again. A year ago, when he first began his program, I assumed that he was a sympathetic "slow" oxidizer, being so skinny, craving carbs, along with moving and speaking very slowly. But the liver dysfunction had greatly impaired his oxidation rates as well. He now could even eat small amounts of animal protein in his diet as well.

With the second pitcher of beer almost gone, I suggested that we should go, as I had a meeting to attend within the next hour or so. Shaking his head in agreement, I noticed that his speech had slowed considerably and he could not focus nearly as well as when we first met earlier in the afternoon.

Then during the short drive back to his apartment, I witnessed the most unusual toxic liver reaction to alcohol that I could have ever imagined. Greg had started talking much slower, then began to slur his words as he rubbed his forehead, as if to soothe an aching headache. Without warning, he then began to sneeze. At first, both quickly and in short bursts. But then, after about twenty or more, he began to sneeze uncontrollably. For the next several minutes, he sneezed at least fifty or more times! As I pulled up in front of his meager apartment, I could see that he was covered with mucus, as well as looking almost *comatose*, as if he had just experienced a seizure. His oxidation rates had completely flipped, as well as his blood chemistry illustrating severe alkalosis.

Quickly, I opened my trunk and pulled out a clean towel, offering it to him so he could possibly clean up all of the gobs of mucus covering his face, neck, and shirt. Sitting in bewilderment, I again mentioned the fact that although he had been on this program for almost a year, he still needed much time to heal and rebuild. That *still* meant refraining from even the smallest amounts of alcohol. Shaking his head in agreement, he opened his door, slowly pulling himself out of the front seat.

"Greg, you need to immediately brew some coffee, do your detox and add as many herbs that you have on hand to the coffee that will help to extract the alcohol from your liver and kidneys!" Shaking my hand, he nodded in agreement, half stepping all the way to the front door. "I will call you Curt, when I can." As I slowly began to drive away, I relived this vivid scene I had just witnessed, praying that Greg would come back to normal within the next few hours.

Later that evening, he called me. Sounding much more like his normal self, I was relieved that he took control of the situation. Greg was a great guy. He was divorced and had a little girl that he shared custody with, as he had been divorced for a while. This had been a temporary setback, but it taught him a valuable lesson!

Just before Christmas of 1993, Z stopped in to visit, so we decided to take a trip to Kansas City and also stop by the state capital in Topeka. I wanted to introduce Z to Governor Finney. When we arrived at her office in the capitol building, Z was hesitant to enter. "Curtis, we don't even have an appointment, so how can we possibly get in to see this lady?"

"I've just got a feeling," I stated, as we were stopped by the receptionist. As we waited for the governor to finish her meeting, Z struck up a conversation with the secretary and discovered that she had dated his younger brother back in the early eighties. It truly was a small world!

Finally, after over an hour, Governor Finney and her security guys suddenly entered the room. As we began to chat, I could see that Z was amazed that we were *really* talking with the governor. When I introduced her to Z, I called him my bodyguard, which was a rather funny remark, but her comeback took us all by surprise. "Are you sure about that, Curtis, or is it the other way around?" For a moment the air was eerily quiet, then we all began to chuckle at her spontaneous and candid remark.

After a few minutes of small talk, she said goodbye and took a few paces toward the main corridor, but suddenly, she slowly turned around, came back and softly kissed me on the cheek and wished me a Merry Christmas. As she left the room, I touched my cheek and smiled as Z stood in amazement. That moment in time stood still for us all and will forever be etched in my mind and soul!

In March of 1994, I decided to move to Las Vegas and set up my clinic again. This city was growing almost exponentially, so it seemed to be the place to relocate. With a major international airport, over a million people and the growing health food industry, it felt like the place to be. Eventually, I could work on my show, *Metabolic Mission*, and hopefully open it somewhere in one of the major casinos!

Before moving to Las Vegas, I traveled with Big Z up to Oregon and Washington. We met with a few potential partners, saw some beautiful sights and spent some time at his late brother's house. His wife was a great lady with very well-disciplined children. Finally by May, I got settled in Las Vegas. It took a few months to adjust to the 115-degree desert heat, but after a while it was easy to handle. The humidity factor was very low so when it was 100 it felt like about eighty-five.

For the next few months, I sang a lot of karaoke and worked part time for a home improvement company. Tammi and I spoke on the phone almost every day, as she was living back in Michigan again. She was going to move out to Vegas with her brother some time in November. She had been on a metabolic program for a year and was doing well, after being diagnosed with polycystic ovaries in March of 1992. She had lost one ovary which had to be removed along with a softball-sized tumor. Tammi's father, a dentist by trade, had tried to treat her with nutritional supplements since she was about the age of ten. She also had been on birth control pills since the age of eleven to try and control her long periods of bleeding during her menstrual cycle.

During the summer of 1994, I met Mario, a promoter that liked my voice and wanted to be my agent. For the next three months, we prepared background tapes for me to take to Tahiti in September to perform at a major hotel. My tour was to last for thirty days and the pay was great, including room and board plus all of the amenities. But Mario had also been working with another singer for several months before me, so I agreed to let him go first. After that first singer came back, we found out that this Tahiti gig was not what it was supposed to be. Besides the fact that "Sonny" had stepped way over the amenities line by running up a huge bar tab while there. Although I was pretty upset at first, I finally cooled off, realizing that there probably would be other similar opportunities, as Vegas was growing in leaps and bounds by the day!

In February of 1995, I was asked to testify in Dallas for the FBI about the $4,000 I had lost to the bogus investment company with the $300,000 bank line of credit. The entire ordeal was quite stressful. After it was all over, the clown that had taken everyone's money was only sentenced to three years in prison. He literally had gotten away with 1.8 million dollars of clients' money from across the country. During the trial, he stated that there was no money left, he had spent all of it! In reality, I'm sure it was tucked away somewhere safe in an offshore bank account.

During my first year in Vegas, my body went through more metabolic changes. Because of the lack of chemicals in the air and the dry heat, my liver began to function at a higher level and I rarely had candida albicans problems. By the spring of 1995, I was right at 200 pounds. I still rarely worked out, instead I walked a lot and did a lot of stretcher exercises. I was considering bodybuilding again but enjoyed the way I felt and looked without all of the time involved in the gym. The Lyme disease I had contracted in the summer of 1990 seemed to be completely gone, although I knew that it was only dormant, as my immune system was functioning so well.

Then in April of 1995, I got lucky on a nickel progressive poker machine and opened my office again. I didn't have much of a bankroll, but my enthusiasm carried me through the tough times. I was starting to advertise and began to get a few calls periodically. As I started running programs again, I would occasionally look through the newspaper for companies that made business loans. Finally, in May, I answered an ad that didn't seem too legitimate but caught my eye. When our conversation was over, I sighed at what I was about to do. Tony, the guy I spoke to, was coming by my office to see about making me a loan.

Before he arrived, I pondered the decision I was about to make. Should I borrow money, especially from a *loan shark*, to market the Healthexcel program I was running? Deep inside, I yearned to again work with Dr. Kelley and follow the *original* metabolic programs that he had designed in the '60s. That was my next goal, to find Dr. Kelley and work with him again.

When Tony and his bodyguard Kenny arrived, with a bag *full* of money at least $50,000 or more in hundreds, I was definitely excited. But at the same time, was a bit apprehensive, knowing that this loan could mark the beginning of a successful business, or the beginning of a *big mistake*! When I asked him about all of the paperwork involved, he just laughed, asked me for a piece of notebook paper and handwrote the note for the loan. In the *blink* of an eye, I was *definitely* now *indebted* to the mob!

As time passed, the 5 percent weekly interest payments on my $7,000 loan began to wear me down. My business was just beginning to pick up again, but it wasn't nearly where it had to be to pay off this crazy loan. Finally, after only six months of operation, I had to move out of my office. The overhead, combined with my $350 weekly loan *interest* payments, was eating my lunch.

Then on Halloween of 1995, while working at home on the computer, I received a call from Tony. "Hey, Curtis, you need to make a payment today, come on by the downtown office." After trying to explain that I wouldn't have any money for a few more days, he started to get agitated. "Maybe I should just send some of the boys over to have some fun with your old lady!" When he made that statement, I calmly told him again that he would get his money, then hung up. As I sat there in silence, my anger began to build to a point that was lethal! Instinctively, I picked up the phone and called Rick, a close friend that was also a retired private investigator. With no answer, I decided to drive to his place and share my anger and frustration. Rick had to be home! He had cerebral palsy and was home most of the time.

By the time I got there, I had mellowed out a little. I knew that Rick had a pistol and had pondered the idea of asking him to borrow it to protect myself and Tammi. But after ten minutes of knocking on his door, I gave up the ghost and drove back home. For the next several hours, I anticipated a knock at the door and a confrontation. The baseball bat behind the front door was about the only viable weapon I could find to defend myself, so I grabbed it and waited! But the knock never came. When I finally looked at the clock, it was already past midnight, so I let out a long sigh of relief put the bat down and made my way to the bedroom.

The next day, I finally contacted Rick. He had fallen asleep in the upstairs bedroom listening to music with headphones on. That's why he never heard the phone or my pounding at the front door!

As he listened to my emotional story, his *first* recommendation was for me to become an investigator and get a concealed weapon permit so I could legally carry a gun and *protect* myself!

Taking his suggestion to heart, I finally decided to look into this private investigator industry. When I got home, I opened the yellow pages and called the first large ad that caught my eye. It also had a sign of the fish, which is a Christian symbol. James T. Born was the guy who answered the phone. He was the owner of "Nevada Investigative Services" in Henderson, Nevada, a suburb of Las Vegas.

"Are you calling in reference to the ad in the newspaper?"

"No, sir, I was advised by a friend to inquire about a job and he told me to start in the yellow pages. You are the first firm that I have called."

"Well, I am looking for an investigator to replace my lead guy, who is retiring, but the qualifications are pretty strict. First of all, do you have any college degrees?"

"Yes, an AA in communications, a BS in psychology, with a premed emphasis, an MS in metabolic therapy, and I will be finishing my doctorate sometime in the near future."

"That's what I'm looking for, but do you have any police or military background?"

"Yes, I was in the Marine Corps from 1973 to 1976 and was a military policeman, guarding nuclear weapons on a Naval Air Station. I also had a secret clearance."

"Hmm, it sounds like you may be what I am looking for, can you come by tomorrow for an interview?"

"Sure, I would be glad to."

The next day, I met James, was hired, got my ID and began to immerse myself into this unusual but very interesting industry. Plus, once Jimmy heard my story about my mob loan, he immediately suggested that we would go to the gun range so I could get my concealed weapon permit.

When I went to make my next payment to Tony, I showed him my investigative ID. At first, he actually thought it was *fake*. But when he realized that it was *legitimate*, I could tell by the look on his face that he wasn't going to intimidate me *nearly* as much as he was accustomed to. Finally, I could breathe a little easier with this crazy loan. Sure, I was going to pay it off, but now I had more leverage in the *harassment* department!

That was the beginning of my new investigative career. I soon became the firms lead surveillance investigator. The hours were long and unpredictable, but each case was different and at times, very unusual. I still worked part time for home improvement companies, knocking doors, setting appointments and spent the rest of my time singing karaoke at several clubs throughout the Vegas Valley. It seemed that I would have to put my consulting service on hold for a while, at least until I was ahead financially.

In November of 1995, after attending an annual conference at the Healthexcel office in Illinois, I stopped back in Winfield, Kansas, trying to find Dr. Kelley. I knew where his mother lived, so I knocked on her door. I was taken by surprise when she told me that he lived right across the street. Knocking on his door, I was anxious to see him again. It had been over eight years since our last encounter. At first, he didn't recognize me, except for my voice. But the last time he saw me, I was still five feet nine inches and 150 pounds. Now I was five feet ten inches and 200 pounds.

For the next day and a half, we talked about everything he had been through over the past several years. It really saddened me. This incredible man had experienced a grave injustice, trying to save and share his incredible gift to mankind, metabolic science.

He had practically starved to death, as well as lived on the brink of homelessness during the past several years. When we talked about Healthexcel, I mentioned how they would always change the subject when I would bring up Dr. Kelley's name, stating that he was not a part of this *new* metabolic typing program. He was a man that had been knocked down but *never* defeated!

The next afternoon, as I prepared to leave for Wichita, Dr. Kelley assured me that his new formulations would soon be made, and I could again work with him as he had cofounded the College of Metabolic Medicine. He and Dr. Carol Morrison had founded this school to both teach new students and again run metabolic programs for people around the world. He also had redesigned his original self-test and narrowed it down to about 400 questions from the original 3,200.

After arriving in Wichita, I called Valerie in Kansas City, as she had moved there a year before I moved to Vegas. But when I called her, the phone had been disconnected. Panicking, I called her father and probed him for information. "Well, Curtis, she is getting married and cutting all her ties to the rest of her family including you." A little freaked out, I asked Joe to give her my hotel number if she called him, so I could see how my son was. He assured me he would tell her.

The next day, my phone rang with Valerie on the other end.

Without even saying hello, she spit out what she had to say, never missing a beat. "Curtis, this is the deal, if you *don't* come back to be with me and your son, I'm getting married. Also, you will *never* see him again, as I'm cutting off child support and changing his name." Stunned, I immediately thought about the guy she was about to marry.

"What about this guy you want to marry, is he aware of this?"

"That doesn't matter! So what are you going to do?"

Hesitating, I thought for several seconds. Then answered quite candidly. "Valerie, I love my son, but you know that we just couldn't live together, not for Ciarston's sake. He deserves better than that."

As soon as I spoke those last words, she hung up the phone. Sitting there in a state of slight confusion, I couldn't believe what had just taken place. Was I dreaming? What she was doing wasn't fair to anyone. As I agonized over the fact that now I may never see my son again, I regained my composure and called my boss in Las Vegas. Being a private investigator for several years, I knew that he could tell me what to do.

After I had explained everything to Jimmy, his advice was to immediately document this in our company files and then notify the FBI. But causing trouble for Valerie and her new husband was the *last* thing that I wanted to do. So we never did go any further than document the event in our company files. It wasn't until over a decade later that I realized Jim was right, we should have documented it at a higher level.

In early December of 1995, I had my final "Come to Jesus" meeting with Tony about my crazy loan. I was behind again on my weekly interest payment, which prompted Tony and Kenny to pay me a visit at my apartment. I had just pulled up in my old BMW, when they both got out of his car and ambushed me at my apartment building. As he began to quiz me about my overdue payment, I finally had reached a boiling point!

Stepping back a few paces from them both, I raised my voice, and shouted directly into Tony's face. "I *know* I'm late again, so just *kill me*! If that will make you any happier! But *dont* break my legs, then I *can't* go back to work!"

For a moment, I think they both were a little shocked! As they looked at each other, then back at me, Tony grinned a little then shook his head. "If we *kill* you, we never get the rest of our money. So how else can we resolve this?" Then as he scratched his head, he started to look at my BMW. Although it was an older model, it still was in great condition. "Is this paid off?"

"Yes, and the blue book on it is around $5,000, if I remember correctly."

As he began to look it over more closely, I began to relax a little, releasing much of the anger and tension that had been building up. "I'll take it and reduce $500 from the principle of your loan."

"You're kidding right? That's only 10 percent of its blue book value!"

"You owe us, dude! It's not like you're in a position to negotiate."

As I hung my head in disgust, I agreed *reluctantly*!

That was a sad and pitiful day, that has *never* completely been erased from my memory. It made my blood *boil* for a very long time, even after the loan was paid off!

In the fall of 1996, I got a job on the strip singing in a gospel show at the "Country Star." Every Sunday, we performed twice, once in the morning and once after lunch. The Country Star was originally owned by Reba McIntyre and Vince Gill but was later bought out by Steve Wynn. I also was trying to promote my song, "Join Hands" which was produced by Rodell Records out of Hollywood, California. It was on a CD along with nineteen other original artists. The CD was a promotional disc that was sent to a hundred of the major labels in the industry. We did have some interest from one label, but nothing ever came of it. A couple of the radio stations in Las Vegas also played my song, but it was hard to promote it by myself. I needed a major label to help me finish my own album and to promote it correctly.

In the Spring of 1997, Z called me early one morning. He knew that I had met Dr. Wallach in the fall of 1994 at one of his seminars in Vegas. He wanted me to call him and see if he would agree to meet with a group of men involved with the upcoming Tyson-Holyfield fight. They were with the World Boxing Organization and wanted Dr. Wallach to contact Evander Holyfield and invite him to a prefight press conference at one of the major casinos. Dr. Wallach was well known for his seminar and audiotape "Dead Doctors Don't Lie." It was his colloidal mineral formulation that had helped Holyfield to overcome his heart problems and actually get back into the fight game again! The press conference was also going to be utilized as a back drop for announcing the birth of the "World Boxing Museum," which was to be built sometime in the future in Vegas off Rancho and the 95 Exit.

I agreed to the meeting, called Dr. Wallach and a few days later we all flew to San Diego. Dr. Wallach was quite an interesting guy. When we all met him in Chula Vista, we followed him up to his beautiful mansion on a mountain that once was a hotel. As we spent the day with Dr. Wallach, I got to know his background and also that of the other men I had come with. The most famous of the group besides Doc was Dick Sadler who, at one time, was a world champion boxer, trainer, and before that a movie star. That's right, he was "Stymie" of the *Little Rascals*. Dick was eighty-three at the time and was still full of a lot of spunk. I'll never forget how hard he and the others laughed when I told them the story of my first Golden Glove fight. My coach had preached to me about running five miles a day and I assured him that I did, but obviously I didn't. I was seventeen and thought I could skip that part, besides, I was a finely tuned athlete, so I thought!

The only thing I remembered after the first bell rang was how many times the kid hit me. I think I threw a couple of wild punches and the rest was a blur! I lasted the entire fight but got the hell beat out of me. When it was over, my coach didn't have to say a word. He already knew. That was the first and last fight I ever lost so pathetically in the ring.

From that moment on, I trained like an animal before each fight. In fact, I won my next fight with a TKO during the first ninety seconds.

We all purchased some of Dr. Wallach's liquid minerals before we left, and I began to notice that they enhanced my current metabolic program. But that was because Healthexcel's metabolic programs just didn't hold a candle to Dr. Kelley's original work, especially his original formulations. Now that I had met with Dr. Kelley again, he kept me informed about his new supplement line being produced, as well as his new streamlined metabolic self-test that was soon to be published.

Dr. Wallach was definitely quite a character, especially when he gave his seminars. He always talked about his favorite hobby which was collecting the obituaries of *famous* cardiologists that died *on the job*! I guess it would be rather frightening to witness your heart doctor passing away right before your eyes.

That summer in Vegas became a *scorcher*, as well as incredibly busy. Our investigative firm was slammed with several new jobs coming in every few days. One day, while shopping for a new car, I test drove a Hyundai Elantra. While talking with the salesman about putting a $1,000 down, my phone rang three different times. All three were my boss, giving me the numbers of potential new clients. By the time we got to the paperwork and payment options, I had called the new clients, set appointments to meet, and assured the salesman that I would have the $1,000 by the end of the day!

Later that week, I experienced an incredible injury to my shoulder, while climbing a wall during an ongoing case. It was a slower day, so I decided to get some sun, relax, and have a few drinks. As the afternoon slipped into darkness, I fell asleep by the pool. Then around 10:00 p.m., my cell phone woke me up. It was a client, tipping me off about her husband, that was about to go out for the night. She was frantic and *absolutely* sure that this was the night he was going to meet with his mystery girlfriend!

By the time I got to their house, he was just leaving. Following him, I was still groggy from all of the sun, drinks, and heat! It must have at least been about 118 that day. Finally, he pulled into a huge apartment complex on the west side of Vegas, right off Desert Inn and Rainbow.

But by the time I meandered through the parking lot, he was already far ahead of me. Parking my car, I jumped out and began a foot chase, as I could still see his taillights across the huge complex.

When he stopped and parked his car, I was suddenly blocked by a dividing wall that was about nine-foot tall. So instead of running another one hundred feet or so around the wall, I decided to just climb it to possibly see which apartment he was going in to. But as I jumped up and quickly pulled myself to the top I heard a tremendous *ripping* and *tearing* sound from my left shoulder, as it was also right next to my left ear! Just as I peeked over the top, I had to let go, as my entire body froze up reacting to the tremendous injury that had just taken place.

With a slight sunburn and consuming a little alcohol that evening, I had set the stage for my body to be in an alkaline state. This, combined with a frame that was now 200 pounds, rather than the 150 that it was, up until age thirty-four, had caused this to happen.

Falling to the ground, I rolled around for a few minutes in sheer agony! My left rotator cuff had *completely ripped*, like a rubber band that had finally *snapped*! Unable to even slightly raise my left arm, I stumbled to my car, oblivious about the case I was working on. I was sweating profusely, as I tried to drive with the use of only one arm!

When I got back to my apartment, I rotated both hot and cold compresses on it, which Tammi made for me. That night was *incredibly* long and painful. The next day, I called my boss and explained what happened. He advised me to go to the hospital, but this was one surgery that I did *not* want to have done! I knew that it would take several months and perhaps years to completely heal without surgery, but I was stubborn like that! With the correct nutrients, I knew that time would help it to heal.

In the Fall of 1997, while doing more investigative work, a recent client's husband was killed by another guy that caught him with his ex-wife. This, combined with another big case we had solved made me stop and think about myself and the future. It seemed that this investigative work was taking up all of my time and energy. I was still working on my second book, but it had been dragging on now for years. This, combined with my father's failing health made me focus more on my book, clinic, and helping others to heal themselves.

Every time that I spoke to Dad on the phone, I could sense that he was getting weaker. One of his carotid arteries was completely blocked and the other about 70 percent. I suggested him doing a program, but the most I could get him to do was to take Dr. Wallach's minerals. His doctor was afraid to operate, assuming that any small fragment of the blockage could travel to the brain and cause a stroke. I also mentioned chelation therapy to him, which he did look into but decided not to try.

It was now already the spring of 1998. Our investigative firm was suffering another slow period and I was trying to catch up long enough to take a week off to go visit Dad. I tried to call him every couple of weeks, just to be sure that he was okay. Then as I began to catch up with work, I realized how broke I still was. It seemed like an endless circle.

Because of a long drawn out case that we finally solved with a local escort/dance service, our business phones had stopped ringing for several months! Another service was trying to buy them out and had *pirated* their phone calls, as well as blocking our phones from getting *new* business. Obviously, they also had deep ties with the local phone company. The *mob* was still alive and well.

With the change of weather, from winter to spring, Tammi and I also decided to call it quits. We had been together since November of 1994 but had grown apart considerably. With my crazy hours as a private investigator, I could feel that our relationship may suffer. We also had a fifteen-year difference between us, which had created a communication gap that we never did completely mend! Our friendship was very strong, but the romance had fizzled out.

As spring turned to summer, I had to do construction work to fill the gaps. The pay wasn't much, but at least I could work any time that I wanted. Then on the weekend of July 18$^{th}$, while house-sitting for a friend, I called an old friend back in Wichita, Kansas. When she answered the phone, she at first was speechless. "Curtis, why did you call today?" Not knowing why, I was startled by the question.

"Did you know that your father passed away?" Shocked by her question, I asked her how she knew.

"We just read it in the paper about an hour ago. He died on Wednesday and the funeral was yesterday."

Still stunned, I asked her if she was sure.

"I'm sorry, Curtis, but didn't anyone call you about the funeral?"

Trying to hold back the emotions, I thought for a moment.

"I recently moved and forgot to call my sisters and give them my new number."

"Something must have made you call here, we haven't heard from you for years."

Fighting back my emotions, I thanked her for the information, hung up and tried to deal with what was now a reality. I had spent the last six months promising Dad that soon I would come home and see him again. But now it was too late. As the waves of emotions overtook me, I cursed my job, myself, and the entire situation. How could this be? He was always so strong, I sometimes thought he would live forever.

As the hours faded into darkness, I found myself sitting alone, still holding my head in my hands. The emptiness inside was so strong that I didn't want to face the future anymore. Slowly lifting my head, I remembered our last conversation which had taken place on father's day.

"Dad, I'll try to make it back soon, so take care of yourself and don't work too hard at the store."

"I won't, Butch, and be really careful out there doing that P.I. work." Then after a moment of silence, "I love you son."

"I love you, too, Dad, I'll see you soon."

With those final words resounding in my mind, I lifted my head and gazed across the valley at the glistening Las Vegas skyline. Another four years of my life gone and now the loss of my father. Would I ever get my business going again? In this town it almost seemed like a craps shoot, with the odds as always, in the house's favor.

# 10

# BORN AGAIN

*For God so loved the world that he gave his one and only begotten son, that whoever believes in him shall not perish, but have eternal life.*

—John 3:16

For the next few weeks, I lost track of time and life. I had been apartment-sitting for a nursing friend and was now without a place to stay. Our investigative firm was getting very little new business, so construction work was all I could do on a daily basis. The work was at times grueling, especially at minimum wage. I resorted to sleeping in my car until I could find another place to live. I still belonged to a health club, so I could work out, swim, and shower each day if I wanted to.

It was the fall of 1998, and although the death of my father was still constantly on my mind, I was starting to sing karaoke again and had rented a room. Every Sunday, I would sing karaoke at Sam's Town Casino, which was just a few blocks from where I was staying. Each time that I showed up, I was approached by Fred Chase, who would always remind me of how much I looked like Vince Gill, as well as had his high-singing range! He was putting an impersonator country show together and wanted me to consider performing as Vince Gill. It seemed like a great opportunity, but I wasn't sure about this Vince Gill guy. I had seen him before on TV and did have his high range, but I never was much of a country singer.

Finally, in December, I agreed to be in their show. Fred also had a room to rent in his house, so it worked out great. Our agent was his mother, which made it more of a family type setting for the group. The show consisted of myself as Vince Gill, Ron Collins as Garth Brooks, a Willie Nelson impersonator, Randy Travis, Charlie Daniels, and I also doubled as a comic character, Jimmy Raye. Jimmy was supposedly Vince Gill's long-lost cousin who always showed up and interrupted the show whenever Vince performed.

Our first show was a full house in Henderson at the MacDonald Ranch Country Club, which was part of the Del Webb community. When I walked out on stage that night, you could have heard a pin drop! This crowd gave us more respect than I was used to. I guess all of the obnoxious karaoke crowds in Vegas and Kansas over the years had made me a bit jaded.

As the fall of 1999 arrived, I began doing more investigative work for the firm and was enjoying my Vince Gill and Jimmy Raye position in our show. I was negotiating with an investment broker for my metabolic clinic and was working on finishing my second book. I had already completed my metamorphosis and was now on a mission, a "metabolic mission."

Once my second book was in print, I was going to market it again via the national and international talk show circuit, both radio and television. Bill Wolcott was about to finish his first book, *The Metabolic Typing Diet*, which was being published by Double Day. I was pretty curious to see this book, as I was sure that it was based on *most* of Dr. Kelley's work. Dr. Kelley needed to get *credit* for all of the decades of incredible research he had done. With his new book coming out, *Cancer, Curing The Incurable*, I knew that it would redeem him, both financially and scholastically. But I was still going to self-publish. I had found a good printer and an artist to redesign my second book cover. We would call ourselves "The Metabolic Press."

With the millennium quickly approaching, I was anxious to finish my second book and start working with new clients on Dr. Kelley's protocol. Dr. Kelley was working hard on his new formulations, as well as finishing the *new* self-test, which was a shorter version of his original 3,200 questions that I had taken in 1985.

Looking back over the past few years in Vegas, I couldn't help but notice that my level of health had *dropped dramatically* while on the Healthexcel program. My thyroid was starting to slow down, as fluid accumulated in my neck, as well as my oxidation rates were being affected. I had to start giving blood again, which was something I had been doing for a decade before I started Dr. Kelley's program. I just couldn't *wait* to get retyped by Dr. Kelley and start on his unique supplements. It was almost like *starting* over again.

I performed on the night of the millennium, as the MC, as well as singing a few songs during the bands' break at the same country club we had first performed at as a group. The only strange thing that happened close to midnight was the power going off, otherwise it was just another New Year's Eve party.

In February of 2000, my agent and Fred moved to Nashville. They wanted me to move also, but I felt compelled to stick it out in Vegas. I had been through way too many trials and tribulations to leave now.

With our group disbanded, I was reluctant to put another show together but a couple of friends encouraged me to give it another shot, so I agreed. This time we had Vince Gill, Travis Tritt, Wynona Judd and John Wayne as MC.

The crowd that night seemed a little temperamental, maybe because of John Wayne's dry humor. Even Tina, a waitress I had been seeing that worked there, thought it was not the caliber of show we had before.

The next year and a half came and went, without much drama. My investigative work was at times sporadic, which finally compelled me to resign and focus on finishing my second book, *Metabolic Mission*, complete my dissertation for my doctorate's and get my PhDs in both psychology and metabolic science.

Then in October of 2001, Dr. Kelley had a three-day metabolic workshop in Weatherford, Texas, where college health stores stocked and sold all of his metabolic formulations. It was great to see Dr. Kelley again and meet other metabolic doctors who were working with him again. I had started his program earlier that year and was going through some *incredible* changes. His *new* enzyme formulations were now known as the *strongest* in the world made to *target* tumors, especially those that were endocrine based. As they had specific receptors that speeded up the process.

He also had perfected all of the twelve metabolic type vitamin/mineral and glandular formulations into one capsule for each. This *combined* all of the elements specifically needed for each type at the cell level. So instead of taking several supplements for each type, you only had to take the one.

When I got back to Vegas, my enthusiasm was suddenly cut short when I called T.J. Parker's house. T.J. was a cousin to Smokey Robinson, that was starting a new television show in Vegas for young singers called *Star Quest*. I was his MC, and we had filmed the first show just before I went to Texas for the weekend.

The day that I called him, his roommate told me that his funeral was to be the next day as he had passed away over the weekend of a heart attack. As I shook my head in disbelief, I kept my composure, offering to sing at the funeral, which was to be a military funeral in Boulder City. Thanking me, she made the arrangements for me to sing "Wayfaring Stranger."

The next afternoon, as I began to sing the first few words of that old spiritual, T.J.'s ex-wife, who was sitting in the first row began to *sob* extremely loudly. I made it through the song, but we all could see that she *really* loved that man, although they had been apart for years. It truly was a sad day, as it seemed that T.J. was once again on his way back up the ladder of success.

The week after the funeral, Tina, the girl I was seeing, explained to me that she had been experiencing some dynamic changes on her program. She had started it almost a year earlier and still could not believe how accurate he was about pinpointing all of her metabolic disorders, especially *without* the benefit of knowing almost *nothing* about her! The day that I had ran her program, I caught him at a very busy time, but he agreed to take some basic information about her and fax me her program the next day. Expecting to give him a lot of medical history info, eating habits, etc. I asked him where I should begin. But instead of rattling off a list of questions, he only asked me *one* question. "What is her first, middle, and last name?"

At first I was taken back by his question, so after I gave him the information, I then proceeded to ask him if he needed all of the other information I had prepared for him. "No, Curtis, this should be enough. I will fax you the results tomorrow, at the number you gave me for another client's program." Still hesitating, I nodded my head, as I thanked him, not quite sure how to interpret his methodology.

The next day, after receiving his fax, I stopped by to see Tina and go over her new program. The diet, juicing, allowable foods, portions, and detoxification all seemed to coincide with her metabolic type, as she was a strong parasympathetic, craving quite a bit of animal protein, fats, and root vegetables in her diet. But as I began to review all of the recommended supplements that he made, I stopped when I came across liquid lithium. As I shook my head, wondering why he even listed this on her program, she asked me what it specifically was recommended for. "This particular mineral is used for neuronal synapse problems, which can create mental deficiencies."

"Like bipolar problems by chance?" Surprised at her statement, I nodded and asked her if that was the case.

"Yes, I have been bipolar for a few years. I used to take medicine for it but haven't for several months now."

"Wow, this is remarkable, I *only* told him your first, middle, and last name and he *actually, somehow* knew that you needed this valuable mineral. This really has me perplexed."

First thing the next morning, I called Dr. Kelley. Thanking him for Tina's program, I couldn't help but ask him the question. "Dr. Kelley, how in the world did you figure out Tina's complete program? Especially right down to *lithium* for her bipolar disease?"

Waiting for his answer I thought maybe, just maybe I had an idea myself but wasn't completely sure. "Curtis, because I had so much to do yesterday and was behind schedule, I didn't have time to get even the basic information about your client. So I prayed for the *Holy Spirit* to give me the information I needed."

For a few moments, I was a bit *stunned*, but it did all make sense, *complete sense*. Dr. Kelley was one of the most spiritual men I had ever known in my lifetime. Although it seemed almost uncanny, it reconfirmed his *genius*, as well as his level of spiritual knowledge and strong relationship with God.

During the next two years, I spent some time in Nashville, finally self-published my second book and again experienced the magic of Dr. Kelley's *incredible*, time-tempered metabolic formulations. It was almost like starting over again. My liver had dropped a level in functioning, as well as my thyroid and immune system. During the first six to eight months, I dropped about ten pounds and my entire physiology was changing taking me to another level, as Dr. Kelley's *original* programs always did.

In the fall of 2002, while in Nashville, I experienced an *unusual* event that could be directly credited to Dr. Kelley and his dynamic formulations. While waiting in line to enter a popular club to sing at an open mic night, I was carded by the young lady at the front door. Laughing, I pulled out my ID to *document* the authenticity of my age, which at the time was forty-eight. As she double-checked my driver's license, the guy standing behind me also got involved. "No way, dude, I'm forty eight! What year did you graduate?"

"In 1972," I exclaimed. Laughing at the entire scenario.

"That's the year I graduated! Wow, whatever you are doing I want some of that!"

Obviously, I *was* going back in time again, thanks to the power of Dr. Kelley's remarkable formulations. But now, not only were they much more concentrated and easier to assimilate, they also were very reasonably priced. The greatest impact that Dr. Kelley had made on the nutritional supplement world, was his *new* pancreatic enzyme formulations, that were by *far* the strongest in the world. With his proprietary formulations, no other company could even come close to making the same products.

On my way back to Las Vegas, I stopped in at Dr. Kelley's place in Texas and spent the next day picking his brain about everything I could think of. I wasn't sure if I would ever get to see him again, so I made the best of our time together. For a man that had been through so much in his life he still was an incredibly humble person.

Funny how life at times can take you by surprise. One day I was in Nashville, checking out the music scene and the next, I was back in Vegas, trying to figure out how to market my book. I was working temporary services again, mostly construction, but could not seem to get enough money to get a decent place to stay, so I opted to live in my car. I was pretty familiar with the aspect of being in my car a lot, as I seemed to *live* in it for all the years I did investigative work. It was the beginning of 2003 and I had quit my investigative work a couple of years earlier, which now could have probably saved me from resorting to this.

As spring approached, I auditioned for a show they were putting together downtown at the World famous Fremont Street Experience. It was an outdoor theater, in the middle of the cinema complex. The show lasted for a few months and gave me a chance to perform a lot of older music that I enjoyed singing, as well as meet several other entertainers in the Business.

It actually turned out to be a pretty busy summer. I would work construction from dawn till early afternoon, shower at the truck stop and perform in the evenings. Guess I always was a pretty good actor, as most of my friends thought that I was doing pretty well financially. If they only knew! Ha!

As summer ended, I spent an afternoon with Trisha, a girl I had seen off and on since 2002. After an early dinner, we stopped just short of her apartment complex, across the street, where we thought it was more secluded. But as the sun began to set, the caliber of people walking by seemed to change as if the day crowd was fading and the "night" people were emerging. Then as we shared some small talk about my book, I noticed a young black fella walking toward us on her side of the car.

He had on a long black leather coat, which was a bit peculiar, as it was still pretty warm out.

When he got within a couple of feet from my Hyundai, he asked Trisha where the strip was. Pointing toward the south, to Flamingo street, she nervously told him it was just about two miles up, going west on Flamingo. Seeming a little nervous himself, he thanked her and slowly turned and began to walk away. But less than a minute later, he turned around and started back toward my car. Anticipating something unexpected, we stopped talking as he again approached her side of the car. This time, he asked us both how to catch a bus to the strip. In response, I again told him to walk to Flamingo, then catch the next bus, as they come by every few minutes.

Then turning briefly to his right, he quickly turned back as he pulled a pistol from under his coat. It looked like a pretty small caliber, either a 22 or just a bit larger. Shoving it in front of her face, he pointed it at me, raised his voice and told me to give him my money. Thinking quickly, I began to laugh quite loudly, which prompted him to nervously look around, as he demanded to know what was so funny. Shaking my head, I reached for my wallet, stating that I was *broke*! "Take your hands out of your pocket, dude," he stated as he waved the gun in front of Trisha's nose. Pulling my hand from my pocket, I stopped laughing and genuinely stated that I really was broke and that Trisha didn't even have her purse with her. I could tell that he was new to Vegas, probably from back East and he just wanted to make a quick buck. He definitely didn't look like a hardened criminal.

Reassuring him that I *really* was broke, I slowly pulled out my wallet and showed him. I had a recent check, but it was in my other pocket. Dropping his head for a moment, he cursed, which prompted me to explain that this neighborhood was a pretty unlikely place to rob anyone, as it was old, with a lot of poor tenants.

Still cussing, he slipped his gun back into his coat and quickly made his way back toward Flamingo Street. As I put my wallet back into my pocket, Trisha let out a huge sigh of relief, then looked at me in bewilderment. "What in the world made you *laugh* when that guy came back?"

"Well, I knew he wasn't a seasoned criminal and doubted that he would shoot me especially if I had *no* money for him anyway. Guess I just followed my instincts."

During the next few weeks, I got another studio apartment and kept working on reestablishing my business. I had an iMac computer a couple of years earlier but gave it to a friend as payment for renting me a room for a while. Then in late 2004, I began to negotiate with a couple of potential partners, attempting to get to the next level with my business. I hired a young guy just out of college to finally begin building my website. It took him quite a while, but the finished product was great. I was just starting to consult with new clients again and was pretty elated about the strength and prices of all Dr. Kelley's formulations. I also had *again* experienced several physiological changes over the past few years on Dr. Kelley's new programs. Reducing his original metabolic questionnaire from 3,200 questions to 400 questions made it much easier for each new client. It still took three or four hours to complete but was just as accurate as the original.

It was the same week in January 2005 that I finally took on my partners with my business that tragedy struck. I had called Dr. Kelley to inform him of my new business structure, when his son John answered the phone. As the words slowly came across the phone line I almost dropped it in disbelief. "He's gone, Curtis, Dad passed away last night. His heart had finally gave out on him." At seventy-nine, Dr. Kelley's heart finally gave in. For a man that had done so much for mankind and struggled so, he finally "gave up the ghost." It was truly a sad day for many.

For the next month, it seemed like the rain would never stop. It *never* rained in Vegas in February, but now it was relentless. With the rain also came my depression. I had been working since 1986 toward this goal and now the *master* was gone. It just couldn't be possible. Finally, by May, I began to pull myself out of the black emotional hole I had fallen into.

During the summer of 2005, I began to knock doors, setting appointments in new housing projects for landscaping estimates.

I was working with one of the oldest companies in Las Vegas. Walking at least four to six miles per day, increased my oxidation rates, keeping my polycythemia in check. As long as I kept my oxygen levels up there was no need to give blood every few months.

It brought back some not so pleasant memories of years past when I gave plasma, to get rid of a small amount of red blood cells, along with some precious minerals and make a few bucks.

In 2006, I went back to Kansas for a few months, but with little work there in Great Bend, I decided to go back to Vegas right before Christmas. I was also still working on my doctorate dissertation and periodically running new programs on clients. I had a university on the East Coast that I was going to finish my doctorate with in both metabolic science and psychology. I had been working on a *new* theory of personality, based on Dr. Kelley's metabolic typing program since 1986.

In 2007, as the housing industry began to crumble, I again worked for my old boss with the landscaping company. But with the housing industry beginning to crumble, getting leads was getting harder and harder. It seemed that every block had more and more foreclosures each week.

Having boxed as a kid in the Golden Gloves, as well as coaching a team before joining the Marines, I had begun to watch the UFC the past couple of years and was amazed at the strength and endurance of many up-and-coming fighters. That's when I got the idea of sponsoring one of the fighters from the *Ultimate Fighter* reality show that was on television. After talking with John Kelley, Dr. Kelley's son, who also ran the supplement company, we decided to offer Gray Maynard a metabolic sponsorship. He was fighting at 155 and was still undefeated.

When I contacted ZUFFA, the company that owned the UFC, they even recommended that we contact Gray. He seemed to be looking for the same thing we were. At our first meeting, Gray was intrigued about our program and agreed to follow a metabolic protocol. In return, we agreed to give him his metabolic supplements and consulting *free* for the life of our sponsorship.

For the next year and a half, Gray won every fight and it was obvious that he was gaining some size, as well as increasing his endurance. He was known as the *biggest* 155-pounder in the UFC, as he walked around weighing close to 180, then would slowly cut weight several weeks before his next fight.

Then in the Spring of 2009, I received a call from Gray, stating that his coach Randy Couture, had contracted with a Doctor that had his own line of supplements and was sponsoring Randy's entire team. We were sad to lose him, but there wasn't much we or Gray could do.

It was about six months later that Gray lost his *first* fight to Frankie Edgar. Gray was a world-class wrestler but tried to fight Frankie standing up, which ultimately cost him the fight. Maybe changing from our nutritional program to another was a contributing factor and maybe it wasn't, but regardless, it was sad to see Gray lose.

By now I had finished both of my PhDs and was working with more clients. In late 2009, I again moved back to Kansas, but the incredibly humid summers and crazy weather conditions always beckoned me to come back to Vegas. I had kept my Lyme disease in check since 1990, but the humidity just cratered my immune system.

While in Kansas, I contacted the Kansas Lyme Association, sharing my experience and knowledge about Dr. Kelley's metabolic science and how it had kept my Lyme condition in check since 1990. They were so excited about the prospect of utilizing our protocol, they invited me to be on their board of directors. Accepting, I was anxious to share the validity of taking a metabolic approach to this rapidly growing disease. There were people that were actually *living* on antibiotics all year long, compromising their immune systems to the point of *collapsing*.

It's sometimes funny but peculiar how people react to a possible new approach to different degenerative diseases. At first, they assured me that *hundreds* of people would be contacting me to start a metabolic program but after several months, not one person inquired about our protocol. I even attended a support group in Wichita, shared my story and invited *all* of the people there who were infected to contact me but to no avail. When I left the meeting that night, I just shook my head and laughed.

This was nothing new to me, I had experienced similar levels of mental lethargy since beginning this program in 1985.

It was just a few days before Christmas 2010, when I finally got to see my son again. He had found my website the year before, and I was anxious to reunite with him. The last time I saw him he was only four. He really had turned out to be a handsome guy. During our brief visit, I tried to explain what had happened between his mother and I so many years ago. Looking back, I knew that I should have pursued finding out where she was but didn't want to disrupt her new life especially with her new husband.

When I initially moved back to Kansas in November 2009, I rented an old house that fifty years earlier had actually been a church. It was small, with a full basement that hadn't been lived in for over forty years, so I just stored some boxes there and locked it up. But after about three months living there, every time the furnace kicked on, it smelled like something dead was in the vent system.

Finally, I decided to go back to the basement and find the cause for the foul odor permeating everything.

When I unlocked the basement door and flicked the light on, I practically fell to my knees. Gasping for breath, I almost puked as I stepped into several inches of black sewage water! As I began to investigate, I found the cause pretty quickly. The bathroom toilet was overflowing with sewage from my upstairs toilet. Every time I flushed or used water anywhere else, the drains would send it all directly to be dumped in the basement toilet and bathtub!

After calling the landlord, I rented a hotel room and waited for the cleanup crew to arrive. Now I also could determine why I was getting headaches and my immune system was so compromised.

The black mold had formed everywhere contaminating the entire house!

For the next several days, the hazardous waste company tried to clean up the basement, but I knew that this house would never be completely free of this toxic mold. In fact, the day before they finished, I spoke with the foreman and shared my experience as a private investigator in Las Vegas during an investigation in 1995 and '96. We had to interview several dozen people that lived in an old apartment complex that had chronic water leakage for years. This had caused a black mold problem that made many people sick, as well as a few even dying. When I mentioned our investigative firm's name, the foreman scratched his head and got a bit animated. "We studied that case in one of our classes last year! That was a *landmark federal* case!" Nodding my head in agreement, I quickly responded.

"Yes, it was, in fact, those people *won* their lawsuit in the early part of 2002! I ran into a lady at karaoke in 2003 that had remembered me from 1995. She was *elated* about winning their Stachybotrys mold case!"

Although the house had been cleaned up you could still smell the sewage and black mold! It was *disgusting*! I probably should also have pursued a legal case but was just glad to still be alive! I moved and tried to put the experience behind me.

While living in Wichita, I reunited with a girl I had dated way back in 1983. Brenda and I had remained friends over the past several years. She had just been diagnosed with a rare bone cancer in her right leg and wanted to take a metabolic approach. I hadn't seen her since 1992, but she was just as pretty as when we first met in 1983. With a handicapped son in his twenties and another son a couple of years younger, she had been a single mother for several years, which had been pretty tough on her.

I was not very familiar with "Special Olympics" and was quite amazed at the structure of their organization. As we grew closer, I began to get involved with Special Olympics and volunteered at a state track meet they held in Wichita, Kansas, during the Spring of 2011. Being an avid runner as a kid, I agreed to help a handicapped black man in his early forties. He had to run a 440 but was not accustomed to running it, as he always ran the 880, or half mile.

With the 440, or the quarter mile race, I instructed him to *sprint* the first 110 yards, *float* the next 220 yards, then sprint the last 110. When the gun sounded, he was off like a shot. Sprinting the first 110, he had already gained a huge lead on all of the other runners. By the time he reached the final 110 yard mark, he was at least seventy-five yards ahead of the second place runner. As he ran past me, I yelled and encouraged him to keep sprinting saying "Go, go, go!" But as soon as he passed me, I could see Brenda waving her arms telling me to calm down.

As he finished in first place, almost one hundred yards ahead of the next runner, Brenda ran up to me, grabbing my arms, telling me to not get so excited. Puzzled, I could not understand her reasoning. "But he just won, by a *landslide*! He did *exactly* what I told him!"

"I understand, Curtis, but we have to cheer for *all* of the athletes, not just one." Pausing for a moment, I began to understand the concept. Special Olympics was about *unity* and equality. As I watched all of the other events throughout the day, I was brought to tears a few times, as I watched athletes that could *barely* walk, still running races and even placing.

Working closely with the Special Olympic people reminded me of a professor at Marymount College who referred to all handicapped people as being only a reflection to mankind, reminding us that we *all* were just as vulnerable and that having a healthy body and mind was a *tremendous* blessing that we all should cherish.

During the next two years, Brenda tried to follow a metabolic protocol, but she still had a few bad eating habits that slowed down the healing process. I tried not to be critical, but it definitely was in my blood after so many years on the program myself. It was pretty hard for her to give up drinking a few cokes every day, although she was aware of the fact that tumors *thrive* on sugar and animal protein.

In the Spring of 2013, I had my website restructured and was working on my third book, which was to be the second edition of metabolic mission. The screenplay for the movie about my story was not quite finished yet, as the screenwriter was a teacher that was still unemployed. He had taken my *true* story, added some fiction and was turning it into a "thriller" type of Hollywood movie. Being on the screenwriters guild in Hollywood was great, but we still needed to have a finished product to show potential directors and film companies. I already had spoken with a few but still did not have a commitment from anyone. In fact, the more I thought about the fiction aspect of my story, the less I liked it! My story was *already* incredible, so why add any fiction to it? There definitely needed to be some changes made to the finished product, before talking with anyone about production.

With summer just around the corner, the owner of a pain clinic in Dallas contacted me, fascinated with Dr. Kelley's program and concepts. I had been teaching a doctor in England via skype, who had told him about metabolic science. He had been working with clients for over twenty-five years, suffering from chronic pain related to cancer, chemo, and radiation therapy. He was sending them to many other doctors around the country for alternative therapy but never saw many positive results.

So Michael began to send me a few new clients, who were in pretty serious pain and had already tried a traditional approach to treating their cancer. They all were in the final stages of their cancer, which created a tremendous challenge to me, as there was not much else traditional medicine could do for them. Dr. Kelley's program worked great for all stages of cancer, but obviously if you were in the third or fourth stages, time was of the essence. That, combined with the strict nutritional parameters of our programs, presented a pretty big challenge to some clients. Altering one's diet extremely, taking many supplements, juicing, and detoxification is at times a *tremendous* obstacle to many people in today's world, especially *here* in America! Old habits, especially for many Baby Boomers, are pretty hard to overcome.

Although I always gave all of my clients their supplements at my wholesale prices, I made an exception when I agreed to take on Michael's referral clients. He wanted to make his profit from selling Dr. Kelley's supplements at standard retail prices. I had offered him a referral fee, which I was going to pay him from my consulting fee, but he wanted to make a continuous profit from selling our supplements. After careful consideration, I finally agreed to do so. I contacted John Kelley and persuaded him to allow Michael to resell Dr. Kelley's supplements. Michael knew very little about Dr. Kelley's metabolic approach but wanted to be the middle man for all supplement sales.

As time passed, Michael agreed that he should take my metabolic science course, so he also could start working closer with clients. This seemed like a good idea, as eventually I wanted to focus on an international talk show tour, as well as teaching other doctors here in America and abroad.

As my business began to grow, I was introduced to an incredibly new amino acid that had been formulated. I had been searching for almost forty years for the right formulation that was not animal based, had a very high concentration of protein per tablet and was quick to assimilate. This was it. The "MAP" formulation was 99 percent utilized by the body, had only 1 percent nitrogen excess and best of all would catabolize and build back up in *only* twenty-three minutes. Fantastic! As I began to add it to my own metabolic formulations, several changes began to take place within my body. The *biggest* change was how it affected my gallbladder and liver. It began to function at a higher level, along with other changes to my musculature, oxidation, and immune system. I still had been slightly protein deficient for years, as it was hard to find a clean and complete form of protein. This was mainly because of the advent of chemical farming, along with all the steroids, growth hormones, and antibiotics added to commercial animals across America.

As I studied all the information about this amino acid, I learned that we only utilize about 16 percent of all the animal protein that we ingest and about 32 percent of any animal or vegetable protein powder that we ingest. It also takes from four to six hours for these proteins to break down and build back up within our physiology. But the Perfect Amino formulation is 99 percent utilized and takes only twenty-three minutes to break down and build back up. Truly a remarkable product to add to any metabolic protocol, especially cancer clients, as they are restricted from eating even small amounts of animal protein.

When I began my metabolic protocol in February of 1985, I was allowed small amounts of animal protein, along with all of Dr. Kelley's array of supplements, including several glandulars. But over the next twenty years, Dr. Kelley had changed the initial protocol for *all* hard and soft tumors, restricting even the smallest amounts of animal protein, as well as glandulars and of course, sugar.

His initial approach for *each* cancer client was very similar, at least in the beginning stages. His methodology was to *first* "put out the *fire*," then begin to address the metabolic type a few months down the road.

## Metabolic Mission

Another factor all clients had to endure when starting a metabolic program was the large amount of supplements that had to be taken. Over the next few decades, Dr. Kelley changed several of his formulations, combining many elements together in one capsule. This was *especially* significant in respect to the twelve metabolic types. By the year 2000, Dr. Kelley had perfected the vitamin/mineral and glandular for each of the twelve metabolic types. So instead of taking several other formulations to meet the specific requirements for that individuals type, these two supplements provided the entire framework for each person's metabolic subtype. These formulations, along with his fantastic pancreatic enzymes, were all *proprietary*, to keep others in the supplement industry from *pirating* them!

With each summer in Kansas, came the extreme humidity! Dreading the effects it had on my immune system, because of my Lyme infestation and with my third book almost finished, I decided to drive back to Las Vegas for a summer working vacation. I wasn't getting many new clients and my old boss with the landscaping company had been calling me, so I agreed to come back and work with him for a while.

Before leaving Kansas, I drove to Great Bend, saw some family and friends, then visited the grave of my old friend Z. I spent over an hour there thinking about all of our adventures that lead up to me moving to Las Vegas. Big Z had done so well on his metabolic program, losing 150 pounds, regaining his short and long-term memory, as well as rebuilding his immune and digestive systems. But the girl he began seeing in the early '90s, being young and beautiful, as well as hooked on *heroin*, lead him down the road of *destruction*. I couldn't help but remember that Spring of '94, when we first arrived in Vegas and he was trying to quit "Cold Turkey." When he finally told me what he had been doing, I was shocked. I tried to get him to concentrate on his program, but Z was as stubborn as they come. The last time I ever saw him was when we flew to San Diego in 1997 and spent the day with Dr. Wallach and the members of the World Boxing Organization.

Roon, Z's closest brother, had told me that Z passed away around memorial weekend in 2004. He had gained all of his original weight back, plus another hundred or so pounds. After so many years of heroin addiction, his body had just been worn out. Besides the fact that he had stopped doing his metabolic program several years earlier. As I wiped the tears from my eyes, I slowly stood up from his grave, brushing the freshly cut grass from my knees and said a little prayer for a guy I truly thought would be around for many more years.

During my 1200-mile trip, I could go back over the last twenty-eight years of my life and try to determine what my next business move would be. I was self-publishing with a print-on-demand company in upstate New York, which also was going to be my fulfillment company for all book orders. My talk show booking agent was in LA and could get me on a few shows per week all year long. I also was talking with a publishing company that could help me to self-publish but split all profits fifty-fifty and get me into bookstores all over the world. They were known as WestBow, a division of the Thomas Nelson publishing company, which was nearly 200 years old. They had published *many* famous authors.

For the next few weeks, I enjoyed the hot but *very* dry climate of the desert and set appointments for the landscaping company I had worked for a few years earlier. I also was consulting with a few cancer clients I had contracted with in the Spring and sang Karaoke in the casinos or at a nearby piano bar almost every evening.

As summer faded into Fall, I packed up and made my way back to Kansas. The thought of fighting with the humidity factor was definitely a deterrent, but I was starting to consider Kansas my home once again.

I also took on another student in metabolic science that was a clinical nutritionist. The previous year, I had instructed a dentist that lived in England. I was checking into the possibility of offering a certification, just like the one Dr. Kelley gave us when I took his course from the International Health Institute in Dallas, back in 1985 and '86. The World Health Organization was Dr. Kelley's sponsor way back then, as they were recognized globally! In fact, during one of our classes back in the summer of 1985, a student asked Dr. Kelley about the WHO sponsorship.

Dr. Kelley simply responded by smirking and stating "Yes, they did *apply* their *holy water* to our institute, when we were first established."

During the next few months, I began to sing more. Although I was not performing anywhere professionally anymore, I enjoyed keeping my voice and emotional memories in tune. Music always did seem to connect my heart with so many wonderful and fulfilling vivid memories. I missed performing with Marshall, as we had put a show together in 2011, with him as Elvis and myself still as Vince Gill. But in 2013 we split, as he put a ten-piece band together that was just for his Elvis act. It always seemed that his "Elvis" impersonation was the highlight of most of the shows we did. Unless of course, it was a "Country" crowd. Then "Vince" was the *star* for the evening. But that was okay, as I had grown accustomed to the many crowds I had performed for over the years.

Then when I *least* expected it, I met Tammy. We were singing karaoke in a small club in West Wichita on a slow weekend night. I wasn't really paying attention, until she stood up to sing. I was instantly impressed by her unique voice, as well as her great looks, along with her full figure! After she finished her song, she strolled over to the bar to get a drink. So without being too conspicuous, I also meandered to the bar and struck up a conversation.

Over the next several weeks, we began a friendship, that was evolving into something much more intense and meaningful. With the cold Kansas winter nights, I enjoyed stopping over at her place, to enjoy the warm fireplace, a glass of Roscato wine, some good conversation and her unassuming personality. As we grew closer together, I could feel that there was something very special about this woman and this relationship.

Although I was not ready for such an intense encounter our time together began to set the stage for exactly that a pretty "intense" relationship.

It was in late March of 2014, that I began a parasite cleanse. Dr. Knackstedt had treated me for liver flukes in 1987 and '88, but that was twenty-seven years ago. There possibly had been eggs left behind that had affected my liver, gallbladder and bile ducts. I still did my gallbladder flushes every few months, as Dr. Kelley felt that as the food chain became much more devitalized, so did our physiology.

During the first few weeks of the cleanse, I was a bit amazed at the bile and other debris that was beginning to pass from my gallbladder. I obviously had parasites in my liver, gallbladder and in the bile duct. Being a ninety-day cleanse, it was a rather lengthy process, but much needed for sure. I was experiencing the Herxheimer effect, just as I did twenty-seven years earlier, when I was having the massive "die off" effect of candida albicans overgrowth. My coffee detox was helping me to eliminate the parasites, eggs, and congested bile that was forming. Even though I still did routine gallbladder flushes, this parasite cleanse was picking up my gallbladder and liver function quite dramatically. My good friend, Mark, who owned Ancient Formulas, had given me the specific formulation for this liver fluke elimination.

One Friday afternoon, I stopped by Mark's office to talk about possibly making some of Dr. Kelley's formulations for my own clients, taking the burden off college health stores. When I started to share my experience with the parasite cleanse, he mentioned an older lady on the East Coast, with Lyme disease, that when retested for the Lyme after the parasite cleanse, was found to be "*free*" of Lyme. I had to admit, I was really feeling good, but did not expect to completely eradicate the Lyme from my body. I guess time would be the judge of that.

In April 2014, I began another metabolic class on Skype with a doctor in the Netherlands. We also had several doctors in Iran, Iraq, and Malaysia that were interested in the course. Mark, who was originally from Iran, had two friends that had agreed to be agents to help sign up all of the potential students for my class.

Once we had several Doctors signed up, my class was expanding, adding two dentists and one MD to our school. Dr. Zeines, who had been a previous client, was going to teach with me, adding all of the specifics of oral health and its relationship to overall metabolic health. The other two Doctors were part of our board of directors. The school was now becoming "The International Metabolic Institute."

Tammy and I also began to see each other more often, as her youngest son went to his father's house every other weekend. Her oldest son was in college pursuing a pharmaceutical career.

Then on Easter weekend, we decided to go camping in my hometown of Reece, on Spring Creek. On Good Friday, we drove to Reece and I gave her the tour of the entire little town, from the two-room schoolhouse, to main street, which now was only a remnant of what once was a grocery store, bank, gas station, and post office. The old little Christian church just down the road a couple of blocks looked like it still was alive and well.

Ironically, Tammy was also working for the Koch oil company in Wichita, who had their ranch on the outskirts of Reece, as well as owning much land surrounding the entire rural community. Spring Creek Ranch had been there since the '40s, as my Grandparents had lived there at one time. Grandpa and Grandma Kuhn were the caretakers, with Grandpa also being the lead rancher.

As the afternoon began to fade into evening, I remembered an old farmstead on the southeast part of town, that had been abandoned for decades. But as we turned down the old dirt road to drive toward the creek, a steel gate with the sign "Koch" stopped us abruptly. A bit dismayed, I decided to look for another spot to pitch our tent for the night.

For the next hour, we drove on the outskirts of Reece, trying to find a good place to camp that also was secluded but easy to get to. With the sun starting to slowly fade away, Tammy suggested we go back to the Reece cemetery, as we had stopped by there earlier to see my grandparents and great grandparents' graves.

A bit confused, I agreed, although I knew that time was not on our side for finding a place to camp near Spring Creek before sunset. Once we arrived at the cemetery, she also instructed me to bring the blanket, as well as the wine and bread we had brought for communion, as it was Good Friday.

Still a bit puzzled, I followed her as we walked back to my grandparents' grave. As she spread out the blanket next to their grave, she looked at me and asked me if I thought that my grandmother would mind us being here as we take communion and share some spiritual vows between each other.

Finally figuring it out, I smiled and agreed that this was even better than down by Spring Creek. What better place to take communion and share some spiritual vows than at my grandparents' resting place.

As the sun began to slowly set behind the beautiful backdrop of the Flint Hills, we broke some bread and drank the wine. Simulating the body and blood of Christ, on this sacred and time-honored day. With tears in our eyes, we both shared our deepest feelings, expressing the spiritual commitment we were making to each other. We had already talked about marriage but wanted to address the spiritual aspect of our relationship first before actually expressing it to the rest of the world.

Although we never got a chance to camp out by Spring Creek, the experience at the graveyard was unforgettable. Never had I ever imagined doing something so spiritual, in such a hallowed and quiet place! It almost had felt like my grandparents *were* there watching everything.

As we drove back to Wichita, Tammy fell asleep, which gave me the opportunity to think back in time, when I first was discharged from the Marine Corps in October of 1975. In a way, it was great to feel *free* again, but at the same time it felt as though I had lost a family that I had become close to over the past couple of years.

I could see myself driving back home to Great Bend, Kansas, from Fort Hays State University. It was early November, with the ground already covered in snow and a beautiful starlit night. I had gone up to see an old friend and was enjoying the pleasant drive, the star-filled sky and the music on the radio. But as I drove deeper into the hills, I lost my radio station. After another few minutes I couldn't get any music stations at all, only a religious station with some kid telling his story.

Reluctantly, I kept the radio on and began to listen to this kid's story. It was strange, but his life had been very similar to mine. He even had a stepmother that he didn't get along with. The more I listened to his story, the more I could identify with his anger. Then he spoke of accepting Christ as his Savior and how all of his anger and hate for others could be forgiven, as also could he forgive them. For the first time in my life I began to ponder the concept of forgiveness. Surely if I could be forgiven for all of my past, I could in turn forgive also.

Reaching the outskirts of Great Bend, I prayed the sinner's prayer and shed tears of both sorrow and joy. For the first time in my life I felt as though a great burden had been lifted from my mortal shoulders. I knew that my life would never be a picnic, but I also felt that I was not alone. Little did I know that it was this faith that would someday compel me to follow a path that possibly *many* others would also someday travel.

During the next few months I finished writing and editing my third book, spent a few weeks on another working summer vacation in Las Vegas and started another metabolic science class.

Then during the second week of October, my stepsister Peggy called me. My stepbrother Jack was in the Hutchinson Hospital. He had recently been admitted, having suffered a near fatal heart attack! Having lost his heart beat and oxygen for several minutes to the brain, he was lucky to still be alive. The nurses also were forced to restrain him, as he was disoriented, having never spent any time in the hospital throughout his entire life! He just wanted to get out of there.

Before we ended our brief conversation, Peggy did say that Jack had been drinking heavily over the past several months. Obviously a precursor to his present condition! He had pretty much kicked the habit a few years earlier, but old habits sometimes do die very slowly!

Peggy asked me if I wanted to take over his guardianship, as they all felt he may possibly need to live in a nursing home, once released from the Hospital. Without hesitation I agreed, as Jack and I were pretty close from grade school, through high school and after. We had an apartment together for a few years after I got out of the Marine Corps, as well as when I graduated from Marymount College.

But during the next week, Jack had another heart attack, then lost his basic lung function and had to be ventilated. It seemed that he was drifting between the realm of this world and the afterlife.

He now was at the mercy of life support. Then while I was at the hospital, Peggy shared the story of when he first had been admitted. A few days after his initial heart attack, when he became conscious, he talked about his long journey to Florida. He also remembered how he had seen so many of his friends from high school that were *deceased*!

He obviously had crossed over to the *other side*, during his time without a heartbeat.

For the next week, I traveled back and forth daily to the hospital. Some days he was conscious and others he wasn't. But even when he could speak, we could not understand anything he would say. His expressions seemed like he knew *exactly* what he was saying and thinking, but it only sounded like he was mumbling. It was both very sad and hard to witness. I knew that he would *never* want to live like that anywhere, anytime!

I spent several hours of each day, waiting for him to become conscious, but it rarely happened. So I began to talk with the nursing staff, sharing some of my knowledge about metabolic science, as well as memories of Jack and myself when we were kids. In fact, I couldn't help but remember how I always called him a "dinosaur" because of his incredibly strong immune system. I was always the "sick" one, while he never seemed to catch any of the lethal bugs that plagued me.

But when I began to probe deeper about my brother's condition, a couple of nurses, as well as one Doctor seemed a little perplexed with his condition. They were just as confused as our family was about his body's ability to still keep going, when taken off the ventilator. It was obvious that his genetic framework was incredibly strong. But there also was one other factor that had to be considered. Jack began a metabolic program in the Spring of 2007, while I was back in Kansas for a short time. After knowing about my profession since 1985, he had finally agreed to give it a try. He had been drinking pretty heavily, was overweight, had some memory issues and even some immune concerns.

He stayed on his program for over three years, lost sixty-plus pounds, got his memory back, as well as his old personality. He was working full time again, as a nurse's aide and spoke pretty highly about our program. Of course, his major concern was the coffee enema, at least in the beginning, but eventually he just called it his periodic "douche." He even had told my sister Peggy, that his good functioning liver could be attributed to his program, as well as *overcoming* hepatitis C, which even baffled his Doctor!

Our last conversation had been just about a week before he had his heart attack. He had called me on the weekend and we had a great conversation. He even expressed how he wanted to start another metabolic program, as he had stopped his when he moved a couple of years earlier. He was anxious to attain the level of health he had achieved several years earlier. I also was glad that he wanted to start another program, as I knew that because of his genetic structure it would *jump-start* his health very quickly. If only I would have known that time really was of the essence. I would have met with him that day! That last phone call will forever be imprinted in my mind!

Finally on Friday, a few of my siblings and I met at the hospital and after many tears were shed, we all agreed to "DNR" on this next attempt to take his ventilator out. They had taken it out a few days before, but had to put it back in, as his autonomic nervous system was not functioning at times. That afternoon, after taking the ventilator out again, he seemed to breathe fairly well on his own. That's when I asked the nurse if she could also give him some morphine, as he looked like his pain levels were pretty high. She agreed and added it to his IV. So after a few more hours, we all agreed to go home and come back again in a day or so. But instead of going home, I went to get something to eat, then came back and stayed all night till late Saturday morning.

During that last night with my brother, I thought back to the fall of 1975, my discharge from the Marine Corps and sharing an apartment with Jack. The week that I had accepted Christ into my life I had left an unusual message on our tape recorder, which was on the kitchen table. I also had left a handwritten note for him to *be sure* and listen to it. Being the eternal prankster I had put together a few verses of Revelation, along with the sinner's prayer, to share my rebirth in the spirit of Christ. I was preparing to start college in the near future and already had my sights on a broadcasting degree, so I decided to put together my *first* sermon! But being a Saturday night, I had neglected to think that he may possibly be in an "altered state."

I had spent the evening at my mother's house in Larned and didn't get back till Sunday afternoon. When I walked through the front door, Jack just shook his head, smiled, raised his eyebrows and told me that

I really "freaked him out!" He had been out drinking and was taken completely off guard with my recording. But it also had made him consider the spiritual realm, especially the possibility of an "afterlife" and the presence of God, his Son and the power of the "Holy Spirit." We always felt that day was a turning point in our lives for us both.

After spending the night at the hospital, I went home late Saturday morning, hoping to get some rest. I slept almost all day Saturday, catching up for the past week. I was going to go back to the hospital that night but had a feeling that he probably would not be lucid enough to even recognize me. When I did call the hospital, his condition was stable, but he was sleeping. The nurse stated that his breathing was very labored but steady. I knew that if his lungs failed again it would probably be in the middle of the night. That's when it had happened twice before.

It was 3:20 a.m., when my phone woke me up. The subdued voice on the other end was my sister Peggy. "Curtis, Jack passed at 2:15 this morning. Rodney and I will make the funeral arrangements tomorrow." Thanking her for the call, I hung up but noticed that a text had also came through a couple of minutes after 2:15. It had been the hospital. I had been so tired I never even heard the buzz of the phone. Laying back down, I prayed for his soul and thanked God for letting him pass on to another realm, one without the pain and anguish that he had been enduring during the past several weeks.

The funeral was on Thursday, in Ellinwood, Kansas. There was a viewing, but instead of being buried in the casket, he had already planned a cremation. He had wanted it that way. Many of his high school friends were there, most of which I had not seen for over forty years. Funny how some people change so dramatically with time, yet others still look just like they did so many years ago.

With the funeral coming to a close, we all payed our respects with many tears being shed by both family, relatives and friends. Jack was always kind to others and would be missed by many. As I said my final farewells to him, I began to recall so many of my childhood memories of us running around together. I will always treasure those times.

Although we were a family of eleven, we truly were blessed with the love that our parents bestowed upon us, as well as for each other.

Slowly walking out of the funeral parlor, I again recalled a recent national talk show that I had guested on and a profound statement that I had made, just before ending the show. "Just as I was willing to *give my life* for my country during the Vietnam War, I also would *give my life* to ensure that Dr. Kelley's research would live on throughout history!"

So it has been this path now for over thirty five years that I have followed. With many winding turns, mountains and valleys, I have pursued this road that Dr. Kelley built over fifty years ago. If someone would have told me in 1975 that this would be my destiny I would have laughed at them, amused at such a strange idea!

But it is so and cannot be changed. After thirty five years, I know that my work is *just* beginning, but at least I am prepared for the unknown. At my forty-year class reunion in 2012, I spoke with a few friends that were preparing to retire. As I shared my own story, I realized that my work was *truly* just beginning. At first, the concept hit me directly in the face but after some thought, I realized that this commission I had taken on was worth it all. My life had evolved *truly* into a mission, a *"metabolic mission."*

Although my story ends here, there still is yet another addition, as life is *ever* changing. In 2017, I reunited with Michelle Wendler, whom I dated back in 1982, in Great Bend, Kansas. When we first met again, I was actually amazed at how she still looked as young as the last time I saw her. But in 1983, I moved to Wichita, seeking answers to all of my myriad of health issues. I never really told her much about my health issues, thus she was confused as to why I moved from Great Bend.

As we all know, Facebook has reunited many people around the world, thus this is what happened to us. In 2018, after a few months of being together again, she flew in to Las Vegas from Utah and we celebrated my birthday at Harrah's Casino on the Strip. My friend Pete, who is an Elvis impersonator, let me perform one Vince Gill song as an opening act for his daily show, especially for Michelle. Then, when I finished, he asked me if there was anything I wanted to ask her. She was still filming with her smart phone when I asked the question, "Would you possibly... marry me?" Not expecting the question, she actually *dropped* the phone and the video blanked out for several seconds, but the audio kept going. With Pete narrating the entire time, she said YES... YES...she did say YES. Since that day, we have moved to Laughlin, Nevada, then Pennsylvania I am pursuing this final chapter of my life. I am very thankful for second chances, both in life and in love.

# EPILOGUE

Now that you have digested my story, take a look around and consider what metabolic typing is *really* all about. Is it but another check and balance man has been forced to utilize because of what we have been doing to our environment over the past one hundred years? Are we not products of our environment? Man is but a mere reflection of what his environment is composed of. Pollute the land and its waters and you sooner or later pollute mankind.

If you are from here in America, you may be aware of the story about the famous actor Steve McQueen. He was treated in 1980 by Dr. Kelley for mesotheleoma, a tumor on the lungs and liver caused by asbestos exposure years earlier. Dr. Kelley had successfully reduced a portion of the tumor, as it was over fourteen pounds. But more importantly, he had completely cut off the blood supply to the tumor utilizing pancreatic enzymes.

When Steve was filming in Southern California and Mexico, Dr. Kelley shared with us how he witnessed a surgeon opening up the area over the tumor and how it suddenly *fell* out on the table, as it had no vascular connection left! But even though he was alive and well, he suddenly passed away the next day mysteriously.

The official report was that his heart had given out but Dr. Kelley always felt that something else had taken place, something *not* so Kosher! Why? Well, for the past several months leading up to this surgery, Steve had adamantly talked about sharing Dr. Kelley's work with the world, as well as exposing the "truth" about cancer research and treatments.

Regardless, he did not make it and we lost a tremendous actor, who was *definitely* a Maverick, just as Dr. Kelley was considered to be. Dr. Kelley also kept Steve's tumor in a large jar, which is *still* in his office today, as a reminder of Dr. Kelley's incredible contribution to mankind.

Another *incredible* true story is based in the movie "Lorenzo's Oil." Filmed in the early '90s, this movie depicts the struggles of an Italian family, whose son is stricken with a very rare disease, called adrenoleukodystrophy, during the early '80s. This rare genetic disease is passed only from the mother to the son. The boy is diagnosed when he is around five, as he was starting to act out in school, displaying an array of many different symptoms.

Because this was considered a neurological disease, it was deemed to have a 100 percent mortality rate for any very young boy that was diagnosed. In essence, it was caused by the livers inability to break down long chain fatty acids. Frustrated with the medical communities approach to trying to cure it, as they were *convinced* there could *never* be a cure, Lorenzo's father began doing his own research. As he was an international banker and could travel to different countries to obtain more information and extend his research.

Not giving up, over the next few years, Lorenzo's father *discovered* a nutritional protocol that *saved* his son's life, as well as thousands of other boys since then, that take the supplement *before* ever showing any symptoms. It is a combination of olive oil and oleic acid. *Amazing*!

After watching that movie, I was *sure* that it would get several awards, just for the fact that this man discovered an *incredible* cure for a *fatal* disease, but that never happened. In fact, it never got the acclaim that it was and *is* still worthy of today. But isn't that rather typical for this entire nutritional *revolution* that has been transcending during the past fifty plus years?

During the last thirty years I have witnessed incredible yet calculated changes in the nutritional industry. People have finally evolved from the "sure I can get all the nutrients I need from the food I eat" to "maybe I should be taking some type of nutritional supplements, as well as eating *organic* foods!"

We all know or should be aware of the fact that our government has *unsuccessfully* tried to control the nutritional industry, throughout the last half of the twentieth century. It has been the mavericks such as Dr. Kelley, and Dr. Wallach along with countless others who have bestowed the wisdom of treating *ourselves* with the food that was always available from the very beginning. It doesn't take an advanced amount of intellectual thought to figure out that food has *something* to do with health, more importantly *quality of health*!

While we are on the subject of our government and healthcare, I would like to share an insight I recently made, while at the V.A. Hospital here in Wichita, Kansas, having some routine blood work done. It seems that with the Obama Healthcare changes, America's veterans are really starting to be taken more seriously, especially those with medical needs.

I am very glad to see this. When I lived in Las Vegas, I worked in construction with many Vietnam Era veterans like myself, that were both *homeless* and suffering from many different medical issues. Now they even have a *hotline* for those veterans that are homeless. This, combined with the much better quality of care they administer today, has definitely affected soldiers across our country, from every conflict since World War II.

Because of this, I have decided to start contributing a portion of all my business profits to the National V.A. Homeless Foundation.

As Americans, we sometimes *forget* that *freedom* is not always *free*. Especially in today's world. The soldiers that are coming back from abroad, suffer from injuries that forty years ago, could *never* had been sustained. Medical technology has advanced incredibly, although at times like a two-edged sword. But regardless, we must not turn a blind eye to the men and women who have offered to *give their lives* for a country that was founded on *freedom* and a much better way of life!

Periodically, when I guest on a talk show or speak publicly, I like to ask a few basic questions before I tell my story. First: How long would it take for one to die if one quit eating food? The answer: about forty-five to sixty days. Second: How long would it take for one to die if one were to quit drinking water? The answer: about a week. Third: How long would it take for one to perish if oxygen were deprived? The answer: a few minutes! Thus we have concluded that food, water, and oxygen *are* the three essential *scientifically based* elements contributing to *life*. Therefore it *must* be apparent that the *quality* of these elements has some relationship to a *quality* of life, correct?

Yet, amazingly there are still those lost souls out there that can't quite figure that out. During my own personal and professional metabolic journey I have encountered many of these *lost* souls and tried desperately to no avail, to enlighten them before they took other drastic health measures. I guess some folks have to take their own wayward journey to eventually stumble upon the *truth*.

In 1995, when I reunited with Dr. Kelley, I was surprised to hear that he had several new formulations that he had been working on. My hat was always off to Dr. Kelley. Here was a man that had successfully helped over 33,000 cancer patients in his lifetime and was still working on new theories.

Another guy that in my book is a true maverick in the holistic movement, was Dr. Wallach. Obviously, his audiotape, *Dead Doctors Don't Lie* had become a national phenomenon. Although his approach to nutrition was nothing near Dr. Kelley's individualized approach, he was educating the masses about the power of minerals and trace minerals in the human body.

This area of nutrition has seen almost exponential growth in the health food and supplement industry. It has helped many individuals on their journey toward better health, but many have suffered the pangs of trying to determine what vitamins, minerals, herbs and etc. they need for maximum efficiency. Without some form of metabolism typing these individuals are at times playing a game of Russian roulette.

Of course we can't forget the advent of *nutriceuticals*, the combining of a certain herb with a pharmaceutical. Like *phen-phen* which was at times lethal to the patient, causing heart problems. One of my clients took it for a while. She looked great until she suffered the *rebound* effect. She not only gained all the weight back but put on several other unwanted pounds.

As of this year 2023, what do you think is the *fastest* growing stock in the world today? *Nutritional supplements*! Although long overdue, this phenomenon has been in the making for the past forty plus years.

Now that it is the $21^{st}$ century I am sure that medical science will eventually begin to look at what we have been doing for fifty years and try to figure it out. The Dr. Oz show is a perfect example of the medical profession suddenly claiming credit for the nutritional industry movement.

As I finish my story, here are a few more statistics gathered on the current health of our nation; The incidence of obesity in the United States increased by 32 percent in the last twenty-five years.

The National Institutes of Health recently reported that over 100 million Americans are now either obese or significantly overweight.

Obesity is a major contributor to heart disease, which now claims the lives of one out of every two Americans.

Cancer, like heart disease, was largely unknown prior to the $20^{th}$ century.

When I began metabolic therapy in 1985, Cancer struck one out of every five people. Today it is almost one out of two. At the turn of the $19^{th}$ century, it was one in every twenty-five people.

The epidemic status of cancer, heart disease, obesity, diabetes and many other chronic ills has resulted in significantly reduced longevity for Americans, who now live an average of five years less than people in other industrialized nations.

Obesity among children in the United States has risen by 50 percent over the last twenty-five years. Over 30 percent of children are now obese or significantly overweight.

Chronic illnesses of all kinds are increasingly common among children and young adults. Today over 40 percent of young people who attempt to enter the Armed Services are rejected due to poor health.

Undoubtedly gloomy statistics but not if we each take control of our own lives and physiological destiny. Maybe the next twenty years will give us time as a nation to take heed and listen to the few brave souls that have been preaching in the desert, the mountains and across the great plains of the Midwest. It's not too late, but time is growing shorter for our planet and its inhabitants. The coming years have much to offer but at the same time we as a planet must pay the price for mistreating mother earth. Only god above knows what the future holds for us all.

During the past thirty years, I have worked with clients from all walks of life, suffering from many different ailments and deficiencies. But over the past few years, it seems that many people with cancer, usually in the fourth stage, have sought out my help. Many had already tried the accepted medical approach of chemo, surgery and radiation, only to be discouraged, finding themselves still looking for other answers. I also have had many people consult with me, who tried other alternative therapies, only to become more discouraged after spending thousands of dollars.

Although putting together a specific metabolic program for each individual is crucial, there are other elements that can be added, that work synergistically with Dr. Kelley's protocol. Bloodroot, Carnivora, B17 and many other herbs and homeopathic substances can work together with a metabolic approach but should be monitored during usage. As science moves forward, we constantly are discovering nutritional factors that accent and help other supplements to function at a higher level increasing the rebuilding factors within the body.

When I began Dr. Kelley's protocol in February 1985, there were almost *no* other choices available. I had spent ten plus years actively looking for answers to all of my severe health questions, to no avail. But then mysteriously in December of 1984, while browsing through a small country health food store in Kansas, I discovered his second book *Metabolic Ecology*. It was this book, along with the gentle nudging of the store owner, who went to *grade school* with Dr. Kelley, that led me down this *metabolic path of truth*. The timing could not have been better, as I had diabetes, polycythemia and a liver-gallbladder dysfunction with malignancy.

Of course, I have *never* been the typical Kansas farm boy. My grandmother taught me at a very young age, to *always* seek the truth and try to live by it. This is why, once I began this therapy and started to experience the incredible results, I *dedicated* my adult life to educating and helping the world to understand and utilize this amazing nutritional discovery.

There is one other factor that I would like to share with you. One that does set me apart from almost every other metabolic Doctor and nutritional practitioner in the *world*! For the past two decades, I have offered *all* of Dr. Kelley's nutritional formulations at my *wholesale* prices. Dr. Kelley and I talked about this and we agreed that this benefit would help many people, as by the time they have contacted me they are usually *broke, very sick,* and need all the help they can get! I do charge a *one-time* consulting fee that covers the first 6 months. As we all know, the supplement industry makes their *living* on selling all supplements at retail prices. Of course, by doing this I have never made much of a living, but many have benefited greatly!

So as you travel through this life, remember what you have learned from my story and seek deeper answers to all of the questions life has given you. If life has dealt you a weak hand, find the answers that will make you a *winner*. You can do it, just as so many others have. I'm only one of many, that have experienced a similar journey, and lived to talk about it.

# A FEW PERSONAL TESTIMONIALS

When I was diagnosed with cancer, multiple myeloma in June of 2013, I started having the conventional treatments. After a couple of months, my wife Blanca realized that the conventional treatment would *never* give me the opportunity to heal and eventually my body would be so toxic that this could even cause a second cancer. She started her long research process, until she found Dr. Curtis Kuhn and metabolic therapy.

That's when my life started to change for the better, giving me hope of living with Dr. Kuhn's holistic healing process. Dr. Kuhn explained to us that cancer is a metabolic disorder, which can be caused by a deficiency in pancreatic enzymes and many other nutrients. Dr. Kuhn helped us tremendously to make the transition from the conventional treatments, without the fear of taking this amazing alternative path. We have come to realize that when the body is given the right raw materials, Dr. Kelley's pancreatic enzymes and all of the other nutrients required, amazing physiological changes begin to take place.

Following this complete protocol, my body has regenerated new healthy cells and the cancer has been reduced considerably. I feel a lot of energy, my immune system is getting stronger, as my body has what it needs to self-heal. Our lives are on the right path with God's Blessings and having Dr. Kuhn to help us.

—Sergio Pinango and Blanca N de Pinango

*****

I have known Dr. Kuhn for a few years. His knowledge and professionalism have guided me through a maze of treatments and helped *save* my life. What more can I say?

—Victor Zeines, DDS
Holistic Dentist

*****

On May 5, 2006, I had twelve biopsies done, eight were positive for prostate cancer. The cancer had already spread and it was number ten, the most aggressive cancer there is. I had lost sixty-eight pounds, being five foot seven inches and 168 pounds, I now weighed only 100 pounds.

The doctor said there was not much he could do, but I told him not to worry about it. *Jesus* was in the healing business. Then I called *all* the Pastors I knew (twenty-five churches) and had their people praying for me. I went home and got on the internet and started researching. In the process I found Dr. Kuhn and his metabolic approach to my illness.

So along with the metabolic approach, I combined several other herbal products, which I took three times each day, along with a particular diet. (No sugar, no fried meats, no dairy products, such as milk and cheese, no red meats and purified water.)

I juiced five different vegetables, along with a habanera pepper three times each day and stayed on Dr. Kuhn's metabolic supplemental support. I also ate plenty of blackened fish, green salads, fruit salads, veggie pizza with jalapeno peppers on the side and plenty of baked chicken.

At the end of seven months, I had a colored doppler test run and it showed *no* cancer. I have not been back to a doctor since May 5, 2006, and did not take any treatments. This has been over five years and I now weigh 160 pounds and feel great at age seventy-eight. Like I said to begin with, *Jesus is in the healing business.*

—Frank S.—Oil Producer
Texas

*****

I met Dr. Curtis R. Kuhn eight years ago, right after I had heart surgery. We became good friends. I read his book and attended his seminar. I'm a registered nurse and cautious about what I put in my body. It took me a while, but I was completely convinced after Curtis worked out my own personal metabolic program. Four years later, my blood tests are normal, my mind is also alert and no one believes that I am seventy-seven years old.

Allow me to share with you the experience I had with an *old* man who was sitting next to me, waiting for a take-out order at one of our local restaurants. In conversation, he said he was at least *fifteen years* older than I was. I challenged him and he admitted he was seventy-five years old. I laughed and told him he wasn't even as old as me. By that time, half of the customers knew my age and heard him say, "Whatever you're doing, keep doing it!" As he walked out, I assured him, "Don't worry, I will."

Thank you, Dr. Curtis Kuhn.

—Shirley L.—Retired R.N.
Las Vegas, Nevada

*****

I would like to thank Dr. Kuhn for his help and advice in working with the metabolic program and enzyme approach that Dr. Kelley designed so many years ago. I would like to report that my PSA has dropped, along with my cholesterol levels. I find that I have more energy and feel better and that my body is detoxifying at a faster rate than ever before. I'm confident that my PSA and other blood levels will return to a normal state, given time, without radical medical therapies and treatments.

—John D., 60
Photographer
Branson, Missouri

*****

"The *best* nutritional supplement program ever designed. Anyone who does this metabolic program will *see* the results. Everything Dr. Kuhn told me about metabolic science is absolutely true. Right down to the specifics of detoxification."

—Joshua W., 30
Registered Nurse
Florida

*****

"It has changed my health considerably. Not only internally, but in my outward appearance as well. No more crow's feet around my eyes. My joints in my feet can bend again, after ten years of stiffness. All joints are pain free, with *no* medication. Now I have mobility in my neck. My hair grows very fast. Got my waist back. Much more energy. Doesn't hurt when I eat anymore. Much better night vision. Even my eyelashes grew."

—Tina S.
Waitress
Henderson, Nevada

*****

Chronic Candida—"This has been an incredible experience. After only two months on the program I feel alive again."

—Lois S.
Housewife Garden Plain, Kansas

*****

"Lost an ovary at the age of twenty-one due to many cysts. Metabolics has rebalanced my body chemistry and given me a second chance. It is correcting my hormonal and thyroid imbalances. Life now has meaning."

—Tammi O.
Designer
Las Vegas, Nevada

*****

Weighed 425 pounds—"Lost 150 pounds. I owe my life to metabolics. It has saved me from the toxins of the world, by taking away the physical and mental sickness I have endured the past ten years."

—Don Z.
Entrepreneur
Salem, Oregon

*****

"To be honest, I assumed that I was in fairly good health before I started Dr. Kelley's metabolic program. After a few months, I now know otherwise. The physical changes have been *remarkable*."

—Phil R.
Commercial Airline Pilot
Las Vegas, Nevada

*****

"Have been plagued with fibromyalgia since 1989. It affected my life severely. Metabolic therapy has given me the tools to live my life again. It has greatly increased functioning of my digestive and immune systems. Also have passed over 2,500 gallstones."

—Terry S.—Accounting Manager
Las Vegas, Nevada

# A COMMENT ON DR. KELLEY'S SYSTEM OF METABOLIC TYPING

During the past thirty years, I have been running programs on clients and have witnessed many remarkable events. Dr. Kelley *always* has strived to take a complex program and make it "user friendly" to the average person. Although I must admit that many of my past client's had some type of advanced education, a fact that suggests to me that inquiring minds are more apt to readily understand and accept this form of healing arts.

Since I began my metabolic journey in 1985, many, many nutritional ideas, concepts and *claims* have come and gone but Dr. Kelley's basic concept of metabolic typing, based on the autonomic nervous system is still working well today. Along with all of the changes in the nutritional industry other companies have claimed to use Dr. Kelley's concepts, products, research, etc. only to line their pockets and cash in on a tried and true science.

I know because when the International Health Institute closed in 1987, I had nowhere to turn except for another company that claimed to use Dr. Kelley's original concepts, as well as *adding* new components to all of Dr. Kelley's work. For a while I agreed to work with them but became disillusioned as time passed and my body did not function nearly as well as when on Dr. Kelley's original formulations. So as you can see I have been on *both sides* of that scientific fence.

It wasn't until reuniting with Dr. Kelley that I *truly* became aware of the politics involved in the healing arts industry. It is sad but true, the *almighty dollar* seems to be a huge motivating factor for many companies involved in this industry. That is one reason why I have given all metabolic supplements at *wholesale* prices to *all* of my clients over the past several years. I have *never* made a nickel in profit on supplements. I also have only charged a one-time consulting fee for the first six months. Granted, at times it has felt like I *truly* did take a vow of poverty, but that was *my* choice.

So as you wander through this life, take a good look around you and consider the facts that have been presented. In fact, by all means check out the competition. *Of course* there will always be "copycats" which usually occurs when some product or service is so good that it is "shoplifted" by the competition. But make no mistake, such a program as this would be incredibly hard to simulate, would take years of extensive research and would cost profoundly! In fact, combined with the fifty years Dr. Kelley contributed, along with all of the other researchers involved, it would almost be impossible. Dr. Kelley's metabolic supplements are just as viable and strong today as fifty years ago, especially his pancreatic enzymes, considered the *strongest* in the world.

That information alone should help you to understand the incredible complexity of metabolic typing and may encourage you to look further for the answers to your own or a loved one's health problems. But remember, once you have taken that first step, and have discovered the basic premise of metabolic typing, the journey will have begun! A journey that many have taken, but *countless scores* of others will someday ultimately experience.

In 2016, when I was teaching a few Doctors in our Metabolic Course, one asked me if I could create a NEW shorter Metabolic Test. This I did, which accurately depicts ones FUNCTIONAL Metabolic Type, along with the Vit/Min, Glandular and Enzyme for the three divisions of the ANS. That first run of Formulas proved to be very effective, although we soon ran out of product. Our current Mission, is to manufacture a much larger amount in our next run. The test is available on my Website, along with a food chart. Once the formulas are available, they will be listed on my site also. Also, we would like to make the test available via a KIOSK in stores, along with the correct formulas for each person's Functional Metabolic Type.

After thirty years of working on my Documentary, we also are preparing to unveil it to the World. It will be filmed, but also available in a "LIVE" show, possibly in a Major Casino in Las Vegas. Keep your eyes and ears open for the Premier of......."METABOLIC MISSION."

# BIBLIOGRAPHY AND SUGGESTED READING

Beard, Howard H., PhD. *A New Approach to the Conquest of Cancer, Rheumatic and Heart Disease*: 1958.

Beard, John, D.Sc.. *The Enzyme Treatment of Cancer and Its Scientific Basis*: 1911.

Benedict, Dirk. *Confessions of a Kamikaze Cowboy*: 1987.

Jensen, Bernard, DC Nutritionist. *Tissue Cleansing Through Bowel Management*: 1981.

Kelley, Dr. William Donald, DDS, MS with FredRohe. *Cancer: Curing The Incurable.* 2005

Sugar Blues, William Dufty, 1975.

Kelley, Dr. W.D. *Dr. Kelley's Answer to Cancer*: 1969.

*Holy Bible, New International Version*: 1978.

*Nutritional Program, Council on Nutritional Research, International Health Institute*: 1973.

Valentine, Tom. *Medicine's Missing Link*: 1986.

von Wimpffen, Dr. Hans Hermann. *ENZYMES: A Drug of The Future*: 1993.

For more information on future seminars, talk shows Dr. Kuhn will be guesting on *His Metabolic Science Class* taught via www.gotomeeting.com, or to order books and seek consulting go to www.TheMetabolicInstitute.com.

You also can reach Dr. Kuhn for consulting at (316) 807–5210.

Title: Metabolic Mission
Genre: Thriller
Synopsis:

A life-hardened ex-Marine struggles with money owed to the Las Vegas Mob while making ends meet as a private investigator. With stress of his debt and his wife on the verge of leaving, he finds his health deteriorating fast. Upon a visit to his doctor, Curtis not only learns that his blood pressure could inflate a blimp, but he has liver cancer. Curtis slugs his way home in a daze, only to find his apartment empty, an eviction notice slipped under the door and a Dear John letter stapled to the wall. Weary, ill, and lost, Curtis calls upon an old girlfriend for help. Becky tells Curtis about metabolic therapy, a cure for disease, developed by a doctor who had a clinic in Dallas.

With a spark of hope and nothing to lose, Curtis looks up the doctor, only to find that his lab has burned down months ago, the clinic has been shut down and the doctor is missing. Pulling in all connections and putting his detective skills to work, Curtis manages to find Dr. Kelley in hiding. The doctor explains that the pharmaceutical companies want him dead to protect their billion dollar-a-year industry. The doctor concedes to help Curtis with his cancer on the premise of protection and getting a *new* identity. Curtis agrees.

Curtis finds he has stirred up a hornet's nest in his search for the doctor and has inadvertently revealed their location. With assassins hot on their heels, the doctor manages to work out a metabolic program on paper for Curtis to heal himself. Soon after, one wrong turn leaves an opening for a killer's bullet. As the doctor dies in a pool of blood, he reveals the secret location of his metabolic formulations—information stored in a chest and locked away in a major casino safe. The doctor's final words plead with Curtis to heal himself then retrieve the chest of information and somehow reveal it to the *world*.

Curtis manages to escape from Vegas. He quietly heads to his childhood home of Kansas, hides in a long-forgotten cabin his grandparents raised him in and begins the long process of rebuilding and detoxifying his body from years of abuse and metabolic debris.

Curtis follows the doctor's recipe to the letter. After three plus years of physical hell and a mental roller coaster of healing, Curtis emerges a new man, stronger than ever before. Having been an avid bodybuilder for the past ten years, he could *never* make any real muscle gains, but as his health came back, he also packed on fifty pounds of bone and muscle. He even was an inch taller, as his calcium deposits on his lumbar spine completely opened up. So he finally heads back to Vegas to fulfill his promise to Dr. Kelley, who had saved his life.

Curtis slips into Las Vegas and finds the casino holding the chest is now owned and operated by the friendly neighborhood *Mob Boss*. In an attempt at retrieving the chest, Curtis is spotted and captured by the Mob Boss's henchmen. As the Mob Boss prints out and hands over a copy of the FBI's most wanted list to Curtis, he explains that Curtis is worth a mountain of money now. Desperate, Curtis negotiates a cut for something more valuable than his head, the *cure* for *cancer*. Intrigued, the Mob Boss agrees. But when the chest is removed from the safe, Curtis finds himself double-crossed. FBI agents appear from the woodwork and assassins fire bullets from every corner. Curtis manages to get his hands on the chest and fight his way to freedom through a rain of bullets. A car chase leaves a trail of destruction down the Vegas strip. In the chaos, Curtis fakes his death and escapes from within an inch of his life.

One week later, Curtis pays his initial doctor a *late night* visit. He wakes him and forces him to run tests on his body, proving his cancer is *really* gone. To the doctor's astonishment, not only has Curtis rid himself of cancer, his numerous other health problems are also nonexistent. The doctor vows to get the cure to the proper authorities. Curtis leaves the chest with the doctor and disappears in the dark of night.

The next morning, as the doctor hands over the chest to the FBI, an audiotape recording of Curtis's final checkup and copies of *cure* appear in the mailbox of every reporter in Vegas.

Curtis smiles as he drives home to Kansas.

Steven Esteb
Writer/Director
Director of the Award Winning Film—*Hate Crime*
Best Picture,
Best Feature,
Best Screenplay,
Best Human Rights and Dignity Film,
Director's Choice Award,
Programmers Choice For Excellence in Filmmaking,
Best Ensemble

Steven Esteb is a versatile filmmaker that has worked as an actor, a Hollywood screenwriter and directed commercials, music videos, documentaries and features. His films include *Dirty Politics*, a dark comedy starring Judd Nelson, Beau Bridges and Howard Hesseman, and *Baller Blockin'*, a rap film for Universal starring Lil Wayne, which hit number one on the Billboard charts in DVD and video sales eventually going quadruple platinum.

Steve's been repped by top agencies like ICM and Paradigm as a screenwriter and worked as a script doctor, coach and screenwriting teacher. And now a professor teaching film and screenwriting at Loyola University in New Orleans. He lived and worked at an AIDS hospice for two years while making the feature length documentary, *Living With…A Film About Love and AIDS*. It premiered at the Santa Barbara Film Festival and traveled the world, contributing to the opening of new AIDS Hospices, his proudest accomplishment. Steve studied film production in the graduate program at Boston University and also has a degree in political science. He now lives in rural Louisiana, his adopted home, with his wife and two kids.

Contact:
gravyfilm@yahoo.com

www.ingramcontent.com/pod-product-compliance
Lightning Source LLC
LaVergne TN
LVHW041916070526
838199LV00051BA/2633